USAF in Sou

Search *and* **R**escue

in Southeast Asia

Earl H. Tilford, Jr.

**Center for
Air Force
History**

1992

The Cover

"Sandy One" by aviation artist Mike Machat, recreates a search and rescue mission along the Ho Chi Minh Trail on February 7, 1970. A Douglas A–1H Skyraider of the 1st Special Operations Squadron orbits overhead, as an OV–1OA Bronco fires smoke rockets and the first of two downed A–6 crewmen is hoisted aboard an HH–53B Super Jolly Green Giant. Courtesy Mike Machat.

Cover Design by Nick Mosura, Headquarters Air Force Graphics.

Foreword

Search and rescue has always been important to the United States Air Force, whose aircrews deserve nothing less than the fullest possible commitment to save them and return them home. The motto of Air Force search and rescue, "So Others May Live," is one of the most compelling of all military mottoes. It embodies this spirit of altruism and, as events have proven, also indicates the service's intention to furnish life-saving SAR for civilian as well as military purposes.

Search and rescue flourished during World War II as lifeguard ships and submarines joined patrolling aircraft in saving lives and sustaining morale, especially in the Pacific Ocean Areas. The rotary-wing, turbojet, and avionics revolutions made modern SAR a reality. Foreshadowed by the Korean War, the helicopter became the principal form of air rescue vehicle in Vietnam. In three major conflicts, SAR forces gained a reputation for bravery, dedication, and self-sacrifice, as they ventured repeatedly into hostile territory to pluck fallen aircrews to safety.

The USAF rightly continues to place a top priority on search and rescue, seeking better ways to perform this function through the use of advanced equipment and aircraft (such as the multipurpose MH-53J Pave Low helicopter) and improved training of personnel.

This reprint of a classic work offers the reader an exciting and exacting history of the evolution of combat search and rescue in America's longest and most grueling war: the conflict in Southeast Asia.

Richard P. Hallion
Air Force Historian

Contents

Photographs

List of Maps and Illustrations

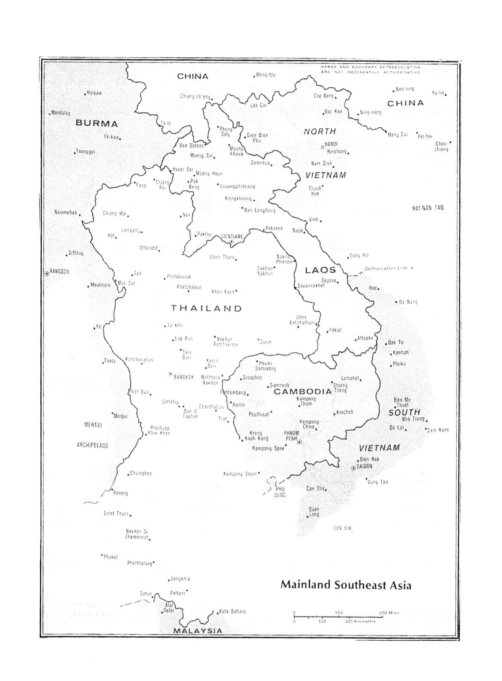

1 Development of Search and Rescue: World War II to 1960

It was the familiar flak trap pattern that developed in the pre-dawn darkness of November 9, 1967. Capt. Gerald O. Young, pilot of the Sikorsky HH-3E Jolly Green Giant rescue helicopter, knew his job would be difficult. The previous day a North Vietnamese battalion had ambushed a combined U.S.-Vietnamese reconnaissance team near Khe Sanh, a large Marine combat base in northern Quang Tri Province. Instead of finishing off the survivors the communists used them for bait for their heavy machine guns which soon brought down a Vietnamese helicopter and a U.S. Army helicopter gunship.[1]

Captain Young was flying backup for another Jolly Green that had been severely damaged while moving in to pick up survivors a few minutes before. Because the ground fire was so intense, rescue coordinators in Saigon authorized Young to abort the mission if he felt it too dangerous. The captain queried his crew, and the decision was unanimous, "Hell, we're airborne and hot to trot!"[2]

As Army helicopter gunships led a renewed attack on the enemy, Young worked his Jolly Green into position for the pickup. Enemy bullets slammed into the armor-plated HH-3 as the large helicopter hovered precariously a few feet above the ground while survivors climbed aboard. Then, as its turbines strained and the aircraft reached upward for darkness and safety, an enemy rifle grenade exploded near the starboard engine, causing a blast that flipped the Jolly Green on its back and sent it rolling down a ravine.[3]

Captain Young fell free of the burning, tumbling wreckage and slid to the bottom of the ravine. In spite of burns covering a quarter of his body, Young climbed back up to the mangled chopper halfway down the steep incline. There he found a badly injured airman and carried him into the bushes to hide from the enemy, while he administered first aid. Since enemy troops might be lurking in the area, Young did not dare risk hauling the injured man back up the ravine to join five other survivors huddled near the wreckage. At dawn a pair of single-engine A-1E Skyraiders, called Sandys, appeared overhead and located the men near the burned-out hulk. Fearing another flak trap, the Sandys made forty low-level passes over the area for a

1

period of two hours . . . a tactic called "trolling for fire." After two hours without enemy fire a Jolly Green moved in to pick up the five survivors.[4]

Although the beeper on Captain Young's survival radio functioned normally, he could not establish voice contact with the rescue force, so they were unaware of his exact location at the bottom of the ravine with the injured survivor. After the Jolly Green pulled away, he figured the enemy would return to use him for flak bait as they had the ambushed patrol. Determined not to allow this, even if it meant his capture or death, Young concealed the injured survivor in the underbrush and struck out through the tall elephant grass hoping to lead the enemy away so that the injured man might be rescued. The trick worked, and the enemy picked up his trail away from the crash site.

Unfortunately, due to the malfunctioning survival radio, the overhead rescue forces were unaware of Young's intentions. Helicopters airlifted a 100-man ground party into the area to pick up bodies and search for survivors. They located the injured man but found no trace of the captain who by this time had led the North Vietnamese several miles away from the crash site. With enemy troops in pursuit, Young stumbled through the bush, sometimes nearly slipping into shock, but refusing to reveal his position to the rescue forces overhead until he was certain a flak trap had not been set up around him. He evaded the enemy throughout the night and finally, on the morning of November 10, he spotted a helicopter circling nearby. The exhausted and injured captain dragged himself into a clearing, was sighted and rescued.[5]

On May 14, 1968, President Lyndon B. Johnson presented the Medal of Honor to Captain Young. Courage such as Young's, and that of his colleagues in the Aerospace Rescue and Recovery Service, resulted in the rescue of 3,883 men who might otherwise have been killed or captured in Southeast Asia.[6]

Brig. Gen. Thomas J. Dubose, commander of the Air Rescue Service from 1952 to 1959, once said, "To me it has always been a source of wonder and pride that the most potent and destructive military force ever known should create a special service dedicated to saving life. Its concept is typically American . . . we hold human lives to be the most precious commodity on earth."[7]

The idea of developing specialized and elite forces to rescue downed aircrews grew from three circumstances. First, the traditional belief in the sanctity of human life. Because of this dedication to the preservation of life, the American military made extensive efforts to protect the lives of fighting men throughout World War II, the Korean War, and the struggle in Vietnam. Secondly, the expense of training a pilot for the United States Air Force surpassed the quarter-million-dollar mark long before the war in Vietnam. As a pilot gains experience and his value to the Air Force increases, so logically everything possible should be done to protect the Air

Force's investment. Finally, from the early days of aerial combat the men who fly and fight performed their duties more efficiently knowing that every effort would be made to rescue them if they were shot down. As a result of these attitudes, rescue evolved into the proud heritage of the Aerospace Rescue and Recovery Service and of the men who labor that others may live.

Captain Young's experiences were no more harrowing than those of many other rescue crewmen who served in Southeast Asia. The U.S. Air Force involvement in the wars there spanned a decade and a half, and exacted a toll of 2,254 Air Force aircraft destroyed in combat and in the course of normal operations. For those flyers who went down, whether in combat or by accident, the best hope for survival was in a quick recovery by air-sea rescue forces. The effectiveness of the Air Force rescue effort depended on many factors including when and where the shoot-down occurred, geography, time of the day, enemy defenses, and the technological state of the art in aircrew recovery. The Aerospace Rescue and Recovery Service was successful in Southeast Asia in saving 3,883 lives, because technological advances, innovation and imagination were applied to overcome the obstacles of an inhospitable climate, rugged terrain, and a persistent enemy.

The search and rescue task force that ultimately made the difference in life or death for Captain Young and his comrades can be traced to World War II. After smashing Poland in September 1939, Hitler turned his attention to the West, occupying Denmark and Norway in April 1940. Then, in May, German forces quickly overran Holland in the north as armored columns raced across Belgium and northern France to the English Channel, where they trapped the bulk of the British Expeditionary Force, plus large numbers of French and Belgian troops, around the channel port of Dunkerque. Despite heavy Luftwaffe opposition, most of these men were evacuated to Britain under the cover of the Royal Air Force. Following the defeat of France in June, Hitler concentrated his forces along the channel coast, apparently ready to invade the British homeland. To prepare for the invasion, Reichsmarschall Herman Göering unleashed the heretofore invincible Luftwaffe against Britain in August 1940. During the intensive air combats of the Battle of Britain, numerous German and RAF flyers bailed out of crippled aircraft over the English Channel. Some were rescued, many were not.

Even before the war began, the Germans pioneered aircrew rescue. Air-sea rescue in the Luftwaffe dated back to 1935 when Lt. Col. Konrad Glotz assumed administrative responsibility for several boats at Kiel. The recovery of downed airmen was one of the many tasks that these boats performed. In 1936 these boats formed the nucleus of a Ships and Boats Group organized by the Luftwaffe at Kiel.[8]

The Germans decided, in 1939, to modify fourteen of the elder

3

-59 (He-59) float planes specifically for the air-sea rescue role. Medical equipment, respirators, electrically heated sleeping bags, a floor hatch with a collapsible ladder, and a hoist to lift the injured were incorporated into the aircraft. To identify their mission, these Heinkels were painted white and marked conspicuously with the Red Cross insignia.[9]

At the outbreak of the war, combat operations were largely restricted to the land campaign against Poland, so that the *Seenotdienst* (air-sea rescue service) was only peripherally involved. A rescue unit, established at Wilhelmshaven on the North Sea, conducted the first air-sea rescue of any appreciable size at the end of 1939. German fighters mauled a British bomber force resulting in many bailouts and ditchings in the North Sea. *Seenotdienst* planes and boats responded quickly and pulled a number of British airmen from the water.[10]

Following the occupation of Denmark and Norway in the spring of 1940, the *Seenotdienst* transferred a number of He-59s from the island of Sylt to Aalborg in northern Denmark. At the same time, units were stationed along the Norwegian coast at Stavanger and Bergen. In many cases, local life-saving societies cooperated with the German rescue crews.[11]

The German rescue units moved into Holland and France after these countries were conquered in May and June. An air-sea rescue center was attached to the Headquarters, Naval Command, at The Hague and a rescue unit was based at Schellingwoude in Holland. Four He-59s and four rescue boats were transferred from Norway to Schellingwoude. In addition, four He-59s and four rescue boats were transferred from Norway to France, where they were assigned to units at Boulogne and Cherbourg prior to the Battle of Britain. In the early autumn of 1940 these units were reinforced with captured and converted Dutch-built Dornier-24 and French Bréguet-Bizerte three-engine seaplanes. Rescue stations were also established at Le Havre, Brest, St. Nazaire, and Royan.[12]

The Germans also pioneered in the development of rescue equipment. Eventually, all combat aircraft, including single-seat fighters, carried an inflatable dinghy. German aircrews used a fluorescein dye to stain the sea a bright green around their dinghies so they could be more easily sighted by rescue aircraft.[13] Also, they introduced large buoy type floats and supplied them with blankets, dry clothing, food, water, flares, and lamps. Capable of accommodating up to four men, these bright yellow floats were positioned in the channel and the North Sea, where they served as a haven for any downed German or British aviator fortunate enough to reach one. British as well as German patrol boats checked these buoys so that a rescued flyer might go home or off to an enemy prisoner of war camp.[14]

Early in the war, the British approach to air-sea rescue was haphazard at best. Their search and rescue system depended upon Royal Air Force high-speed boats, any surface vessels that were in the vicinity, and whatever aircraft might be available either from the Coastal Command or the home squadron of the missing plane. There was some improvement in March 1940 when a communications system was established that gave priority to distress messages.[15]

Between July 10 and August 10, 1940, the Royal Air Force lost 220 men killed or missing, most of these over the English Channel.[16] A fortnight later the Germans began a two-week campaign to destroy the Fighter Command. In this period 102 pilots were killed or missing and another 128 seriously wounded. Out of a total strength of only about 1,000 trained pilots, more than twenty-five percent were lost. Winston Churchill wrote, "Their places could only be filled by 260 new, ardent, but inexperienced pilots drawn from training units, in many cases before their full courses were completed."[17] As the Battle of Britain reached its climax in the late summer of 1940, the RAF could not afford the loss of a single trained aviator.

The losses in the channel and North Sea made it evident that an improved rescue capability was needed. A start was made in late July when Air Vice Marshal Keith R. Park, Air Officer Commanding No. 11 Group of the Fighter Command, succeeded in borrowing twelve Lysander single-engine patrol aircraft from the Army Co-operation Command. These planes worked together with launches and other boats in locating and retrieving downed airmen.[18] On August 22, Air Vice Marshal Sir Arthur T. Harris, Air Officer Commanding No. 5 Group of the Bomber Command, called a meeting at the Air Ministry in London to draft a plan to coordinate rescue efforts. The result was the establishment of a joint RAF/Royal Navy rescue organization, with the Royal Air Force responsible for organizing and performing aerial searches and the Navy for making the actual recoveries.[19] A Directorate of Air-Sea Rescue was formed at the Air Ministry to develop and coordinate rescue methods. In the months following the Battle of Britain, though much progress was made, responsibility for rescue was still divided among a number of authorities until, in August 1941, executive control for all air-sea rescue operations was vested in one person, the Air Officer Commander in Chief, Coastal Command, Air Chief Marshal Sir Philip B. Joubert de la Ferté. The Directorate of Air-Sea Rescue at the Air Ministry became part of the larger Directorate-General of Aircraft Safety, and Sir John Salmond, ex-Chief of Air Staff, was given command.[20]

The growing interest in rescue operations was reflected in an improved record. While the rescue of a flyer downed off the coast in the summer of 1940 was a rarity, between February and August 1941, of the 1,200 aircrew members who went down in the Channel or North Sea, 444 were saved.[21] During the same period the *Seenotdienst* picked up 78 other downed British flyers.[22]

Like Great Britain, the United States entered World War II with almost no air-sea rescue capability. Prior to the war, the U.S. Army Air Corps was responsible for investigating aircraft accidents that occurred on land while the Navy and Coast Guard were charged with rescue at sea. The individual services were responsible for training their aircrews in survival techniques as well as providing them with the appropriate equipment.[23] On land, with no rescue procedures defined, any search for a missing aviator was conducted in a random fashion.[24]

Aircrew casualties began to climb as soon as the U.S. entered the war. General Henry H. "Hap" Arnold, Commanding General, United States Army Air Forces, became increasingly concerned with the need for rescue. This concern led to a conference with the Royal Air Force and, in September 1942, the two services agreed to begin coordinated rescue efforts in the North Sea and English Channel area. Although the British dominated this rescue program, the Army Air Forces initiated an aircrew training program to instruct airmen in emergency and abandonment procedures. Survival following a bailout or ditching and subsequent rescue depended upon many variable and complex factors: the coolness and skill of the individual confronted with the emergency, his physical condition, the ditching characteristics of the aircraft, weather conditions, and even luck. The aircrew training program was successful in making aircrews more aware of rescue procedures.[25]

Much of the flying done in World War II was over water. Bombers and transports flew across the Atlantic to various stations in Europe and Africa. To reach targets on the European continent, combat aircraft crossed the English Channel, the North Sea, the Mediterranean, or the Adriatic. After their missions over Europe, these aircraft, often battle-damaged, returned over water before landing at their home bases. Rescue from the European landmass remained highly improbable as long as German troops occupied most areas. In the Pacific theater aerial combat was over or near the water. The U.S. Navy contributed immensely to the rescue efforts throughout the Pacific. Navy planes, surface vessels, and submarines recovered many Army and Navy flyers.[26] The concepts and capabilities of rescue were, therefore, developed primarily for water recovery. Fortunately, aircraft developed during the decades prior to the war proved suitable for this mission.

The first successful water-takeoff of a "hydro-aeroplane" was made by Glenn H. Curtiss on February 17, 1911.[27] Seaplanes were used by both sides during World War I for scouting, antisubmarine patrol, and bombing. After the war, in the late 1920s, the Consolidated Aircraft Corporation developed the PY-1 for the U.S. Navy as a patrol and rescue craft. Flying boat technology was advanced in the 1930s by the quest for air routes to the Far East, with the Boeing Company, Glenn L. Martin Company, and Consolidated making valuable contributions. In 1935 Consolidated tested the PBY-1 Catalina, an evolutionary improvement on the PY-1. The high-wing, twin-engine Catalina was destined to be the mainstay of search and rescue in World War II.[28] The Catalina's cruising speed of 120 knots made it slow enough to conduct thorough searches. Unfortunately, it was not rugged enough to land and take off in any but the smoothest seas, and its 600- to 800-mile radius of action limited its effectiveness.[29]

The B-17 provided one answer to some of the Catalina's problems. With twice the range of the Catalina and loaded with life rafts and other rescue equipment, modified B-17s accompanied bombers to the enemy coast, orbited, and awaited the return of any damaged aircraft from the target area. Improving on the Luftwaffe practice of dropping inflatable dinghies to downed pilots, American engineers developed a twenty-seven foot mahogany-laminated, plywood boat to fit under the belly of the B-17. The boat was stocked with food, water, and clothing, and its two small air cooled engines provided an eight-knot cruising speed and a 500-mile range. Thus equipped, the rescue version of the Flying Fortress was redesignated the SB-17. The first operational drop was performed in April 1945, just before Germany surrendered.[30] Meanwhile, the air campaign against Japan continued as B-29 Superfortresses carried the war to the Imperial homeland from bases in the Mariana Islands. These strikes necessitated long, eight- to ten-hour over-water flights, but the SB-17s had neither the range nor the speed to keep pace with the B-29s. A rescue version of the Superfortress, the SB-29, met these requirements, but the war ended before its full potential as a rescue aircraft was realized. Both the SB-17 and SB-29 remained in the rescue inventory into the next decade.

Although rescue from the water dominated search and rescue activities in World War II, rescue from land areas received increasing attention as the war dragged on. In the China-Burma-India theater much of the aerial fighting was over jungle and mountain areas. A unit dedicated to rescuing aircrews down in the jungle was established at the village of Chabua in eastern India in 1943. When an aircraft went down in the jungle, an element of this unit traveled overland to the crash site. If all went well, the victim might be located in a matter of a few days or weeks and returned to civilization.

The need for a land rescue capability led to the development of the helicopter as a rescue machine. The first squadron to use helicopters in rescue operations, the 8th Emergency Rescue Squadron, was formed in China in May 1945. Equipped with Sikorsky R-6 helicopters, this squadron had the exclusive mission of rescuing aircrews down on land. In the first six months of operation, 110 land rescue missions were attempted and 43 airmen were saved. In one instance three R-6s, though limited to a 135-mile combat radius, were employed in locating and recovering a crew that had parachuted into a dense jungle. The helicopters took only a few hours to make a rescue that would have taken a ground party weeks.[31] The development of the helicopter came too late in the war to have a significant impact, but the implications for the future of rescue were immense.

Organizational arrangements of rescue activities were fluid and, until

7

1943, not auspicious. Rescue was first subordinated to the Director of Traffic Control during the reorganization of Headquarters, Army Air Forces, in March 1942. In April the job moved over to the Director of Flying Safety, headed by Lt. Col. S.R. Harris. In March 1943, in a third headquarters reorganization, air-sea rescue was placed under the Flight Control Command located at Winston-Salem, North Carolina. On August 25, 1943, it was returned to Washington, as the Emergency Rescue Branch commanded by Lt. Col. J.W. Burgand, subordinated to the Assistant Chief of Air Staff for Operations, Commitments, and Requirements under Brig. Gen. H.A. Craig.[32]

The success attained in air-sea rescue operations varied according to the theater of operations, local climatic conditions, and the period of the war. A total of 1,972 American airmen were saved from the North Sea, English Channel, and waters surrounding Britain through March 1945. The rescue chances for an Eighth Air Force crew forced to ditch in European waters increased from twenty-eight percent in 1942 to forty-three percent by April 1943. In the nine months of B-29 Pacific missions flown from the Marianas after November 1944, 654 of 1,210 crewmen reported down were rescued.[33] Considering the absence of a rescue capability in the Army Air Forces at the beginning of the war, these figures indicated great progress. By 1945 air rescue had improved to the point where chances of rescue were good, given adequate planning and advantageous positioning of the force. Vastly improved rescue and survival equipment, though developed slowly, was available by mid-1945. Throughout the war nearly 5,000 Army Air Forces crew members rescued were eloquent testimony to the improved conditions in air-sea rescue. By the end of World War II, combat crews could reasonably expect to be picked up if they were shot down.[34]

The question of rescue responsibility emerged after the war. The United States Coast Guard, supported by the U.S. Navy, claimed that since 1915 air and sea rescue had traditionally been its responsibility.[35] The Army Air Forces, on the other hand, believed that its air rescue capability should be expanded to meet the enlarged role and scope of global air power. Lt. Gen. Hoyt S. Vandenberg, Assistant Chief of the Air Staff for Operations, Commitments, and Requirements in 1945, suggested a compromise solution. Vandenberg recommended that the Air Transport Command be given the responsibility for air search and rescue over land and along ATC's oversea air routes. He proposed a plan whereby the Air Transport Command would reorganize its rescue units to meet the needs of the various Army Air Forces commands and establish liaison with the Coast Guard on matters pertaining to search and rescue over land masses and along the coastal waters of the United States.[36]

General Vandenberg's proposals led to the establishment of the Air Rescue Service in March 1946, and its assignment to the Air Transport Command on April 1, marking the birth of the Air Rescue Service in a form recognizable today.[37] Conceived at a time of budget cuts and military reductions, the Air Rescue Service was originally authorized 1,135 officers and men. On July 1, 1946, it had only a limited number of aircraft available for rescue in the continental United States. These included thirty-three C-47s, thirteen SB-17s, and twelve OA-10 Catalinas in the "heavy" category. For low-level and short-range search, the rescue service had thirty light-weight L-5 liaison aircraft and nine AT-11s. The Sikorsky H-5 helicopter was only just coming into the inventory with a mere seventeen available for duty. Cutbacks reduced the number of aircraft based overseas. Because of their high rate of fuel consumption, only a few SB-29s remained in the Air Rescue Service inventory.[38]

During the five short years of peace the Air Rescue Service suffered from the same budget cuts and force limitations endured by the whole Air Force. These constraints compelled centralization to conserve available resources for the most effective employment. The benefits of this were realized later when men and material had to be moved rapidly to yet another war, this time in Korea.

On June 25, 1950, units of the North Korean People's Army crossed the 38th Parallel into South Korea.[39] Two days later, President Harry S. Truman ordered American air, ground and naval units stationed in South Korea, Guam, Okinawa, and Japan to aid the South Koreans. On the first day of fighting, North Korean Yak fighters destroyed an American C-54 transport during a strafing attack on Kimpo Airfield northwest of Seoul. On June 27, five U.S. Air Force North American F-82 Twin Mustang fighters intercepted five Yaks over Seoul downing three of them. Later that afternoon four Lockheed F-80 jets from the 35th Fighter-Bomber Squadron joined battle with eight IL-10 "Shturmovik" propeller-driven attack planes, shooting down four of the Russian-built aircraft. From the first it was evident that airpower would play an important role in the war.[40]

The 2d and 3d Air Rescue Squadrons were responsible for rescue in the Far East Air Forces. The 2d Air Rescue Squadron, based on the Philippines and Okinawa furnished SB-29s for long-range rescue escort missions to and from the coastal ingress/egress points where aircraft crossed into enemy territory and where rescue aircraft could orbit, just off the enemy coast, while bombers carried out their missions inland. The 3d Air Rescue Squadron, headquartered at Johnson Air Base, Japan, with detachments at Yokota, Misawa, and Ashiya had various allocations of SB-29s, SB-17s, SC-47s, SA-16A amphibians, and L-5 liaison aircraft, along with nine Sikorsky H-5 helicopters.[41] On July 7, the 3d Squadron dispatched two L-5s to Korea where the mountains and water-filled rice paddies negated their effectiveness. These obstacles did not hamper the first H-5s that arrived at Taegu on July 22, 1950.[42]

Within hours of their arrival, the H-5s were engaged in the medical evacuation of wounded soldiers from the battlefront. These helicopters

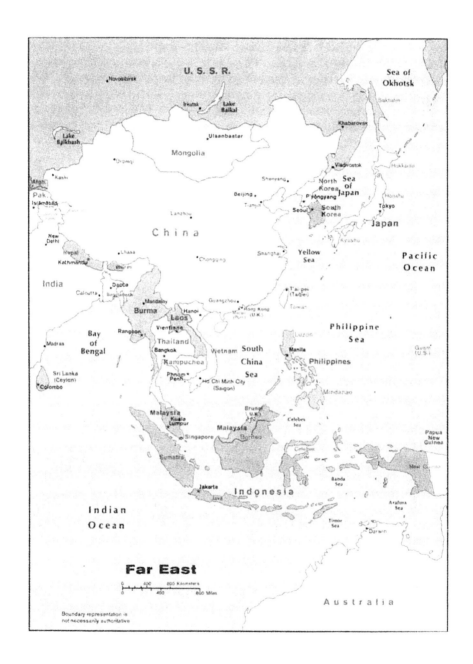

Far East

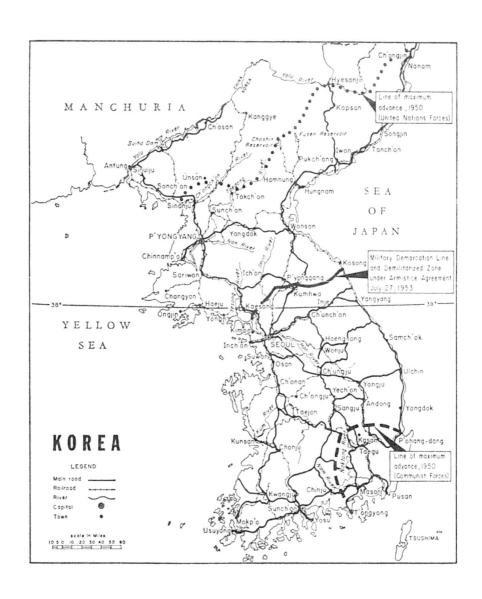

KOREA

LEGEND

Main road	——————
Railroad	—·—·—·—
River	~~~~~~
Capital	⊚
Town	•

scale in Miles
10 5 0 10 20 30 40 50 60

Line of maximum advance, 1950 (United Nations Forces)

Military Demarcation Line and Demilitarized Zone under Armistice Agreement July 27, 1953

Line of maximum advance, 1950 (Communist Forces)

MANCHURIA

SEA OF JAPAN

YELLOW SEA

TSUSHIMA

11

proved so effective that by mid-August the 3d ARSq had dispatched nine H-5s to Korea. On August 14 General George E. Stratemeyer, Commander, FEAF, requested twenty-five H-5s for the medical evacuation role, of which he got fourteen.[43] On September 14, 1950, Detachment F of the 3d Air Rescue Squadron was formed at Taegu. United Nations forces surged up the Korean peninsula following the amphibious landing at Inchon and the breakout from the Pusan perimeter in mid-September 1950.[44] The 3d Squadron moved with the flow of battle into North Korea, then retreated back to Taegu and finally stabilized itself at Yongdungpo near Seoul airport. There it was augmented with personnel required to man a rescue control center and Detachment 1, 3d Air Rescue Squadron was formed on June 22, 1951.[45]

As the war progressed the helicopter demonstrated its value in the medical evacuation role. The rough Korean roads made the evacuation of wounded by land vehicle slow and arduous, while helicopters transported the injured from the battlefield to the Mobile Army Surgical Hospitals (MASH) smoothly and quickly. The 3d Squadron's choppers were in constant demand for this mission from the earliest days of the fighting. In testament to the effectiveness of the helicopter, Dr. Elmer Henderson, a past chairman of the American Medical Association, said that the mortality rate among wounded in Korea was half that of the previous war largely because of the rapid medical evacuation provided by Air Rescue Service helicopters.[46] Throughout the war the Air Rescue Service carried 9,680 military personnel to safety, with helicopters carrying 9,216 of these cases. There were 8,598 medical evacuations from the front line units.[47]

The value of the helicopter in the air evacuation role was emphasized when, on November 11, 1951, Marine Corps choppers lifted 950 troops to the front and brought back an equal number of wounded. General Matthew B. Ridgway, Commander in Chief of the United Nations Forces, was so impressed by this operation that he recommended four Army helicopter battalions be made available to the Far East Command.[48] As the war progressed, it was the Army that assumed the dominant role in medical evacuation, though the USAF continued to perform a limited number of front-line evacuations.[49] The first Army medical evacuation helicopters arrived in Korea on November 22, 1951, and this unit was soon joined by others. Throughout the war, Army choppers carried 19,946 patients from the battlefield to various MASH units.[50]

The helicopter demonstrated its great versatility by performing other missions important to the United Nations' effort. One of these missions was the evacuation of troops trapped behind enemy lines. On October 22 and 23, 1950, two H-5s teamed with three L-5 light liaison aircraft to evacuate forty-seven paratroopers from surrounded drop zones at Sunchon and Sukchon deep in enemy territory near Pyongyang. On March 24 and 25, 1951, a single Sikorsky YH-19 helicopter worked with H-5s to evacuate 148 paratroopers from the Munsan-ni drop zone north of Seoul.[51]

As deep interdiction targets were struck further north, Air Rescue Service helicopters took up positions on Paengnyong-do and Cho-do islands located off the west coast of Korea. From these islands a number of highly effective rescues were made as the helicopter established itself as a unique vehicle capable of performing aircrew recoveries from behind enemy lines.[52] Considering that in World War II an aircrew member downed behind enemy lines was virtually certain of capture or death, the Korean War record of H-5 and H-19 accomplishments in aircrew recovery was particularly impressive. Between June 1950 and the cease-fire of July 1953, 1,690 USAF crewmembers went down inside enemy territory. The Air Rescue Service saved 170 (ten percent): 102 by helicopters, 66 by SA-16 amphibians, and 2 by liaison planes. Additionally, 84 airmen from the other United Nations Command air services were plucked from behind enemy lines. These included 11 Navy, 35 Marine and 5 Army flyers as well as 33 airmen from allied air forces. Within friendly territory, ARS picked up 86 aircrewmen.[53] Of the 40 aces of the Korean War, 4 were saved by the efforts of Air Rescue Service, including Capt. Joseph C. McConnell, Jr., leading ace of the Korean War.[54]

The H-5 helicopter had several operational limitations. It had no armor, its range was limited, and it carried only four people including the pilot and copilot. These factors made missions behind enemy lines precarious. Lack of range caused the first helicopter loss of the Korean War. On July 25, 1950, an H-5 tarried too long on a rescue mission, ran out of fuel, and crashed before it could reach its home base. The first helicopter loss due to enemy action again demonstrated the vulnerability of the H-5. On October 1, 1950, an H-5 returning to allied lines was flying along a road at 300 feet when its rotor wash detonated an enemy anti-tank mine. The explosion blew the whirly bird into a hillside.[55]

The H-5 was an early helicopter, and its limitations reflected the technical state of the art. Fortunately the Sikorsky engineers were at work on a more advanced design, the H-19, which first flew in November 1949. It had increased range, better altitude and speed capabilities, and carried ten passengers besides the pilot, copilot, and medical attendant.[56] The combat performance was favorable, and in February 1952, H-19s began replacing H-5s in the rescue inventory.[57]

The development of the helicopter dominated the rescue experience in Korea. Fixed-wing aircraft, however, rescued sixty-eight Air Force aircrew members, two Navy, four Marine, and nine allied flyers. All but two of these saves were accomplished by the amphibious SA-16A.[58] When enemy night fighters threatened B-29s flying night missions, 37th Air Rescue Squadron SB-29s from Komaki, Japan, flew long-range rescue-escort missions for the Superfortresses. Following the same patterns used in both Europe and the Pacific during World War II, SB-29s trailed the last bomber of a stream then orbited just off the coast to provide assistance if needed when the bombers returned.[59]

The Grumman SA-16A Albatross, which first flew in 1949, provided a new amphibious addition to the rescue inventory. In the rescue configuration the Albatross was capable of carrying ten passengers in addition to its pilot, copilot, and navigator. It was designed to operate from both land and water areas, with one version equipped with skis for landing on snow and ice. The Albatross combined this versatility with an endurance of twelve to fourteen hours on extended search missions.[60] These characteristics proved advantageous as the air war ranged farther north and the SA-16s orbited north of Cho-do Island awaiting mayday calls. The Albatross did a creditable job but was limited in that it could not land in seas running more than five feet, and icing problems hampered takeoffs from the water during the extreme winter.[61] Nevertheless, the SA-16A performed well in Korea and served in the Air Rescue Service, as the modified SA-16B, through much of the Vietnam conflict fifteen years later.

The Korean War ended on July 27, 1953. The Air Rescue Service survived its baptism under fire and emerged with an enviable reputation. The 3d Air Rescue Squadron was the first unit to be awarded the Presidential Unit Citation during the Korean War. Additionally, its members received more than a thousand personal citations and commendations.[62]

While the United Nations forces were engaged in Korea, the French continued their fight, begun in 1946 in the jungles and rice paddies of French Indochina, against the communist-led Viet Minh guerrillas. The French approach to this unconventional war was prosaically conventional, but they did promote the military use of the helicopter.

The first two Hiller 360 light helicopters arrived in Saigon in 1950 for use by the medical service of the French Air Force, Far East. By 1952 ten helicopters were engaged in medical evacuation missions necessitating the construction of a heliport at Tan Son Nhut Airport near Saigon.[63] By the end of the war forty-two choppers, all of American manufacture, had been delivered to the French forces. These included Hiller 360s, carrying only a pilot and one passenger, Sikorsky H-5s (S-5/S), and Sikorsky H-19s, which were introduced toward the end of the war. The little Hillers lacked power except for operations in the Delta area around Saigon and in the flatlands around Hanoi. The H-5s had greater capacity but could not fly at the higher altitudes required for operations over the mountains and karst that covered most of Indochina. The H-19s, capable of flying anywhere in the war zone, replaced the H-5s and compiled an impressive record. Of the helicopters that served the French, virtually all were hit by enemy small arms fire, but only two were known to have been shot down. Realizing the vulnerability of the slow moving helicopters, the French took certain precautions. A minimum cruise altitude of 3,000 feet was required to keep helicopters well out of range of most rifle and machinegun fire. Whenever possible, French pilots flew along secure roadways to their destinations. And, if available, fighters escorted the choppers over hostile territory.[64]

Medical evacuation of the wounded was the primary function of the helicopters. During the French Indochina conflict, they carried 10,820 sick and wounded men. Because of the relatively limited air activity, aircrew recovery played a small role; only thirty-eight pilots were rescued after bailing out of their aircraft. Helicopters also were used to locate and pick up ground force stragglers, eighty of whom were brought to safety after the staggering defeat of French forces at Dien Bien Phu in May 1954.[65]

In response to the crisis in Indochina, the Air Rescue Service delayed a planned force reduction and alerted its detachments throughout the Pacific to provide rescue coverage for supply flights to the French.[66] Following the 1953 Korean armistice, the United States Air Force flew an increasing number of overwater airlift sorties from Clark Field in central Luzon to Hanoi and Haiphong. After the defeat at Dien Bien Phu, troop carrier planes evacuated 502 French foreign legionnaires.[67] Douglas C-124s picked up the casualties at Saigon and transported them to Tokyo via Clark. From Tokyo, Boeing C-97 transports carried the men to Travis Air Force Base, California, and then across the continental United States to Westover AFB, Massachusetts before continuing to Algeria and France.[68] Air Rescue Service units monitored these flights from departure to arrival at their destinations. No mishaps occurred so rescue missions were not required. The conclusion of the Geneva Agreement on July 21, 1954, brought some stability to Southeast Asia. Accordingly, Air Rescue Service terminated its precautionary alert.[69]

When the war in Korea ended, the United States Air Force had planes based all around the world to counter the perceived threat from the Soviet Union and the People's Republic of China. The Air Rescue Service correspondingly assumed a world-wide responsibility — the "global" search and rescue concept. Nevertheless, budget cuts and fiscal restraints limited the Air Rescue Service in its mission and development. A restricted budget dictated a reduction in the size of the 7,900-man ARS force from fifty squadrons in 1954 to eleven squadrons (1,600 men) in 1961.[70]

The mission of the Strategic Air Command (SAC) dominated the Air Force of the 1950s. The recovery of SAC crews downed behind enemy lines should a nuclear war occur, was the responsibility of that command. The 8th Emergency Rescue Squadron, the first squadron to use helicopters for aircrew recovery in World War II, was activated and, on October 21, 1950, assigned to the 3904th Composite Wing (SAC) at Camp Carson, Colorado. Stead AFB, Nevada, became the permanent home of the 3904th on September 1, 1951. SAC assigned the survival training mission to the 3904th while the 8th ARSq assumed responsibility for the rescue of SAC crews if and when extended missions over the polar region into the Soviet Union or across the Pacific against Communist China were required. Helicopters, limited in range, had no role in this kind of rescue operation. The 8th Air Rescue Squadron flew SC-47s specially equipped with detachable skis for landing in the icy polar regions or the flat snow-covered expanses of the central Eurasian landmass.[71]

Ranking officers at Air Training Command proposed that the training function of the 3904th be integrated into their command. Likewise, the Air Rescue Service took the position that the mission of the 8th Air Rescue Squadron properly belonged within its force structure. Finally, the Inspector General of the Air Force conducted an operational readiness test to determine who would control the Eighth. The Air Rescue Service matched the 14th Air Rescue Group against the SAC squadron. The carefully studied results of the exercise showed that the Air Rescue Service was capable of performing the mission of SAC aircrew recovery.[72] The Inspector General, consequently, transferred the 3904th to the Air Training Command, and, effective September 1, 1954, established the 8th Air Rescue Group as a part of the Air Rescue Service.[73]

The mission of Air Rescue Service in the 1950s was world-wide in scope. Rescue service units rushed to the scene of floods in Kansas and participated in rescue efforts for downed aircraft in the Pacific. Squadrons of the Air Rescue Service were stationed around the world from Dhahran to Okinawa. The responsibilities of the rescue service included support of the Air Force's world-wide operations as well as inland search and rescue within the United States under the administration of the Continental Air Command as provided for in the National SAR Plan of March 1956. The overseas unified commands administered the theater rescue mission through joint search and rescue centers, and after 1960, the Air Rescue Service acquired the local base rescue mission from the different Air Force commands.[74]

In the late fifties military planners, reacting to Soviet and Red Chinese expansionist rhetoric, assumed that any future wars would involve an exchange of nuclear weapons with either or both of these communist nations. Air Rescue Service units, stationed around the world, were in a position to extend operations to cover any eventuality. Under the global concept, the peacetime role of search and rescue extended to wartime requirements. An Air Rescue Service directive for reorganization published on September 25, 1958 stated:

> ARS will be organized, manned, equipped, trained, and deployed to support peacetime air operations.
> No special units or specially designed aircraft will be provided for the sole purpose of wartime search and rescue (SAR).
> Wartime rescue operations will be dictated by the capabilities of equipment used for peacetime SAR, and will be conducted in accordance with JANAF [Joint Army, Navy, Air Force] and Standard Wartime SAR procedures.[75]

The global search and rescue concept provided a practical and workable concept for the 1950s. It was practical because of its compatibility with the equipment available for SAR at that time. This concept demonstrated its viability during crises that broke out in Lebanon and Formosa in 1958. When the United States reacted to these emergencies by moving a variety of contingency forces to the troubled areas, Air Rescue Service SA-16s provided coverage for air transport and tactical fighter units flying into the troubled locations.[76]

Some important aircraft changes and acquisitions were made between 1954 and the Vietnam conflict. The Air Rescue Service obtained the necessary aircraft to meet its world-wide search and rescue commitments. In 1953 ARS replaced its SB-17s and SB-29s with a version of the C-54 modified to increase its range, cargo capacity, and with an external configuration making it more suitable to the rescue mission. The redesignated SC-54 carried four MA-1 rescue kits, each kit containing a forty-person inflatable life raft that weighed only three hundred pounds and could be dropped more safely to victims in the water than the fourteen-man wooden boats carried under the SB-17s and SB-29s. Thus, each SC-54 was theoretically capable of saving 160 lives as compared to 14 for the older converted bombers.[77]

The SC-54, lacking amphibious capability, after locating victims, dropped whatever assistance was necessary. Korean-war vintage SA-16As provided the amphibious capability. In 1956 the Grumman SA-16B began replacing the SA-16A in the rescue inventory where it remained until mid-1968. It was an early participant in the Vietnam war during which it compiled a distinguished record.[78]

Helicopters, though recognized as optimum recovery vehicles during the Korean War, were somewhat limited in use by the global search and rescue concept requirement that rescue vehicles be compatible with the mission of long-range transports and jet bombers. Helicopters suitable for the extended recovery missions were not developed until the mid-1960s. By 1955 all H-5s were phased out of the rescue inventory leaving the SH-19 as the backbone of the rescue service helicopter fleet. In 1956 the Air Rescue Service acquired the Piasecki SH-21B to serve as an arctic rescue chopper.The SH-21B carried twelve stretcher patients and a medical attendant. The rescue version modifications included a hoist, two large windows, a jettisonable auxiliary fuel tank, a self-sealing main tank, and special rescue paint. However, insufficient range and a low cruising speed of about 100-miles-per-hour limited its effectiveness.

In the late 1950s the Air Force, and the nation, saw a new era of space exploration and travel just ahead. Orlando Air Force Base, Florida, was the scene of a September 1958 conference convened to determine the requirements for an Air Rescue Service aerial recovery force capable of locating, rendering aid to, and retrieving nose cones, space capsules, and personnel.[80] Two months later, a plan outlining concepts and needs for a system capable of safely recovering astronauts after an ocean splashdown was submitted. In response to Project Mercury, the first U.S. manned spaceflight program, a planning group met at ARS headquarters to coordinate and plan all phases of the recovery requirements.[81] As a result, the Air Force embarked on a SCUBA [Self Contained Underwater Breathing Apparatus] training program for all pararescuemen, jump qualified rescue personnel who first conducted pararescue operations in the China-Burma-India theater during World War II. Pararescuemen were formally organized as a part of the Air Rescue Service in July 1947, and the first class of SCUBA qualified pararescuemen graduated in September 1960.[82]

The consolidation of all rescue functions under one command was a major tenet of the global search and rescue concept. In conjunction with this, in December 1960, the Chief of Staff, USAF, transferred the local base rescue mission from the jurisdiction of the various commands to the Air Rescue Service.[83] One week later, the ARS prepared and published a plan for implementing this mission.[84] Throughout the Air Force seven types of helicopters were in use in local base rescue. The Air Rescue Service planned to utilize the H-43B, H-19B, and H-21 with the H-43B as the primary aircraft.[85]

On October 1, 1961, the Air Rescue Service integrated seventy local base rescue units into its structure. These included sixty-nine H-43Bs, seventeen piston driven H-43As, fifty-eight H-19Bs, and four SH-21Bs.[86] Under the ARS concept for local base rescue each unit consisted of two helicopters, four officers, and seven airmen. One helicopter and crew were on twenty-four hour availability. By late 1961 an Air Rescue Service local base rescue unit was stationed at every major Air Force installation in the world.[87]

The need to recover space program hardware and astronauts from ocean landings, the long range concepts of strategic warfare, and the existing state-of-the-art in rescue technology, had influenced the ARS toward a water-oriented role. Acquisition of the local base rescue mission proved to be a windfall for the Air Rescue Service. An enlarged helicopter force enabled the service to develop and expand rescue concepts as well as to acquire valuable experience in helicopter operations over land areas.

From World War II until 1961, the primary mission of the Air Rescue Service remained that of saving lives. The technological orientation was toward meeting the needs of equipment recovery in the space program as well as search and rescue on a world-wide scale. The unforeseen requirements imposed by climate, geography, and a stubborn enemy in the jungles of Southeast Asia would make much of the equipment inadequate and nullify many of the tactics previously used by ARS crews. A spirit of determined and imaginative innovation, however, which had become traditional in the Air Rescue Service, would be applied to meet and overcome the difficulties of rescuing men in Southeast Asia.

AEROSPACE RESCUE AND RECOVERY SERVICE

Emblem of the ARRS

Gen. John P. McConnell, Chief of Staff,
congratulates Capt. Gerald O. Young,
recipient of the Medal of Honor; lower
photo: HH–3E helicopter, of the type flown
by Capt. Young, escorted by a pair of A–1E
Skyraiders.

Heinkel He–59 used in 1940 for German air-
sea rescue; lower photo: PBY Catalina
operating over the waters of N. Africa.

22

Left: SB-17 with a lifeboat attachment, flying over Alaska; center; SB-29 equipped with a drop boat for rescue; bottom: drop boat parachuting from an SB-29.

P. 24: H–5 helicopter in Panama; lower photo: ski-equipped C–47.

P. 25: SH–19 helicopter demonstrating a rescue.

Above: SC-54 air rescue plane converted from a C-54 transport; left: MSgt. Ira M. Chichester in the port scanner's seat of an SC-54.

Above: SA-16 Albatross, often called "Dumbo," takes off for a search mission in Korea; right: an H-5 rescue of an engineer from a Korean river.

Top photo: parajumpers drop
from a C-47; center: H-19
helicopters in Puerto Rico; left:
H-21 helicopter in Alaska.

Left: Kaman H–43B Huskie; center: C–124 used to evacuate French legionnaires from Haiphong; bottom: USAF flight nurses with French wounded from Dien Bien Phu.

NORTH
VIETNAM

LAOS

HO CHI MINH TRAIL
INFILTRATION ROUTES

JANUARY 1971

GULF
OF
TONKIN

DMZ
DONG HA
QUANG TRI

TCHEPONE

THAILAND

DA NANG

SOUTH
VIETNAM

CAMBODIA

NHA TRANG

GULF
OF
THAILAND

CHUP
SNUOL
PHNOM
PENH
MIMOT

SAIGON

KOMPONG SOM

Base Areas

30

2 Genesis of Search and Rescue in Southeast Asia

Although commonly called the Vietnam War, the fighting in Southeast Asia actually involved several wars. In Laos there was a three-way civil war between rightists, Neutralists, and the Pathet Lao. There was an insurgency in South Vietnam guided and eventually dominated by North Vietnam. The United States conducted an air war against North Vietnam, another against the infiltration system along the Ho Chi Minh Trail, provided air support to the forces in South Vietnam and, after 1970, carried out an air war against the Khmer Rouge in Cambodia. These interrelated conflicts each posed different problems in rescuing and recovering aircrews shot down in enemy territory. The required rescue tactics differed according to the location of the survivor, the nature of the terrain, enemy defenses, and the technological state-of-the-art in rescue at the time of the shoot down. For the U.S. Air Force the wars of Southeast Asia began in the kingdom of Laos.

Laos, a land-locked country, in 1959 shared a common frontier with six other nations. The People's Republic of China and the Democratic Republic of Vietnam, along the north and northeastern frontiers, had been dominated by the communists since 1949 and 1954 respectively. Bordering Laos on the southeast and south were the Republic of Vietnam and Cambodia. Anticommunist Thailand formed the southwestern frontier while neutral Burma lay along the northwestern border.[1]

Laotian land area totals 91,400 square miles, approximately the size of Great Britain or the state of Idaho. Sixty percent of Laos, particularly the north, is covered with dense tropical rain forest and humped-back mountains, some of which rise to over 7,000 feet. In the frontier areas especially, the Laotian people are ethnically similar to their neighbors. This similarity is most apparent along the northern border with Vietnam where inhabitants on both sides look the same and speak similar languages. Communist cadres found the geography and the social circumstances along the border areas well suited for infiltration and subversion.[2] The lowland areas of Laos lie primarily along the Mekong River, which itself runs practically the length of the country and serves as the border with Thailand for most of its length. The major towns of Laos, including Luang Prabang the Royal capital and Vientiane the administrative center, grew up along the Mekong because it

31

provided the main trade artery from China to Cambodia and Vietnam.

The monsoon climate determines the weather patterns for Laos and provides three overlapping seasons. There is a rainy season lasting five months from May through September. In October, the rain tapers off, and the cool season begins and continues through January. March brings warmer humid weather with temperatures that reach a high of ninety-five degrees in April, the hottest month. Dust and haze dominate the dry season, when the Lao farmers practice their slash and burn agriculture.[3]

Laos is a nation of pronounced ethnic and linguistic as well as geographic diversity. Even in 1975, at the end of many years of revolution, invasion, aggresssion, and foreign intervention, when the people of Vientiane and the major towns turned out to welcome the victorious Pathet Lao armies, Laos was not a state in the traditional sense. No central government had ever successfully administered the entire nation. Political, national, and ideological concepts meant little to a people whose existence was marked by poverty, famine, disease, and war.

In 1960 the interests of the United States, the Soviet Union, the People's Republic of China, and the Democratic Republic of Vietnam converged and conflicted in Laos. Domestic politics in Laos, when divorced from East-West ideological, political, and military rivalries, followed a traditional pattern of competition among a few ruling families, including the Souvanna (Souvanna Phouma and his half-brother Souphanouvong, the Pathet Lao chieftain), Phoumi, Champassak, Sannikone, and Somsanith.[4]

On August 9, 1960, most members of the Royal Laotian government were in the Royal capital of Luang Prabang, a hundred miles north of Vientiane, attending funeral ceremonies for King Sisavang Vong. Capt. Kong Le, a paratrooper battalion commander, disgusted with the continuing civil war, used this opportunity to take control of Vientiane, dissolve the right-wing cabinet of Prime Minister Prince Somsanith, and invite Prince Souvanna Phouma to form a neutralist government.[5]

When news of the coup reached Luang Prabang, Gen. Phoumi Nosavan, a right-wing military leader who dominated the Sannikone government, flew to his home in Savannakhet. There, with most of the conservatives in the National Assembly, he established a "Committee Against the Coup d'Etat". The U.S. government began backing the Savannakhet group with money and arms while maintaining formal diplomatic relations with the Vientiane government under the Neutralist Souvanna Phouma. In late November Phoumi's troops marched northward up National Route 13, reaching Vientiane in early December. A battle raged around the city for three days before Kong Le retreated northward to the strategic Plain of Jars with the remnants of his followers.[6]

Kong Le, already in a temporary and tenuous alliance with the Pathet Lao and North Vietnamese Army units operating in northeast Laos, began, in early December, receiving arms and supplies from a Soviet airlift. Later that month his forces, with their communist allies, attacked Royal Laotian Army units on the Plain of Jars.[7] On December 16, 1960, the American Air Attaché, Col. Butler B. Toland, Jr., photographed a Soviet IL-14 dropping supplies to the Kong Le forces near Vang Vieng. A few days later, on December 23, Toland, while flying the American Embassy's VC-47 on a reconnaissance flight over the Plain of Jars, was fired upon by Kong Le and Pathet Lao troops. A .50-caliber machine gun bullet wounded Colonel Toland's radio operator. This was the first U.S. Air Force aircraft fired at by the communists in the Southeast Asia conflict.[8]

President John F. Kennedy held a televised news conference on March 23, 1961, at which he announced that the Soviet airlift for the Kong Le Pathet Lao forces had passed the 1,000 sortie mark.[9] Meanwhile, on March 23, Capt. Stanley P. McGee, Jr., pilot of a specially modified intelligence-gathering SC-47, took off from Vientiane for Saigon with his plane loaded with passengers bound for a rest and recuperation visit to "the Paris of the Orient". Before heading for Saigon, McGee turned north toward Xieng Khouangville, a Pathet Lao stronghold on the eastern edge of the Plain of Jars. The crew, experienced in intelligence collection, planned to use their radio-direction finding equipment to determine the frequencies being used by Soviet pilots to locate the Xieng Khouangville airfield through the dense fog that often blanketed the region. Suddenly, shells from a Pathet Lao antiaircraft gun slammed into the aircraft, shearing off a wing and sending the plane plummeting toward the jungle. A U.S. Army major who always wore a parachute when he flew, jumped from the falling aircraft and was captured by the Pathet Lao. He spent seventeen months as a prisoner in Sam Neua, the Pathet Lao headquarters near the North Vietnamese border, before being repatriated after the signing of the Geneva Agreements on Laos in 1962. This shoot-down marked the first American plane lost to enemy action in the war in Indochina.[10]

Had this incident occurred a few years later, a large armada of Air Force rescue helicopters, fighter escorts, and airborne controllers would have responded in an attempt to save the lone survivor. However, in 1961 the Air Rescue Service had no units in Southeast Asia. According to the Department of Defense National Search and Rescue Plan of 1956, search and rescue in the Pacific was the responsibility of the Commander in Chief, Pacific who was, in 1961, Adm. Harry D. Felt. He, in turn, assigned the search and rescue mission to the service or major area commanders: the Commander in Chief, Pacific Air Forces; the Commander, Naval Forces Philippines; or the Commander, Hawaiian Sea Frontier. They, in turn, directed their search and rescue duties to the sub-area or numbered Air Force level. In early 1961, the Thirteenth Air Force was assigned the search and rescue mission for the Saigon, Bangkok, and Rangoon Flight Information Region. Later, the Thirteenth Air Force gave the search and rescue task for this area to 2d Air Division.[11]

Doctrinal considerations made it difficult to identify a role for the Air Rescue Service in Southeast Asia. In 1958, Headquarters USAF withdrew the wartime mission clause from the National Search and Rescue Plan and substituted a precept whereby "wartime SAR" became an extension of peacetime operations. Rescue techniques developed for certain geographical areas were neglected in favor of a standardized approach to rescue that was consistent with the global concept. A crew stationed in Europe, for example, was trained to use the same techniques as a crew based in California. With no official wartime mission, the Air Rescue Service did very little, if any, planning for a combat role.[12]

Even before McGee's SC-47 was shot down, problems in Laos were dominating President Kennedy's attention. At a White House meeting on March 9, 1961, the President directed that certain specific actions be taken to demonstrate American resolve in Laos to the Soviet Union.[13] On March 21, the 315th Air Division (Combat Cargo) started a three-day airlift of Marines from Okinawa to an old Japanese airstrip near Udorn Thani, Thailand, a provincial capital fifty miles south of Vientiane. Kennedy did not, however, want to commit American soldiers to combat in Laos. Therefore sixteen Sikorsky H-34 "Choctaw" helicopters were provided to Air America, a company with government contracts, to fly men and material in Southeast Asia.[14] These helicopters, although flown by civilian crews, were available to fly rescue missions should the need arise. The Air Rescue Service, however, would not have been involved.

Rescue activities increased in importance as the U.S. covertly sent reconnaissance and combat aircraft to Thailand while the North Vietnamese moved more antiaircraft weapons onto the Plain of Jars. The survival of the Neutralist government in Vientiane depended on the acquisition of useful intelligence about enemy activities, so aerial reconnaissance became increasingly important. The Royal Thai Air Force had been providing reconnaissance support to Laos with their RT-33A jets, but in February 1961 Thailand's military dictator Marshal Sarit Thanarat withdrew that support. The loss of the American SC-47 on March 23 further weakened the reconnaissance capability. Only the air attaché's VC-47 remained available for Laotian reconnaissance, and it could hardly be expected to survive in the increasingly dangerous antiaircraft environment that was developing on the Plain of Jars.[15]

From the time of Sarit's withdrawal of Thai reconnaissance airplanes the Joint Chiefs of Staff had been recommending an Air Force reconnaissance unit be sent to Thailand. President Kennedy vetoed the suggested use of U.S. Air Force RF-101 jets, and suggested instead that Admiral Felt borrow RT-33s from the Philippine Air Force, paint them with Laotian markings, and use Air Force pilots to fly reconnaissance missions over Laos.[16] On April 24, 1961, the first American-piloted RT-33 sortie flew from Udorn under the code name "Field Goal".

Meanwhile, the Air Force mission in Thailand and Laos continued. Additionally, on April 16, six F-100 Super Saber fighters, under the code name "Bell Tone", flew from the 510th Tactical Fighter Squadron at Clark AFB, Philippines to Don Muang International Airport outside Bangkok, Thailand to provide air defense.[17] The Royal Thai Air Force agreed to provide search and rescue services to this unit. However, their rescue capability proved too limited to meet the needs of either Air America or the Air Force.[18]

On the political front, President Kennedy and Soviet Premier Nikita Khrushchev realized their two countries were on a possible collision course in Laos.[19] In April 1961, the United States and the Soviet Union agreed to defuse the situation by arranging a cease-fire and calling for an international conference to work out a political solution to the Laotian problem. The Geneva Conference on Laos opened on May 16, 1961, and lasted through July 23, 1962. While the Geneva talks proceeded, the three Lao factions − Neutralists, Pathet Lao, and rightists − alternated armed conflict with separate negotiations until all factions, in Laos and in Switzerland, finally agreed on a delicate settlement. As a result, Prince Souvanna Phouma established a coalition government which lasted from July 1962 until fighting resumed in April 1963. During this period the focus in the Indochina conflict shifted to South Vietnam where U.S. support for the Saigon government was evidenced by a growing American military presence, an increasing number of combat deaths and, in early 1962, the assignment of Air Rescue Service personnel.

In May 1959, at its fifteenth meeting, the Lao Dong (communist) party of North Vietnam, decided to take control of the infant insurgency in South Vietnam and guide its growth. Southern cadres, who had gone north for indoctrination and training, trekked south along a network of footpaths soon to be expanded into the Ho Chi Minh Trail.[20] These footpaths ran north to south along the Annamite mountains and fanned out into the jungles of South Vietnam. This terrain favored unconventional warfare. The guerrillas could hide in the monsoon forest and jungle that covered sixty percent of the nation. The forest canopy rose as high as 200 to 250 feet above the jungle floor − a factor that complicated the efforts of rescue forces whenever a plane was shot down in tree-covered areas of Vietnam or Laos.

Much of South Vietnam is mountainous. The Annamite chain runs southward from North Vietnam, straddling the Laotian border on the west and extending to the South China Sea on the east. These jungled mountains and limestone outcroppings, sometimes rising to 8,500 feet, presented a hazardous obstacle to low flying planes. Following bail-out some pilots were killed when they landed on the jagged karst and others suffered broken bones as they came down through the branches of the multi-layered jungle canopy. Disaster often resulted when helicopters attempted to rescue a downed airman from a tree-shrouded peak because the higher altitudes overextended their limited hover capabilities.[21]

The southern third of South Vietnam consists of flat lands and the Mekong River delta. One of the great rivers of Asia, the Mekong provides the southern part of Vietnam with 26,000 square miles of delta, 9,000 miles of which can be cultivated. Nowhere is the land higher than ten feet above sea level. The southernmost tip, the Ca Mau Peninsula is covered by thick jungles and mangrove swamps. Rescue forces, therefore, had to prepare for operations that ranged from mountainous jungles to swamps.

South Vietnam's climate was as debilitating as its geography was rugged and hostile. The temperature in Saigon occasionally reached 104 degrees Fahrenheit and rarely dipped below 80 degrees, while the humidity was always high. Major air masses blew from the northeast in the winter bringing dry weather to most of Southeast Asia. From May through October, however, the winds blew from the southwest frequently bringing more than forty inches of torrential rainfall. During this period most of South Vietnam experienced heavy precipitation, low cloud ceilings, chronic fog, and poor visibility. When the rains came, equipment often became inoperable, roads impassable, and flying nearly impossible.[22]

Before the war, South Vietnam was a place of exotic beauty. The streets of Saigon, its capital, bustled with crowds of hawkers, vendors, and taxicabs each adding an ingredient of charm to the city. Saigon was the administrative capital of the Republic of Vietnam but, for all it shared with the countryside, the city might as well have been situated on the banks of the Seine as on the Mekong. In contrast to the busy charm of Saigon, the countryside possessed a bucolic beauty. There the peasants passed their lives unaltered through successive generations until politics, revolution, and military technology brought them misery, privation, and death.[23]

The Viet Cong intensified its guerrilla war against President Ngo Dinh Diem's regime early in 1961. By March, U.S. intelligence analysts estimated that the guerrillas were killing, assassinating, or kidnapping five hundred pro-government village officials, teachers, and soldiers every month. Secretary of State Dean Rusk reported at a Washington press conference on May 4, 1961, that the Viet Cong had grown to 12,000 in number and had killed or kidnapped more than 3,000 persons in 1960.[24] Although the rebellion in South Vietnam was originally an indigenous revolt against the Diem regime, its stepped-up pace after 1959 was the result of North Vietnamese intervention.[25]

On October 11, 1961, President Kennedy authorized the sending of a U.S. Air Force unit to South Vietnam. The following day, a detachment of the 4400th Combat Crew Training Squadron, code-named "Farm Gate", flew to South Vietnam. Stationed at Bien Hoa Air Base just north of Saigon, the 4400th CCTS flew combat modified T-28 fighter-bomber trainers, SC-47s, and B-26s, redesignated "Reconnaissance Bombers"

(RB-26s) in deference to the 1954 Geneva Conventions prohibition against the introduction of bombers into Indochina. On December 16, Secretary of Defense Robert S. McNamara authorized participation in combat operations, provided a Vietnamese crewmember was aboard the strike aircraft.[26]

On November 15, 1961, Detachment 7 of the Thirteenth Air Force was established at Tan Son Nhut Airfield, Saigon. Five days later Brig. Gen. Rollen H. Anthis, Vice Commander of the Thirteenth Air Force, became Commander, Detachment 7, 2d ADVON (Advanced Echelon). On December 1 he was named Chief, Air Force Section, Military Assistance Advisory Group/Vietnam.[27]

Air activity increased as the American presence grew during the early years. On January 13, 1962, Farm Gate T-28s flew their first Vietnamese forward air controller directed mission, supporting an Army of the Republic of Vietnam outpost that was under Viet Cong attack. On January 29, T-28s and RB-26s struck targets from Saigon north to Quang Tri Province near the demilitarized zone. By the end of the month Farm Gate crews had flown a total of 229 sorties.[28] Meanwhile, the detachment's SC-47s were used in transport missions, leaflet drops, psychological warfare broadcasts, and flare drop operations.

When the U.S. Air Force began flying combat missions, American casualties were inevitable. Were Air Force planners remiss in not securing adequate search and rescue forces for Vietnam prior to the commitment of American units? Throughout Southeast Asia several factors, political and technological as well as doctrinal, complicated the campaign for adequate search and rescue support.

The same doctrinal considerations that made it difficult to send the Air Rescue Service to Thailand in support of air operations in Laos, also made it difficult to assign rescue units to Vietnam. Furthermore, the leadership at Air Rescue Service headquarters was not convinced that it had a legitimate wartime rescue mission.[29] Because their approach was for peacetime search and rescue and because they had no official wartime mission, Air Rescue Service planners had not planned for a wartime situation.[30]

In South Vietnam political considerations also hindered the early involvement of rescue units. Farm Gate's role in combat was semi-covert and politically sensitive. Since U.S. aircrews were supposedly conducting training missions only, there should have been little chance that anyone would be shot down. The presence of regular search and rescue forces, however, complete with helicopters and HU-16 amphibians, would have advertised the existence of air operations with a casualty potential far greater than that to be expected in the course of normal flight training.[31]

The rescue vehicles in the 1961 Air Rescue Service inventory were ill-suited for search and rescue in jungles and mountains. The rescue concepts and limited fiscal resources of the late 1950s had forced the ARS to give up most of its helicopters. Acquisition of the local base rescue function restored some choppers, but these HH-43 "Huskies" were primarily used in fire-fighting and picking up pilots who had bailed out in close proximity to an air base.

In December 1961 the Commander of the Pacific Air Rescue Center sent three officers and two enlisted men to Saigon to establish a Search and Rescue Center in the Air Operations Center at Tan Son Nhut Air Base. The rescue personnel arrived at the operations center the next month only to find that there were no phones, desks, or chairs available for them in the prefabricated Jamesway huts that served as the control center for air strikes in Vietnam. After gathering the necessary phones, tables, and chairs, these men began operating as a coordinating center for rescue activities. In order to limit the magnitude of the U.S. involvement in Vietnam, no provision had been made for the use of Air Rescue Service aircraft. To overcome this limitation the rescue coordinators contacted Army advisors in each of the four corps areas and obtained agreements whereby U.S. Army helicopters could be used to assist in 2d Air Division rescue efforts, provided they were not needed elsewhere.[32]

The first Air Force casualties in Vietnam occurred when a twin-engine Fairchild C-123 Ranch Hand crop defoliation airplane crashed on February 2, 1962. Capt. Fergus C. Groves, Capt. Robert D. Larson, and SSgt. Milo B. Coghill died in that crash.[33] There was no record of any search and rescue effort. Nine days later the first Farm Gate aircraft was lost. Shortly before dawn on Sunday, February 11, a Farm Gate SC-47 with eight U.S. Air Force and Army advisors plus two Vietnamese left Saigon on a leaflet-dropping mission. At eight-thirty in the morning a province chief reported a twin-engine aircraft had crashed in the mountains near his village, about seventy miles northeast of Saigon. The Saigon search and rescue center arranged for a helicopter to carry a Vietnamese Army ground party to the crash area to locate the wreckage and search for survivors. They arrived by mid-afternoon and reported that the wreckage was the Farm Gate SC-47 and that all on board were dead. The next day a combined Air Force-Army search team at the crash site was puzzled to find only nine bodies instead of the ten manifested for the mission. Further investigation revealed that one of the two Vietnamese had decided, at the last minute, not to make the flight.[34]

The number of U.S. and Vietnamese Air Force combat sorties increased rapidly in early 1962. At the beginning of the year the Vietnamese Air Force combat inventory consisted of twenty-two A-1 Skyraiders. Under the Military Assistance Program, thirty T-28s were delivered in early March. This increase in Vietnamese Air Force strength enabled Saigon to mount a fifty plane raid on a Viet Cong headquarters in the central highlands on May 27,1962. During this same period, A-1 sorties increased from 150 in January to 390 in June.[35]

As the Farm Gate T-28s and RB-26s pressed their low-level attacks, the

Viet Cong improved their countermeasures. The principal Viet Cong antiaircraft weapons were the 12.7-mm Soviet or Chinese-built heavy machinegun and small arms.[36] In the last four months of 1962, the enemy scored 89 hits against Farm Gate and other U.S. Air Force planes. In the first four months of 1963, this figure jumped to 257 as the Viet Cong increased their accuracy. The pilots found the enemy fire most deadly as they pulled out of their bomb runs below 1,000 feet.[37] Before the year ended the Air Force had lost six aircraft to enemy action.[38]

In response to the increasing pace of air activity, the three officers and two noncommissioned officers at the search and rescue center at Tan Son Nhut were officially established as Detachment 3, Pacific Air Rescue Center, on April 1, 1962.[39] This lent a certain legitimacy to the first Air Rescue Service cadre and gave a sense of permanency to the rescue effort in Vietnam. Nevertheless, considerably more rescue personnel and helicopters were needed to pick up downed aircrew members, yet these were not forthcoming. The rescue controllers at Tan Son Nhut had to rely on the resources available: Farm Gate aircraft and a few Army H-21 and Marine H-34 helicopters. The Vietnamese Air Force possessed a limited chopper inventory which was available for rescue work, but the Vietnamese had no trained rescue personnel.[40]

To facilitate rescue operations, South Vietnam and the United States signed the Joint Vietnamese/U.S. Search and Rescue Agreement in 1962. It established policies for mutual coordination and control of search and rescue efforts within the Republic of Vietnam.[41] According to the agreement, the Vietnamese were responsible for civil search and rescue and for rescue operations for their own forces. Search and rescue efforts in support of U.S. forces became the responsibility of the Commander, U.S. Military Assistance Command, Vietnam, and the Commander, 2d Air Division.[42] This agreement also defined procedural matters and emphasized the importance of cooperation and prompt action by any agency "to relieve distress wherever found."[43] This document meant little to the men flying combat missions in 1962 since both Vietnamese and American forces were ill-equipped to fulfill their responsibilities under the terms of this agreement.[44]

Rescue operations varied greatly, with geography, weather, time of day, and the disposition of friendly and enemy forces as contributing factors. However, a general search and rescue pattern developed early in the Vietnam war. When an aircraft was overdue at its destination, this was reported to Detachment 3, Pacific Air Rescue Center at Tan Son Nhut. The rescue controller then asked the senior controller to have all available aircraft search for the crash site. As soon as the wreckage of the missing plane was found, the commander of Detachment 3 marshalled whatever forces he could for the rescue effort. As noted earlier, the Army and the Marines had agreed to make their helicopters available whenever they were not needed elsewhere. Usually, American forces were used for these rescue attempts, but if they were unavailable, the search and rescue commander had to rely on the Vietnamese. Once the rescue force was on the way, the Detachment 3 commander would then fly to the crash area by chopper. If the site was located more than a hundred miles from Saigon, he took whatever transportation he could muster, usually a C-47 or C-123 to a base nearby.[45] He then assembled a small force and flew by helicopter to a clearing near the wreckage. Occasionally a Vietnamese Army company or even a battalion was required to secure the area before a landing party could be set down near the downed aircraft — the survivors or the bodies were carried back to the helicopter landing zone.[46]

Some of the problems encountered during rescue attempts in the period before Air Rescue Service helicopters and trained rescue personnel reached Southeast Asia were illustrated in a rescue operation that occurred in October 1963. On the afternoon of October 8, GRAD OK 01 and GRAD OK 02, a pair of Farm Gate T-28s, rolled in on a target in the mountainous jungle area near the Laotian border west of Da Nang. The American pilot of GRAD OK 02 bore in low on his bomb run unaware that it was to be his last. The second pilot watched as GRAD OK 02 went out of control near the end of its dive and disintegrated upon impact. GRAD OK 01 returned to base and at the mission debriefing reported the aircraft down in the jungle near a swollen stream that flowed into the Buong. Maj. Alan W. Saunders, Commander, Detachment 3, Pacific Air Rescue Center, was notified at his office in Saigon. Saunders gathered the members of his rescue team, a two-man explosive ordnance detail, a flying safety officer, and a photographer. Within the hour they took off for Da Nang on a C-123.

When Saunders reached Da Nang he assumed the role of on-scene-commander. Briefers told him that two U.S. Marine H-34s had flown to the crash site only a few hours earlier and disappeared in an area known as "V.C. [Viet Cong] Valley". This upped the ante.

At dawn Marine helicopters lifted two Vietnamese Infantry companies to the area of the downed aircraft. As the helicopters landed, enemy troops firing from the surrounding hillsides wounded three U.S. Marine crewmen and killed a Vietnamese soldier. Farm Gate T-28s, B-26s and a Vietnamese Air Force propeller-driven A-1 Skyraider responded by strafing the enemy positions. An American L-19 light observation plane directing the strike aircraft took a hit that punctured a fuel line and wounded the Vietnamese observer. The American pilot nursed his crippled craft with its suffering Vietnamese observer back to a forced landing in friendly territory. Meanwhile, the Vietnamese Army force landed and began hacking out a larger landing zone to facilitate future landings. When that task was finished the troops started working their way to the site of the H-34 crashes. They reached the downed helicopters the next morning, October 10, only to find the remains of 10 of the 12 persons who had been aboard the two aircraft. The other two, if they survived, were probably carried off by the Viet Cong.

On October 11 Marine helicopters airlifted Major Saunders and his rescue team to the landing zone where they encountered heavy fire from hostile forces located nearby. The pilots diverted to a clear area along the stream about two-and-a-half miles northeast of the T-28 wreckage. Saunders then led his party through the dense jungle underbrush rather than along the trails to lessen the risk of encountering Viet Cong booby traps. It was several hours before they hacked their way to the partially submerged wreckage of the T-28. They found a wing partially under water at the edge of the swollen stream and a horizontal stabilizer on the opposite bank. The rest of the debris was either under water or strewn out along the opposite shore. The photographer made pictures while the flying safety officer cut a spar from the wing to document the location of the crash.

The Marine helicopter crew, not wanting to fly after dark, radioed Saunders to be back at the landing zone no later than 1700, or risk spending the night in Viet Cong territory. Still fearful of communist booby traps or ambushes along the jungle trails, the tired party started cutting their way back through the tangled jungle underbrush. The flying safety officer sprained his ankle jumping a ravine and had to be carried, further slowing their progress. The hot sun was moving closer to the horizon when Saunders radioed for a thirty-minute extension on the pickup deadline. Reluctantly the marines agreed, and the exhausted men struggled on through the stifling heat and binding bush, reaching the landing zone with only ten minutes to spare. The first helicopter appeared overhead promptly at 1730. The flying safety officer and one of the explosive ordnance detail members had just climbed on board when enemy fire ripped into the engine, putting the H-34 out of commission. The crewmembers, the flying safety officer, and the man from the explosive ordnance detail scurried from the damaged chopper to seek cover along the edge of the landing zone. While a U.S. Army Bell UH-1D "Huey" helicopter and a pair of T-28s bombed and strafed the ridge line, Saunders crept back to the disabled H-34, and determined it was impossible to fly. As soon as the hostile fire was silenced the second H-34 set down and snatched the Americans to safety. The 120 Vietnamese Army troops in the clearing spent the night in Viet Cong territory before being lifted out the next morning.

Meanwhile, Saunders returned to Saigon to check on business at Detachment 3 and file reports on the search and rescue effort. On October 14 he flew to Da Nang once again, this time to organize a return to the T-28 crash in an effort to find any clues as to the fate of the crew. He arranged for a Green Beret team to lead a Vietnam Army ranger unit providing escort. At dawn a Marine H-34 carried Saunders, the Green Berets, and the rangers back to the landing zone originally cut out of the jungle on October 11. Some enemy resistance slowed their progress, so that they did not reach the T-28 wreckage until the following day. The unexamined portion of the debris rested on the opposite side of the swollen stream, so the Green Berets led the Vietnamese rangers across the swiftly flowing water. Viet Cong ambushers opened fire on the party as it emerged from the stream but were soon silenced as the Vietnamese Army pressed ahead with its clearing operation. The night passed quietly, but the communists attacked at dawn forcing the South Vietnamese rangers to take up positions on a ridgeline overlooking the crash site. After the area finally was cleared, Saunders organized an intensive search that lasted for three days. Other than the pilot's headset, no sign of the missing men was ever found. Saunders believed that either the Viet Cong had killed the two men, or they had been carried away in the fast moving waters of the swollen stream. A helicopter then extracted the team without further incident.[47]

Saunders' efforts in the GRAD OK 02 mission underscored the fact that combat rescues required more than a crew, a helicopter, and good intentions. During this "dark age of SAR", men often died in attempting a rescue simply because the available crews lacked rescue training and were ignorant of proper recovery procedures. There was a misconception on the part of some Army helicopter crewmen, shared by their Marine and Vietnamese counterparts, that rescue entailed nothing more than flying over a downed crewman and picking him up. In each case, problems encountered in mountains, jungles, and water pickups required specialization, as the following cases illustrate.

On March 9, 1963, an Army OV-1 "Mohawk" twin-engine reconnaissance aircraft crashed near the top of a 6,000-foot mountain in the central highlands. Two Marine H-34D helicopters attempted to land a four-man American-Vietnamese rescue team at the crash site. One of the helicopters hovered over the tall jungle canopy while a Vietnamese airman was lowered on a cable. The short cable forced the helicopter to hover close to the tree tops. Suddenly it stalled and fell through the trees killing the dangling Vietnamese. The crewmembers crawled from the burning craft before it exploded; however, the severely burned copilot died during the night. The next morning, a second Marine helicopter, attempting the same pickup, met with the fate of its predecessor. This time two crewmen were injured, but no one was killed.[48] Nevertheless, two men died and two others were injured during the rescue attempt.

There were other rescue fiascos. Darkness was closing in on the coast of Vietnam on a November day in 1963, when a U.S. Army helicopter pilot lost his bearings and flew his Huey into the water off the fishing village of Nha Trang. The next morning the copilot was found, cold, tired, with his arm broken, but alive near the beach. At the debriefing, he said that after plowing into the water all four men on board successfully abandoned the sinking helicopter. Though caught in an outgoing tide, optimism heightened when other Army helicopters appeared overhead and an Air Force C-47 dropped flares to make it "bright as day." With the shore clearly in sight, the men waited in the water for a quick pickup. Instead of dipping in to snatch the men to safety, the circling choppers formed a line and flew off into the dark. The four men struggled with the outgoing tide as they watched the coast line grow dim in the eerie green light of the flare swinging rhythmically toward the waiting water. The copilot found that, with a broken arm, he could not fight the merciless tide. He rolled on his back and concentrated on conserving his energy while his comrades flailed at the water, only to exhaust themselves and disappear into the murky depths. Finally, the tide turned and washed the pain-racked copilot onto the shore. He managed to drag himself off the beach to hide in the bushes until dawn when he felt safe from the local Viet Cong. Shortly after sunrise a Vietnamese Army search party found the shivering, but still-living copilot. At the debriefing he asked why the helicopters flew away when rescue seemed so close. He was told that the local U.S. Army commander decided that since one pilot lost his bearings and dumped his machine into the sea, others might do the same in the darkness.[49]

In early January 1964, four Americans, a Vietnamese crewmember, and a Royal Air Force wing commander flying as an observer, were aboard an armed Huey that crashed into the mouth of the Mekong after being hit by Viet Cong small arms fire. The helicopter sank rapidly, carrying two trapped crewmen to their deaths. The pilot, copilot, Vietnamese crewman, and the British officer escaped, treading water while another Huey circled in for the pickup. The helicopter dipped low and came straight up to the waiting men. As it hovered over the water, the rotor wash created a frontal wave that drowned the hapless pilot. With the pilot dead, the would-be rescuer wheeled his helicopter around to aid another survivor. A crewmember had the man by the hand, and was hauling him to safety, when an Army H-21 that was circling overhead, radioed instructions to clear the area so Mae West life vests could be dropped. The crewmember loosed his grip and watched the horror-struck face of the victim slip beneath the muddy water. The other two men were rescued, and two bodies washed up on the shore the following morning.[50]

Alan Saunders was not the sort of person who could accept the grim outlook resulting from the lack of adequate rescue forces. In the absence of trained search and rescue personnel, he worked to give some specialized training to Army helicopter crews. A helicopter "cockpit" was placed at the edge of the swimming pool at Bien Hoa Air Base, and helicopter crewmen were strapped into this contraption and dumped into the water. They had to unstrap themselves, get out of the cockpit, inflate their life vests, swim to a raft and climb into it.[51]

Detachment 3 personnel made other attempts to improve their overall search and rescue capability. The procurement of mobile communications equipment improved the rescue control capability of the on-scene commander. Litter baskets, medical kits, and homing devices were obtained and put into use, and more Army chopper crews started carrying 200 to 250-foot ropes to haul downed crewmen out of the jungle.[52]

Throughout the mid-fifties and into the early 1960s, the Army suffered in the acquisition of sophisticated military hardware in comparison to the Air Force and Navy. The Air Force had its ever-improving bomber force and its increasingly more sophisticated fighters. New supercarriers and ballistic missile firing submarines came into the Navy's inventory. Together, the Air Force and the Navy dominated the Army in the cold war period. Vietnam breathed new life into the Army as it latched onto the helicopter as the vehicle to salvage its position in the interservice rivalry.[53]

U.S. Army commanders in Vietnam fostered the interests of their service from the beginning of the Southeast Asia buildup. The Army had the dominant voice at MACV because they held not only the commander and deputy commander positions, but also four of the six staff positions.[54] The Army used its dominant position to advantage as American aviation in Vietnam expanded between 1961 and 1964. Leading the way, the Army increased its aircraft inventory in Vietnam from 40 helicopters and planes in 1961 to over 100 in 1962 and 325 in 1963. The Air Force, on the other hand, had 35 aircraft in Vietnam in 1961 and two years later, had only 117 airplanes.[55]

Army aircraft in Vietnam in the early 1960s included the OV-1 intelligence collection plane, the C-7 light transport, as well as the H-21 and UH-1 helicopters. The UH-1s were used as transports and for suppressive fire missions on occasion. Choppers rapidly became the mainstay of Army aviation in Vietnam. By 1963, the Army had a virtual monopoly on helicopters in the escalating war and they had no intention of relinquishing it.

On November 27, 1961, Secretary of Defense Robert S. McNamara established the position of Commander, U.S. Military Assistance Command/Vietnam (COMUSMACV), as a four-star Army general's post, and by 1963 the Army had six of the nine top officer positions on the MACV staff. The Air Force held only one position, that of Director J-5 (Plans). The Air Force, the Navy, and the Marines combined had only 135 of the 335 staff positions at MACV in 1964 while the Army filled 200 slots. Of the approximately 16,000 U.S. military personnel in Vietnam at the end of 1963, roughly 10,000 were Army, 4,600 were Air Force, 1,200 were Navy and Marines, and 200 were in the Coast Guard.[56]

A message from Headquarters, Thirteenth Air Force in PACAF in October 1962 indicated the increasing tension between the U.S. Army and the U.S. Air Force as the Vietnam commitment grew in the early sixties:

> USAF interests are suffering in SEA. The trend toward an Army dominated and controlled COIN (Counter-insurgency) effort is clear. Because the USAF position in COMUSMACV's structure is weak in both numbers and rank, the Army is able to impose their will . . . Their case will cost the USAF in roles and missions and will cost U.S. lives in future actions. Army people are, in effect, being trained to consider our tactics

ineffective and our capability limited, while being oversold on Army organic air. [57]

After Major Saunders arrived to take command of Detachment 3, Pacific Air Rescue Center, in June 1963, he embarked on a campaign to secure Air Rescue Service forces for Southeast Asia. He began a study of search and rescue requirements in late August which led to a report recommending that an Air Force rescue force be assigned to Vietnam. [58]

At the time Saunders wrote his report, nine Air Force planes had been shot down and nine others lost to unknown or non-hostile causes. [59] Nineteen airmen were dead or missing and six others had been injured. The Army sustained even higher losses: 26 aircraft shot down, 32 lost for non-hostile reasons, and twenty Army aviators killed. [60] Saunders feared the worst still lay ahead. His study cited the annual movement of 14,000 American military personnel through Vietnam, and the possible consequences of a crash involving a transport carrying 100 or more people. Saunders believed if this happened in the jungle, "We would be helpless . . . it would be a disaster." [61]

The study emphasized that U.S. Army, Marine Corps, and Vietnamese aircraft were not always available for search and rescue missions. Furthermore, they were subject to recall at their respective commander's discretion. In any event, as Saunders noted, these helicopter crews had no formal rescue training. [62]

Saunders completed the search and rescue study in September and submitted it to the commander of the 2d Air Division, Maj. Gen. Rollen H. Anthis. Saunders suggested that after the study was endorsed it should be sent to Adm. Harry D. Felt (CINCPAC) via the Thirteenth Air Force and PACAF to preclude MACV interference. He believed MACV wanted to make use of the fact that the Air Force was using Army helicopters in its search and rescue effort as justification for obtaining additional choppers. General Anthis submitted the plan as Saunders suggested, throwing his full support behind it by enclosing a letter to PACAF in which he stated, "The SAR requirement exists and increases daily." [63]

PACAF concurred with the study, but Admiral Felt insisted on coordinating it with MACV before sending it to the Joint Chiefs of Staff. Consequently the study came back to MACV where it remained until Saunders followed it up in February 1964. His queries were not well received by the Army leadership at MACV. According to Saunders one U.S. Army colonel admitted he was sitting on the report because he thought the Army's helicopters could handle the search and rescue requirements, provided they made a few equipment modifications and instituted a rescue training program. [64]

The 2d Air Division study bounced back and forth between MACV and CINCPAC for the next three months. During this time PACAF, the Air Rescue Service, and the Air Force began planning for the first rescue units.

SEARCH AND RESCUE

Back in September 1963, when the search and rescue study was completed, Brig. Gen. Adriel N. Williams, commander of the Air Rescue Service, told Gen. Joe W. Kelly, commander of the Military Air Transport Service, that the Air Rescue Service lacked sufficient equipment to perform the Southeast Asia mission as outlined in the Saunders study. He pointed out that the only helicopter in the rescue service's inventory was the short-range HH-43B helicopter used to fight fires and rescue aircrews from crashes either on the runway or near the air base. General Williams asked for six of the new, longer-range, higher-speed, Sikorsky CH-3 helicopters, which he believed would be able to meet the requirements of aircrew rescue in Southeast Asia. But, the CH-3s programmed into the Air Force were already allocated to the space vehicle and astronaut recovery mission. As an alternative, the Air Rescue Service decided to modify the HH-43B to make it better suited for combat aircrew recovery. Modifications included the addition of armor plate, installation of a larger self-sealing fuel tank, a bigger engine, and gun mounts. The modified version would be redesignated the HH-43F. However, Kaman Aircraft Corporation indicated these improvements would not be completed before October 1964.[65]

Meanwhile, the need for some sort of rescue helicopter in Southeast Asia increased. In March 1964, six HH-43Bs, three from PACAF and three from Air Force units in the States, were obtained for Southeast Asia through an agreement between Maj. Gen. Jamie Gough, Director of Operations at Headquarters, USAF, and Maj. Gen. Glen W. Martin, Deputy Chief of Staff, Plans and Operations at PACAF.[66]

Squabbling between CINCPAC and MACV, however, delayed arrival of these helicopters through April. Two issues formed the basis for contention. First, Air Force involvement in Southeast Asia was semicovert. Search and rescue forces would underline American participation in secret operations like Farm Gate and the controversial Ranch Hand defoliation program. Additionally, to keep these operations covert, strict manpower ceilings were imposed on the Air Force. The introduction of search and rescue units would increase the number of Air Force personnel in Vietnam by eighty-six men. Second, there was the question of conceptual differences between the Army and the Air Force and their fight over the use and mission of helicopters. In May the Joint Chiefs of Staff resolved these issues by assigning the Southeast Asia rescue mission to the Air Force. From that point events moved rapidly with CINCPAC approving the introduction of Air Force search and rescue helicopters and crews into Vietnam and the Joint Chiefs directing the Chief of Staff of the Air Force to deploy rescue units.[67]

Meanwhile, immediately following the signing of the *Protocol to the Declaration on the Neutrality of Laos* on July 23, 1962, American activity slackened as the United States reduced its military presence to conform with the requirements of the Geneva Convention. This respite in hostilities left the North Vietnamese and their Pathet Lao clients in control of more than half the country. North Vietnamese Army porters continued to hustle arms and supplies down the eastern Laotian corridor trails to South Vietnam while the Pathet Lao recruited new followers and steeled themselves for future struggles in northern Laos.[68] In response to these flagrant violations of the Geneva agreements, the United States conducted RF-101 reconnaissance flights under the code name "Able Mable" to check on activity along the infiltration routes and in the Plain of Jars area. Though no U.S. Air Force planes flying over Laos were lost to enemy activity during this respite, the communists did fire on American reconnaissance missions. On August 14, 1962, an Able Mable RF-101, flying near Phong Savan on the eastern edge of the Plain of Jars was hit by 37-mm and 57-mm antiaircraft artillery fire. The pilot brought his crippled aircraft back to Don Muang and made a successful wheels up landing.[69] One week later another RF-101 pilot reported 100 to 200 rounds of 37-mm or 57-mm antiaircraft fire directed from the same area. The cloud cover and 10,000-foot altitude of the RF-101 suggested the probable use of radar-controlled antiaircraft weapons — a significant escalation in the Laotian air war.[70]

This increase in enemy antiaircraft weapons heightened the threat to American aircraft. Although the Air Rescue Service had no helicopters in Southeast Asia to respond to rescue situations, there were plenty of choppers throughout the region. Air America, Continental Air Service, and Bird and Son, air transport companies with U.S. Government contracts, made their helicopters and light planes available to meet rescue requirements as they arose. The pilots who worked for these companies acquired many hours of flying experience and had an intimate familiarity with the peculiarities of Laotian terrain and climatic conditions.[71] Additionally, the Royal Thai Air Force had a very limited search and rescue force composed of a handful of Sikorsky H-19s and two Kaman HH-43B Huskies delivered at the end of June 1962.[72]

Political agreements reached at Geneva proved too weak to keep together the tenuous coalition that made up the Royal Laotian Government. Sporadic fighting continued on the Plain of Jars and throughout south central Laos, as Pathet Lao, Neutralists, and rightist elements vied with each other to gain the upper hand. Throughout the summer of 1963, while Souvanna Phouma tried to convince his communist-influenced step-brother Souphanouvong to reenter the coalition government, Pathet Lao and North Vietnamese units continued their offensives. By the end of 1963 flagrant communist violations of the 1962 agreements made it apparent that a more forceful American demonstration was appropriate. On March 5, 1964, Secretary of Defense Robert S. McNamara approved the assignment of Detachment 6, 1st Air Commando Wing, to Udorn Royal Thai Air Force Base. Known by the nickname "Waterpump", its mission was to train Laotian and Thai pilots and maintenance personnel. Not coincidentally, this unit also provided a readily available source of U.S. controlled aircraft to augment the tiny Royal Laotian Air Force. Although formally attached to the 2d Air Division in Saigon, in reality Detachment 6 was responsible to U.S. Ambassador Leonard Unger in Vientiane.[73]

On March 16, 1964, all semblance of peace in Laos vanished as the Pathet Lao, with North Vietnamese backing, attacked across the Plain of Jars. Neutralist and Royal Laotian Government forces evaporated in the path of the enemy advance. In response, the United States resumed RF-101 reconnaissance flights on May 19 under the nickname "Yankee Team". U.S. Navy RF-8A and RA-3B reconnaissance planes from the Seventh Fleet in the Gulf of Tonkin joined in this effort with Air Force RF-101s from Detachment 1, 33rd Tactical Group based at Tan Son Nhut Air Base, Republic of Vietnam.[74]

Photo interpreters scrutinizing Yankee Team pictures found that the Plain of Jars was bristling with antiaircraft artillery with sixteen 37-mm and 57-mm antiaircraft sites on or around the plain. These guns, capable of firing 150 rounds per minute, were effective up to 4,500 and 15,000 feet respectively. Since most Yankee Team missions flew at minimum altitudes (below 1,500 feet), the 12.7-mm and 14.5-mm heavy machine guns, with an effective range of 1,800 and 3,000 feet and a high rate of fire, also presented a hazard.[75]

Yankee Team missions made the presence of a professional search and rescue force even more important, since the capture of an American airman in Laos would have had an adverse international political effect. Although the Joint Chiefs of Staff had approved sending Air Rescue Service helicopters to Vietnam, this force was not in place. Even stationed in Vietnam, the short-range HH-43s would have been of no use for rescue missions in northern Laos. Air America's limited search and rescue capability was considered inadequate to meet the potential danger. The Commander of 2d Air Division, Maj. Gen. Joseph H. Moore, recognized these limitations, and on May 29 moved to correct them by asking PACAF for permission to use Air Force aircraft for search and rescue in Laos.[76]

During the first week in June, General Moore traveled to Udorn to confer with the Deputy Commander of 2d Air Division, Col. Jack Catlin. The subject was a search and rescue conference scheduled to begin on June 15. While visiting Udorn the rescue problem in northern Laos was vividly and tragically illustrated for General Moore.

A few minutes after noon on June 6, Eagle Green, a Royal Laotian Air Force T-28, picked up a mayday call from Corktip 920, a Navy RF-8A Yankee Team reconnaissance plane piloted by Lt. Charles Klusmann. Corktip 32 reported his wingman down south of the village of Ban Ban deep inside communist-controlled territory and only twenty miles from the North Vietnamese border.[77] An Air America C-123 cargo plane also heard the call for help and flew to the general area to assume the role of on-scene commander. An Air America U-10 single-engine aircraft also joined the search, and within an hour they located the pilot. Three hours after the call for help went out, two Air America helicopters arrived at the crash scene, but as they approached to make the recovery, the entire area erupted in gunfire. The enemy had employed a tactic he would use often during the next ten years: the flak trap. While allowing the injured survivor to call for help, enemy gunners positioned themselves to wait for the arrival of the vulnerable helicopters. In this case both Air America choppers were hit and two men were critically wounded. The helicopters abandoned their efforts and headed for the nearest Lima Site (landing strip and base area in Laos).[78]

It was evident to General Moore that the rescue forces faced heavy opposition. He contacted Gen. Jacob E. Smart, Commander in Chief, Pacific Air Forces, who authorized the use of Air Force aircraft and pilots in combat operations to rescue the downed Navy pilot. Meanwhile, Lt. Col. Robert Tyrrell, U.S. air attaché in Vientiane, dispatched four T-28s from Wattay Airport outside the capital. These Thai-piloted Laotian planes failed to find their target, so General Moore ordered three more T-28s, some with American pilots, from Wattay. It was too late. When these planes arrived over the crash site there was no sign of Klusmann who had been hauled off to captivity. With the weather deteriorating, General Moore ordered the search called off shortly before sunset.[79]

The following day Pathet Lao and North Vietnamese gunners brought down a second Navy fighter. Old Nick 110, an F-8D piloted by Cdr. D.W. Lynn, was hit while escorting an RF-8A reconnaissance plane in the same area where Corktip 920 went down. Old Nick's wingman called the mayday at approximately two in the afternoon, reported that the commander's chute had opened, and passed coordinates to controllers at the Air Support Operations Center at Udorn. The controllers there passed the information to the Air Operations Center in Vientiane, and to Detachment 3, Pacific Air Rescue Center at Tan Son Nhut.[80] Air America H-34 Choctaws and Laotian-based T-28s responded in a rescue attempt that included an area search three miles either side of a point given as the downed pilot's location.[81] However, Lynn's reported position was incorrect. Moreover, the search forces did not know that the Navy used a homing beacon transmitted on a different frequency from the one employed by the Air Force. Air America C-7 Caribous were equipped with compatible receivers and located the downed airman before darkness postponed the rescue. A low overcast covered northern Laos the next morning as the Air America Caribous flew back to the search area with their receivers open for a signal. When they picked up the signal, the downed pilot's exact location was pinpointed about forty miles south of the originally reported position. When Commander Lynn heard the drone of aircraft above the foggy mist, he fired a flare. An Air America H-34 helicopter dipped beneath the clouds and snatched the weary pilot to safety.[82]

SEARCH AND RESCUE

President Lyndon B. Johnson, Secretary of Defense McNamara, and the Joint Chiefs of Staff shared a keen interest in Yankee Team reconnaissance missions. Accordingly, Gen. Curtis E. LeMay, Chief of Staff of the Air Force, took a close look at existing arrangements for the use of Thailand-based aircraft in search and rescue efforts. The American Ambassador to Thailand, Graham Martin, reported that he had called a high Thai official as soon as he heard of the shootdown of Corktip 920, on Saturday, June 6. The Thai official granted permission to use Air Force aircraft based in Thailand to support search and rescue operations in Laos, but asked that the Thai Government be kept informed.[83]

The loss of two American aircraft within twenty-four hours over northern Laos made the June 15 meeting at Udorn, attended by General Moore, Colonel Catlin, and Colonel Tyrrell as well as representatives from Air America, even more critical to future operations. At the conference a plan evolved whereby Air America assumed responsibility for rescue coverage on the Plain of Jars during all Yankee Team missions. The Deputy Commander of the 2d Air Division became responsible for all Air Force search and rescue operations in Laos subject to the rules of engagement established by the American Embassy in Vientiane.[84]

Meanwhile, in accordance with the Joint Chiefs of Staff directive in May, directing the Air Force to send search and rescue units to Southeast Asia, two ARS HH-43Bs, their crews and mechanics, were sent from the 33d Air Rescue Squadron at Naha Air Station, Okinawa, to Bien Hoa. Because of the Yankee Team rescue requirements, they were diverted and rerouted to Nakhon Phanom Royal Thai Air Force Base on the Thai-Laos border. Arrangements also were made to have two U.S. Marine H-34s placed on alert at Khe Sanh in northern South Vietnam whenever a Yankee Team mission flew over Laos. Simultaneously, the 33d Air Rescue Squadron at Naha sent two HU-16Bs to Korat Royal Thai Air Force Base to perform as airborne rescue control ships during search and rescue missions. During this same period, the 31st Air Rescue Squadron, Clark Air Base, Philippines, sent three HU-16Bs to Da Nang for rescue duties in the Gulf of Tonkin.[85]

Since the 6,000-foot pierced-steel planking runway at Nakhon Phanom could not handle loaded C-97 cargo planes, the plan was to land the unit at Udorn, have the helicopters unloaded, assembled, and then fly them to their final destination. Major Saunders flew up to Udorn to make final arrangements and to greet the men. Unfortunately, he failed to obtain the necessary support items such as JP-4 fuel, bedding and rations for the men at either Udorn or Nakhon Phanom. Consequently, when the rescue unit reached Udorn on June 17 and began unloading and assembling their choppers, Saunders discovered there were no facilities to accommodate the men for that night. Saunders had the men flown to Nakhon Phanom for the night, where he assumed there were suitable facilities. Only a few rickety, open-sided sheds awaited the tired crewmen when they reached the dusty, riverside base. The exhausted party made a campfire, barbecued their C-rations, and slept under the stars. At dawn most of the men returned to Udorn where they continued assembling their choppers. By the following morning the helicopters were ready to fly to Nakhon Phanom, but then the crews discovered that the fuel had not arrived. Another day was spent in securing fuel, but finally, late on the afternoon of June 20, the HH-43Bs reached Nakhon Phanom.[86]

During the next few weeks, barely liveable conditions continued at Nakhon Phanom. Officers and enlisted men endured a lack of suitable latrine facilities, electric power, and even potable water. On June 27 an Air Force electrician arrived from Bangkok and installed a generator and some wiring for lights. Three days later four Thai carpenters began refurbishing the sheds and building a kitchen. Meanwhile, the rescue personnel worked at putting in a latrine and constructing a shower. Such as it was, Nakhon Phanom was the only base in the world with an Air Rescue Service officer as its American commander.[87]

Substantial problems remained, but at last Air Rescue Service helicopters were entrenched in Southeast Asia. Pilots who flew over Laos had trained Air Rescue Service forces to support their mission. The effect on morale was favorable, though not entirely warranted. The HH-43B was limited to a relatively small radius of action that varied between 125 to 140 nautical miles. Due to this range limitation the Nakhon Phanom based Huskies were not able to provide search and rescue services for the Plain of Jars or areas southeast of Pakse in the Laotian panhandle. An aircraft damaged by enemy fire over the center of the Plain of Jars had to be flown at least fifty miles south to be within range of any Nakhon Phanom based Air Force rescue choppers. Fortunately, Air America planes and helicopters were available to provide search and rescue support when needed.

The need for their services increased when, throughout June 1964, the communists continued their offensive across northern Laos. By July the tempo of Air Force and Navy air operations over Laos was beyond the limited capabilities of the Air Rescue Service unit at Nakhon Phanom. Although additional rescue forces were scheduled to arrive, the urgent problem in Laos required an immediate remedy. The fleet of sixteen H-34s turned over to Air America at Udorn in March 1961, had decreased to four. These helicopters provided search and rescue support, in addition to their normal functions, for both the Royal Laotian Air Force and U.S. combat missions. In July 1964, Air America asked for four additional H-34s from Department of Defense resources. CINCPAC protested that all Navy and Marine H-34s in the Pacific had operational commitments. It was suggested that the Royal Thai Army be asked to lend Air America the needed choppers. Ambassador Martin, fearing an adverse Thai reaction, rejected this suggestion.[88] The Secretary of Defense solved the controversy by instructing the Chairman of the Joint Chiefs of Staff to order CINCPAC to loan the four helicopters to Air America.[89] Admiral Felt then took the H-34s from the Fleet Marine Forces, Pacific, and turned them over to Air America.[90]

These additional helicopters were soon put to use. On August 18, 1964, during the Neutralist withdrawal from their stronghold in the northwestern corner of the Plain of Jars, communist gunners brought down a T-28 engaged in a close air support mission. The wingman notified the Air Support Operations Center at Udorn, and the controllers there, following rescue procedures established at the June 15 Udorn conference, contacted the Air America Air Operations Center at Vientiane. An H-34 took off from Wattay Airport and U.S. Air Force F-100 fighters scrambled from Takhli to form a Rescue Combat Air Patrol. Pathet Lao gunners zeroed in on the approaching helicopter and shot it out of the air. As the F-100s strafed suspected gun emplacements, the enemy scored hits on one of them. The pilot wrestled his crippled craft up to a safe altitude and turned south toward Udorn. He managed to nurse the plane to the Mekong River, then ejected and landed on the southern outskirts of the Thai river town of Nong Khai. An Air America helicopter soon picked him up and flew him to Udorn.

In Vientiane, six T-28s took off from Wattay to escort a second H-34 search and rescue attempt. Meanwhile, the Air Force jets continued blasting suspected enemy positions with rocket and cannon fire. When the guns fell silent, the chopper darted in and picked up a badly burned Air America helicopter pilot. A Filipino crewman died in the helicopter crash, and the two Thai T-28 flyers, objectives of the original rescue, were last seen scurrying into the bushes, where they disappeared.[91]

In the next two days enemy gunners bagged two more T-28s and the crews were not rescued.[92] From the earliest days of the air war in Southeast Asia it was apparent that search and rescue had to be timely and well organized if it was to succeed. To improve the rescue capability, Ambassador Unger asked the State Department for discretionary authority for use of Air America helicopters and planes for search and rescue whenever he felt the situation warranted such action. The Air Rescue Service HH-43Bs at Nakhon Phanom were limited in range, therefore limited in their usefulness. Royal Laotian Air Force rescue capabilities were negligible, and language differences would have made proper coordination among rescue forces, airborne controllers, the Air Support Operations Center in Udorn, the Air Operations Center in Vientiane, and the downed pilot impossible. Additionally, Air America pilots had a knowledge of flying conditions in Laos that came from years of experience.[93]

There were no formal agreements between the United States and Laos that allowed for placing Laotian T-28s under American control during rescue efforts. During the August 18 search and rescue missions, the Royal

Laotian Air Force cooperated with Colonel Tyrrell on an "unofficial" basis. However, with human lives at stake, this was not sufficient for future contingencies. Ambassador Unger wanted to offer the pilots assurances that they were not going to be abandoned. Following Unger's request to the State Department to permit use of U.S. piloted T-28s in search and rescue operations in Laos, Secretary of State Dean Rusk discussed the request with President Johnson. The President realized the problem's bombshell potential. What if an American pilot flying an airplane that took off from a base in Thailand were shot down and captured? But he also understood that human lives — American and allied — were being risked in a mutual fight against communist expansion. On August 26, the President advised Ambassador Unger of his authorization for use of U.S. pilots in T-28s for rescue operations, when it was absolutely essential to the successful completion of the search and rescue mission.[94]

Following the Gulf of Tonkin Incident (August 2-4, 1964), President Johnson, among other actions, sent additional U.S. Air Force units to Vietnam and Thailand. The arrival of additional jet fighters in Southeast Asia placed added demands on the Air Rescue Service. Pacific Air Forces rescue resources were already stretched following the commitment of the Naha local base rescue unit to Nakhon Phanom. However, in response to the early August crisis, Detachment 4 of the 36th Air Rescue Squadron at Osan Air Base, Korea, an HH-43B unit, was assigned to Takhli on a temporary basis.[95] Because Pacific area rescue forces were already thin, local base rescue detachments in the United States were told to prepare for short notice temporary assignments to Vietnam and Thailand. On August 6 the unit at Maxwell Air Force Base, Alabama, received orders to leave immediately for Southeast Asia. Capt. Philip Prince, the detachment commander, worked his crew through the night dismantling and loading their two HH-43Bs on board two C-124 transports. By noon the following day they were on their way to Thailand. Prince's unit reached Korat on August 14 and was soon performing local base rescue services for both the Air Force F-105 unit and the Royal Thai Air Force flying school.[96]

With the U.S. Air Force publicly committed to an active combat role in Southeast Asia, the mission of rescue forces was less sensitive that it had been in the period of convert operations. It became easier to get Joint Chiefs of Staff and Headquarters, Air Force approval to send the necessary Air Rescue Service units. On September 9, 1964, the chief of staff of the Air Force, General Curtis LeMay, approved sending six HH-43Fs to Vietnam as soon as they were delivered by the Kaman factory. Pacific Air Forces requested that the HH-43Bs stationed at Bien Hoa and Da Nang, as an interim measure, be moved to Nakhon Phanom and Takhli to replace the Osan and Naha detachments. In November the local base rescue detachments were transferred from the Republic of Vietnam to Tahiland, and the temporary units at Nakhon Phanom and Takhli returned to their parent units.[97]

SEARCH AND RESCUE

By November 1964 the Air Rescue Service commitment in Southeast Asia included units at six bases in Thailand and Vietnam. However, the HH-43Bs at Korat and Takhli were useless for aircrew recovery missions in Laos. The Nakhon Phanom local base rescue unit, although designated for Yankee Team search and rescue, lacked the range necessary for effective coverage in northern Laos or the Bolovens Plateau area west of Attopeu in the south. In these places Air America still carried the burden of aircrew recovery.[98]

The first large-scale search and rescue effort of the Indochina war took place on November 18 and 19, 1964, and involved Air Force, Navy, and Air America aircraft. It began when Ball 03, one of two F-100s escorting a Yankee Team reconnaissance mission, was shot down while trading fire with an enemy antiaircraft gun position.[99] Ball 03's wingman called "dropkick" (a distress signal used in place of mayday to confuse any listening enemy troops) to the Air America Air Operations Center in Vientiane at 11:27 in the morning. Ball 03 crashed just south of Ban Senphan in central Laos near the North Vietnamese border. The Air America operations officer at the Air Operations Center diverted one of their C-123s to reconnoiter the area and act as airborne controller until Air Force HU-16s arrived from Korat. Once in position, Tacky 44 (call sign for the H-16 control ship) asked that U.S. Navy A-1E Skyraiders fly to the Ban Senphan area to join the search for the wreckage and pilot and to suppress enemy opposition if it were encountered. Pansy 88 and 89, Air Rescue Service HH-43s at Nakhon Phanom, were put on alert.

Within minutes of their arrival on the scene, the Navy Skyraiders were hit by antiaircraft fire from Pathet Lao emplacements located near the place where the F-100 was believed to have been shot down. The A-1s attacked the enemy guns, took some flak and small arms fire, but escaped major damage. During the action, one of the Skyraider pilots spotted what appeared to be a burning crash site in the jungle approximately five miles away from the coordinates originally furnished. Tacky 44 ordered the HH-43s at Nakhon Phanon to take off.

The Navy Skyraiders met Pansy 88 and 89 east of Thakhek and escorted them to the crash site. After carefully surveying the burning jungle, the chopper pilots found no wreckage and decided that the fire was probably of natural origins. Pansy 88 and 89 returned to Nakhon Phanom, ending the first Air Rescue Service chopper sorties into Laos.[100]

Before darkness temporarily ended the rescue efforts, the HU-16 coordinated thirteen F-105s, eight F-100s, six Navy A-1Es, two Air Rescue Service HH-43s, and a pair of Air America H-34s in a concerted effort to find and rescue the downed pilot.[101] The coordination and control of these diverse elements provided a preview of search and rescue efforts that would be conducted over the next decade.

Airborne at first light, Tacky 45, another HU-16 from Korat, and four

F-105s returned to the Ban Senphan area. At mid-morning the aircraft commander of Tacky 45 sighted the downed pilot's parachute and the wreckage on a rocky outcropping only fifty yards from the nearest antiaircraft position. As the F-105s attacked the gun position, the on-scene commander contacted Nakhon Phanom and ordered helicopters and their propeller-driven escorts. However, poor weather conditions kept the helicopters grounded for nearly two hours before a pair of Air America H-34s took off and joined four American-piloted T-28s out of Savannakhet to provide escort. Tacky 44, a second HU-16, relieved Tacky 45 as the on-scene commander and began to control the pickup attempt. Upon arrival at the crash site the copilot of one of the Air America choppers was lowered on a cable. He found that the flyer had apparently died of injuries sustained when he landed on the karst.[102]

On November 21, an RF-101 on a Yankee Team mission was lost forty miles east of Thakhek. The pilot ejected and came down in a tropical rain forest. An Air America H-34 happened to be in the area and recovered the survivor within an hour. Within thirty-six hours the Air Force was forced to rely on Air America twice to perform aircrew recovery missions. At the end of 1964 it was evident that the Air Rescue Service was not able to handle the rescue mission in Laos.[103]

In the last months of 1964, American casualties, both on the ground and in the air, increased as the fighting in Southeast Asia intensified. In October and November additional HH-43B/F rescue helicopters were sent to Vietnam, but the limited range of these choppers restricted their usefulness. Industry, employing the latest in helicopter technology, was only beginning to respond to the urgent need for an improved aircrew recovery aircraft. Tactics were emerging to meet the challenges presented by enemy opposition, the climate, and the diverse geographic features of Southeast Asia. Nevertheless, in late 1964, flyers continued to fly missions without the kind of search and rescue support they — and the Air Force — would have liked to have had.

Right: scramble for a rescue mission; below: HH–43 with fire suppression kit for fire fighting; bottom: HH–43 plucks a pilot from Puget Sound.

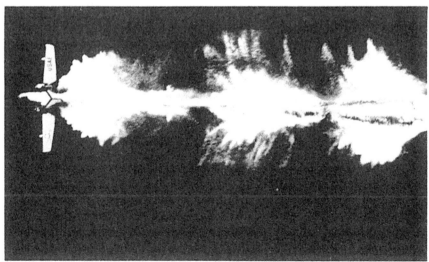

Top: RB–26 at Tan Son Nhut, 1964; center: HU–16B Albatross of the 37th ARRS at Da Nang Air Base, 1966; HU–16 lands in the Gulf of Tonkin for a rescue, June 1966.

3 Period of Escalation: 1964-1966

The May 1964 directive from the Joint Chiefs of Staff ordering the introduction of search and rescue forces and plans to deploy those units, inaugurated air-sea rescue service in Southeast Asia. However, orders and plans alone did not meet the needs of combat aircrews. They needed a rescue force capable of aircrew recovery missions far inside enemy-held areas of Laos and South Vietnam and in North Vietnam, and this was not forthcoming for another year. The short-range local base rescue Kaman HH-43 Huskie helicopters, sent to Bien Hoa in June but diverted to Nakhon Phanom Air Base, Thailand, had yet to pick up their first survivor. In Laos, Air America remained the backbone of rescue throughout 1964 and into 1965.[1]

The frenzied force buildup that began in mid-1964 placed new demands on the Air Rescue Service. The Pacific Air Rescue Center did not have the resources to meet these demands, making it necessary to order stateside rescue units to Southeast Asia from the Eastern, Central, and Western rescue centers on a temporary duty basis. In addition to the Pacific Air Rescue Center units, the Naha local base rescue detachment sent to Nakhon Phanom in June, and two HU-16s from the 31st Air Rescue Squadron at Clark Air Base, Philippines, sent to Da Nang in July, the Air Rescue Service dispatched HH-43s from five continental U.S. detachments. These were: Detachment 10, Eastern Air Rescue Center, Maxwell Air Force Base, Alabama; Detachment 1, Central Air Rescue Center, Glasgow Air Force Base, Montana; Detachment 2, Central Air Rescue Center, Minot Air Force Base, North Dakota; Detachment 4, Western Air Rescue Center, Paine Air Force Base, Oregon; and Detachment 5, Western Air Rescue Center, McChord Air Force Base, Washington.[2]

In late August men and helicopters from these units began reaching Southeast Asia to join the Maxwell unit that had reached Korat on August 14. Detachment 1 (Provisional) was formed at Bien Hoa and Detachment 2 (Provisional) at Da Nang.[3] Meanwhile, Air Rescue headquarters notified two units in the United States of a permanent change of station assignment to Southeast Asia. The Air Rescue Service selected the crews on the basis of rescue experience and professional qualifications, which included training at the jungle survival school in Panama. In September 1964, the crews reported to Stead Air Force Base, Nevada, for a thirty-day training period. At Stead the pilots put their HH-43s through their paces, subjecting them to maneuvers never attempted in their normal local base rescue duties. They hovered the Huskies at altitudes above 3,000 feet, made steep approaches, and did autorotational descents where they killed the power to the rotors and let the helicopter settle to earth on the lift of the still rotating blades. One chopper crashed in these initial training exercises.[4]

Personnel, equipment, and organizational changes occurred rapidly in the first months in Southeast Asia. The units from the states, which in August formed Detachment 1 (Provisional) at Bien Hoa, and Detachment 2 (Provisional) at Da Nang, were sent to Takhli and Nakhon Phanom respectively in November 1964. Pacific Air Rescue Center temporary units at these latter bases were returned to their parent units. Duties at Bien Hoa and Da Nang were assumed by Detachment 4 and Detachment 5 of the Pacific Air Rescue Center which were created by Military Air Transport Service Special Order G-131 on September 16, 1964, and established on October 20. These two units were equipped with the HH-43F combat modified helicopter.[5]

The HH-43F represented a significant improvement over the B-models and provided the Air Rescue Service with a limited combat aircrew recovery capability. Kaman delivered the first two F models on September 25, 1964. Six additional machines were in the Air Rescue Service inventory by Thanksgiving. To protect the aircrews and passengers, the new model carried 800 pounds of titanium armor distributed in half-inch sheet around the crew compartment and over the engine cowling. The F model engine, a Lycoming T53-L-11A shaft turbine, produced 1,150 horsepower, 400 more than the engine in the standard Huskie. To extend the combat radius from 75 to 120 nautical miles, a 350 gallon self-sealing fuel tank was installed. The B model had been equipped with an ultra high frequency radio. Combat-modified F models carried both very high frequency and frequency modulation sets which provided the helicopter crews with improved communications aids to coordinate rescue activities. Finally, Kaman engineers, in response to the need to be able to reach survivors through jungle canopy, developed the jungle penetrator. This device incorporated spring-loaded arms that parted jungle foliage as it was lowered to the survivor who, after strapping himself to the penetrator, released a set of spring-loaded arms at the other end to protect himself as he was hauled up through the branches of trees. The jungle penetrator was used throughout the war and was responsible for saving numerous survivors from the Southeast Asian rain forests.[6]

Stationed at Da Nang and Bien Hoa, the first HH-43Fs were responsible for aircrew recoveries throughout Southeast Asia. Air Rescue Service headquarters personnel knew that the HH-43F could not fly very far into North Vietnam or Laos from bases in South Vietnam. Indeed, the commander of the Pacific Air Rescue Center, Col. Walter F. Derck, did not want the HH-43Bs modified for the combat aircrew recovery mission because, along with Air Rescue Service headquarters, he wanted any available money applied toward a more capable aircraft designed specifically for the combat aircrew rescue role. However, Derck realized that the immediate needs of the men flying combat missions in Southeast Asia left no other alternative.[7]

A Pacific Air Forces study in late 1964 identified the requirements for an extended range aircrew recovery vehicle for Southeast Asia units. Pacific Air Forces expected the Air Rescue Service to have this capability and criticized them for not having it. While a Pacific Air Forces study conducted in December 1964 conceded that the HH-43 performed satisfactorily in the local base rescue role, it was judged ". . . not adequate to perform the majority of recovery missions."[8] Six months would pass before the first Sikorsky CH-3C helicopters, on loan from the Tactical Air Command, would arrive in Thailand. Meanwhile, the rescue units did the best they could with the tiny, vulnerable HH-43Bs.

A total of thirteen HH-43B/Fs, two each at Nakhon Phanom, Takhli, Pleiku, and Korat and three located at Bien Hoa and two at Da Nang were dedicated primarily to the local base rescue mission. Normally these aircraft operated in a non-hostile environment; however, all were available to pick up downed aircrews. The F models at Da Nang and Bien Hoa had a primary aircrew recovery mission but retained the local base rescue capability which included fire-fighting.[9]

Still, the rescue mission in Southeast Asia suffered from inadequate forces, nonexistent doctrine, and ill-suited aircraft. Moreover, Air Rescue Service leaders knew that rescue had failed to meet the urgent needs of aircrews in combat. On October 31, 1964, Air Rescue Service headquarters published a revision to ARS OPLAN 510 (Air Rescue Service Operations Plan 510) which stated: "A requirement exists for an Air Force helicopter capability to support world-wide rescue and recovery contingencies."[10] The plan established a method for rapidly forming and deploying Local Base Rescue Contingency Force units. Each of the rescue centers was directed to maintain the capability for forming one contingency unit of two HH-43Bs to be prepared for missions of up to 700 miles from the parent units within two hours of notification. Additionally, the plan called for a capability to go anywhere in the world within twelve hours notice.[11]

Half a world away from Air Rescue Service headquarters in Orlando, Florida, in the predawn hours of November 1, a hot war got hotter as the Viet Cong carried out a sneak attack on Bien Hoa Air Base. Raiders infiltrated the outskirts of the base and mortared the flight line, killing five Americans, destroying five Martin B-57 jet bombers and one HH-43F. Thirteen B-57s and the remaining HH-43Bs and HH-43Fs were damaged.[12] The next day when one of the damaged HH-43Fs was repaired, it flew its first night mission picking up a Vietnamese A-1 pilot shot down in an attack on the Viet Cong Zone D headquarters in Phuoc Thanh Province northwest of Saigon. For the first night aircrew rescue conducted by an Air Rescue Service unit in Southeast Asia, the pilot received the Vietnamese Air Force Distinguished Flying Cross with a gold star.[13]

With the limited number of helicopters available for aircrew recovery missions, rescue personnel at both detachment and headquarters level felt that combat should be avoided. Kaman provided gun mounts for the M-60 machine gun, but there was not enough room in the HH-43B/F for a gunner. The parajumper was usually too involved with getting the survivor aboard to man a gun. Additionally, the Air Rescue Service did not want their rescue choppers to become gunships. Therefore, the machine guns were rarely mounted. If a situation demanded suppressive fire from their rescue choppers crew members usually fired an AR-15 or M-16 rifle from the door or out the window. In an effort to conserve the available choppers, rescue crews refused to take off on recovery missions until a survivor had been located. Rescue headquarters supported these decisions.[14]

Further developing the argument that Air Rescue Service could not afford needlessly to risk helicopters in search missions, Brig. Gen. Adriel N. Williams, commander of the Air Rescue Service, in a letter to the chief of staff of the Air Force, Gen. Curtis E. LeMay, cited ARS Programming Plan 563 which estimated that the HH-43B/F force would suffer a forty percent attrition rate in the first year of combat operations. Williams also noted that whereas the plan called for a minimum of nine HH-43Bs to be modified as F models, in fact Air Force headquarters directed only six modifications.[15] Attrition rates matched the estimates as three HH-43Bs and two HH-43Fs were either damaged or destroyed during the Viet Cong attack at Bien Hoa. In May 1965 an F model sustained battle damage and on June 3, enemy gunners brought down one of the beefed-up Huskies on a recovery mission.[16]

Helicopters, because of their slow speed and the mechanical complexity of the gearing in the exposed rotor system, have always been vulnerable to antiaircraft and small arms fire. Initially ill-prepared to meet the demands of aircrew rescue in Southeast Asia, rescue personnel had to develop tactics and doctrine. It was during this time that the Search and Rescue Task Force evolved.

In late 1964, due to the limitations of the HH-43 helicopter, Air Rescue Service units were not providing dependable aircrew recovery. In Vietnam, Army and Marine choppers often picked up their own downed flyers. In Laos, Air America pilots, thoroughly familiar with the nuances of terrain and weather, still performed most of the aircrew recoveries. For instance, between June 1964 and June 1965, Air America helicopters picked up twenty-one downed aircrew members. Air Rescue Service choppers rescued only five flyers downed in Laos.[17] Nevertheless, it was in this period that

HU-16 control ships, HH-43 helicopters, and A-1 rescue escort aircraft began working together to form the rescue task force.

Rescue in a hostile environment required control and coordination of many elements. First, the downed airman had to be located, his position verified and his physical condition determined. Enemy presence and disposition had to be determined. If rescue appeared feasible, helicopters (two if available) were sent. Rescue escort planes, slow-moving propeller-driven aircraft and a jet fighter escort, had to be coordinated according to the particular situation.

The airborne command and control function included relay of search and rescue communications to ground controllers in rescue centers in Thailand and South Vietnam as well as actual control of rescue forces. The airborne mission controller's function evolved and changed as the war progressed, but basically involved acting as a focal point for search and rescue operations. Primarily, the air missions controller determined what forces were needed, briefed them on the location and condition of the survivors and the disposition of enemy forces, and then worked with the on-scene commander to direct the forces in the recovery operation.[18]

Early in the war it was evident that, due to limitations in communications imposed by geographical features and the presence of a large amount of radio chatter, an airborne on-scene commander would be needed to conduct a rescue mission properly. Air Rescue Service planners knew this, and when the first HH-43Bs reached Thailand in June 1964, two HU-16 control ships, jury-rigged with communications gear, were sent from the 33d Air Rescue Squadron at Naha to Korat.[19] Normally used as water rescue aircraft and pressed into service as control ships on an emergency basis, the HU-16s were not entirely suited to the command and control mission. Rescue controllers and crewmen reported experiencing discomfort in the cramped, unpressurized, unheated interiors.

The mission of the HU-16Bs included not only command and control but also search and, whenever possible, water rescue. With a limited electronic search capability, the venerable "Albatross" was able to remain above 4,000 feet — out of the range of small arms fire — while searching for a survivor. Operating over water, the crew could conduct both electronic and visual searches. Furthermore, if the search was over the Gulf of Tonkin, the Albatross often became the primary rescue vehicle. Once a survivor was spotted, the amphibian would, sea conditions permitting, make a water landing to pick him up. If water and wind conditions precluded a water landing, the parajumper could drop a rescue kit which included an inflatable rubber raft and other survival equipment. If the survivors were unable to reach or use the rescue kit the parajumper could parachute into the water to lend assistance. If all else failed, the HU-16 would call for help from U.S. ships or submarines operating in the area.[20]

In 1965, as air strikes intensified over Laos and North Vietnam, it became more difficult for the HU-16s, with their limited communications capability, to control effectively the search and rescue task force. The previous year the Air Rescue Service decided to order modified C-130 transports for airborne rescue command and control. However, these aircraft would not be ready until 1966. The Boeing HC-97 four engine transport, serving the Air Rescue Service in limited numbers, had the range, performance, and communications gear. However, these aircraft were already committed to the space vehicle recovery mission.[21]

The Douglas SC-54 "Rescuemaster", a modified version of the C-54, became part of the Air Rescue Service inventory in October 1955. Auxiliary fuel tanks enabled the SC-54 to stay aloft for up to eighteen hours, and it carried some of the latest electronic and communications equipment. Moreover, its added room increased personnel comfort and boosted the efficiency of individual crewmembers. Also, the four engine Rescuemaster, although as slow as the twin-engine HU-16, could operate at altitudes above most antiaircraft fire with full pressurization and heating for the crew.[22] However, the SC-54, designed for the global search and rescue mission of the 1950s was not entirely suited to the unique demands of aircrew recovery in a combat situation. For instance, the command console, installed for peacetime rescue control and space vehicle recovery, lacked the latest communications equipment necessary to control effectively the many diverse elements of the search and rescue task force. Additionally, there was no backup communications equipment. Nevertheless, it offered an interim capability until the HC-130 could be built, tested, and put into service.[23]

In June 1965 three SC-54s, on temporary duty from the 79th Air Rescue Squadron at Guam and the 36th Air Rescue Squadron at Tachikawa, were sent to Udorn. The HU-16s, which had recently moved from Korat to get closer to northern Laos and North Vietnam, were transferred to Da Nang. From there the Albatrosses flew rescue missions over the Gulf of Tonkin for the next two years.

Rescuemaster operations in Southeast Asia were short-lived and not entirely satisfactory. Brig. Gen. John R. Murphy, 2d Air Division's deputy commander, considered the SC-54 the weak link in the search and rescue task force because of its lack of adequate backup communications equipment. The SC-54 served only six months in Southeast Asia, until December 1965 when two HC-130Hs arrived as replacements. Subsequently, the Rescuemaster was removed from the Air Rescue Service inventory.[24]

The airborne mission controller, whether in an HU-16, SC-54, or HC-130, was responsible for controlling the choppers and the various fixed-wing aircraft that made up the search and rescue task forces. During the course of the war, fixed-wing aircraft used most extensively for rescue escort included the T-28, A-1 and, toward the end of the conflict, the A-7 jet fighter. If the survivors were located in an area where north Vietnamese Migs posed a threat, fighters like the F-4 Phantom flew rescue combat air patrol.

The Germans developed the rudiments of coordinated rescue operations during the Battle of Britain when twin-engine Bf-110s escorted He-59 float planes on rescue missions over the English Channel. British and American rescue forces, using whatever fighters were available, did not develop rescue escort to the same extent.[25] In the Korean War, P-51s sometimes escorted H-19s and Grumman Albatrosses on rescue missions behind enemy lines, while F-86s kept Mig-15s at bay. This was done informally and ten years later, when the first Air Rescue Service choppers arrived in Southeast Asia, the concept of using fighters for rescue escort and rescue combat air patrol had not been formally recognized within the Air Force.

South Vietnam, North Vietnam, and Laos each posed unique problems for rescue forces. The search and rescue task force not only had to overcome enemy opposition that varied in intensity with location and time of the war, but also had to deal with the difficulties of terrain and climate. The problem of rescue escort first focused upon Laos where aircrews who went down in enemy territory faced capture and almost certain death, if not picked up quickly. Very early in the war the North Vietnamese and their Pathet Lao allies became adept at setting up flak traps, which proved very dangerous for helicopter operations.

In late August 1964, President Johnson gave the American Ambassador to Laos, Leonard Unger, permission to use U.S. pilots in T-28s for rescue escort on a case by case basis.[26] The T-28, used by the air forces of Laos and South Vietnam as well as by the U.S. Air Force's Detachment 1, 1st Air Commando Wing, was a beefed-up version of an aging trainer. These planes had good loiter capabilities and operated well at slow speeds while carrying up to 4,000 pounds of ordnance.[27] Based at Udorn and stationed throughout Laos, the slow moving T-28s were especially well matched with the HH-43B/F helicopters operating out of Nakhon Phanom. Rescue escort, however, was only an additional mission for the T-28s, and for most of the war, from August 1965 through 1972, the Douglas A-1 Skyraider provided rescue escort.

Provisions for rescue escort and rescue combat air patrol began informally and remained informal until 1965. At first the senior controller at the Air America operations center in Vientiane obtained whatever aircraft he could for this mission. For example, on August 18, 1964, when a T-28 was shot down off the northwestern edge of the Plain of Jars, the operations center in Vientiane requested four F-100s from Takhli to provide patrol and escort for an Air America rescue effort. Totally untrained for these missions, one of the pilots lost a "shoot out" with a Pathet Lao antiaircraft gunner. He managed to fly his damaged plane back over Vientiane and across the Mekong where he ejected and parachuted into the Thai border town of Nong Khai.[28] Several times, notably in a November 1964 rescue attempt south of Ban Senphan in central Laos near the North Vietnamese border, the Navy provided a flight of A-1Es for rescue escort. And, in Vietnam,

HH-43Fs at Bien Hoa and Da Nang often relied on U.S. Army and South Vietnamese UH-1 Huey gunships for rescue escort.[29]

The Douglas A-1 Skyraider, with its 7,000-pound bomb load, four 20-mm cannons, heavy armor plating, and excellent loiter capability, met the needs of rescue escort better than any other aircraft. On May 30, 1964, six A-1Es arrived at Bien Hoa for duty with the 1st Air Commando Squadron as replacements for the T-28s and B-26s which had been operating there since 1961. The Skyraiders soon showed themselves to be rugged, hard-hitting aircraft, well suited to the counterinsurgency role and rescue escort.[30]

In early 1965 the Navy agreed to provide A-1Es for escort duty and stationed from four to six of these planes at Udorn on a rotating basis. Unfortunately, the Navy could not always meet this commitment because of other operational considerations. Attempts to fill the rescue escort need in Laos by flying A-1s from carriers in the Gulf of Tonkin proved unsatisfactory due to the relatively slow speed of the Skyraiders. This forced the newly appointed American Ambassador to Laos, William H. Sullivan, to request more use of U.S. pilots in T-28s than he liked. He, like his predecessor Leonard Unger, dreaded the possible political repercussions.[31]

Sullivan's fears were never realized. In August 1965, to meet the needs of rescue escort over northern Laos and North Vietnam, the 602d Fighter Squadron (Commando) rotated its A-1Es from Bien Hoa to Udorn. Two TAC CH-3Es had, meanwhile, arrived at Nakhon Phanom on July 5, and two HH-43Bs moved up from the Mekong River town to Udorn where they were joined by two factory-fresh HH-43Fs. The addition of the A-1Es meant that with the HC-54s in place, and the HU-16s operating out of Da Nang to cover the water rescue mission, a full search and rescue task force was in Southeast Asia. Over the years equipment improved and aircraft changed but the search and rescue task force of 1965 closely resembled that of 1973 in doctrine, tactics, and procedures.[32]

Because of the limitations of the HH-43B/F, the Air Force rescue capability in Southeast Asia still left a lot to be desired. Nevertheless the Air Rescue Service had come a long way from the days when the rescue controller in Saigon had to depend on whatever Army, Marine, or Vietnamese choppers might be available for a rescue effort. In fact, by June 1965 rescue missions were being performed which only a year before would have been all but impossible.

A typical search and rescue for the period occurred on June 23, 1965, when Maj. Robert Wilson's F-105 was hit by ground fire while on a mission over southwestern North Vietnam. Wilson could not fly his damaged Thunderchief over a ridgeline, so he ejected. After a normal descent he found himself suspended upside down in a tree 150 feet above the jungle floor. Wilson managed to swing into a crotch of the tree where he wiggled out of his parachute harness. He then took out his survival knife and cut a small branch from the tree. Wilson used the branch to snag his seat pack which contained all his survival equipment. After drawing the pack over to where he stood, he retrieved his URC-11 survival radio. Wilson contacted the HC-54 airborne rescue command post called "Crown" which, in response to his mayday, had moved off its orbit along the Thai-Laotian border and now flew nearby. Half an hour later four Air Force A-1 Skyraiders droned into view and contacted the survivor. Soon the pilots spotted Wilson's chute and, after radioing the downed pilot's exact position to Crown, flew to an orbit several miles away so as not to reveal Wilson's location to any enemy troops that might be lurking nearby. Had Wilson or the A-1 pilots spotted the enemy, the A-1s would have attacked them with 20-mm cannon fire, rockets, and fragmentation bombs. Ninety minutes after Wilson's ejection, an HH-43, from a forward operating base in Laos, showed up. Wilson fired off a small flare that was part of his survival equipment. The Huskie pilots spotted it and moved their chopper directly overhead while the parajumper lowered the penetrator through the foliage. Wilson grabbed it, strapped himself on, and began his ascent to the helicopter. A few hours later, safe at the Nakhon Phanom officer's club, Wilson set up drinks for the chopper pilots. The next day he returned to Korat.[33]

Of course not all HH-43 rescue missions went so smoothly, and the enemy sometimes bested the search and rescue task forces. On September 20, 1965, Capt. Willis E. Forby's F-105 was hit by large caliber antiaircraft fire while attacking a target near Vinh, North Vietnam. Forby turned his damaged F-105 toward Laos and ejected a few minutes later. His wingman circled until he received a signal from the downed pilot's survival radio indicating he was alive. Then Crown launched two HH-43s from a Lima Site. All seemed normal as Captain Forby dispensed smoke to mark his exact location and make voice contact with one of the rescue choppers piloted by Capt. Tom J. Curtis. Forby did not know that enemy troops had hidden themselves in the jungle all around to make him the live bait on a flak trap. Captain Curtis was concentrating on holding the chopper in a hover near the survivor when several black clad figures stepped from the underbrush and fired their automatic weapons. The helicopter shivered as bullets impacted, then it dropped into the trees. In an almost automatic response, the pilot of the second helicopter, orbiting above as part of the search and rescue task force, moved in to pick up any survivors as A-1s blasted the surrounding area. Again the troops opened fire forcing the backup chopper to pull up and return to the Lima Site. Crown called for a massive rescue task force but the armada of A-1s failed to find any trace of the downed men. Tom Curtis spent the next seven years as a prisoner of war in North Vietnam. His copilot, 1st Lt. Duane W. Martin remained a prisoner of the Pathet Lao. Martin escaped captivity a year later. He was, however, murdered by a Laotian peasant before he could be rescued.[34]

SEARCH AND RESCUE

Throughout the war there were several ways a downed aircrew member might be rescued. Helicopters performed most recoveries; however, if a survivor was down at sea he might be picked up by either a chopper or, until they were phased out in 1967, an HU-16 Albatross, or even a friendly surface vessel. These methods were useful in recovering aircrew members immediately — usually within a couple of hours — after the shootdown. If the rescue operation dragged on for several days and, for some reason, the survivor lost contact with the rescue forces, he still had cause to hope. He still might be found through the efforts of clandestine operations.

Clandestine operations, too, played a part in search and rescue. The U.S. mission, working through Air America, could and often did, put together an entire rescue operation. For example, on May 14, 1965, Air America assembled a search and rescue task force consisting of one C-123 twin-engine transport acting as an airborne rescue control ship, two H-34 helicopters, and six T-28s for escort. This task force was to retrieve a team which had been operating deep inside Pathet Lao territory near the North Vietnamese border. A radio report from this team stated that they had spotted a bound American pilot being marched along by a Pathet Lao platoon. The team said they followed the pilot and his captors to a cave in the village of Sam Neua. While three team members remained around Sam Neua to check on guards and prison routine, the other agents slipped away to the rendezvous point. These men reached the designated site just as the Air America armada arrived. An H-34 hovered above the ground while the men scrambled aboard, but before the helicopter could clear the trees, 37-mm antiaircraft fire erupted from the surrounding jungle. The chopper was hit but managed to get back to a Lima Site. Meanwhile, the C-123 control ship directed the T-28s in an attack on the gun emplacements. Enemy fire severely damaged one of the planes, but the pilot elected to stay with the aircraft rather than eject deep inside enemy territory. The pilot made a "dead stick" landing at Lima Site 36 where the T-28 careened off the end of the runway and flipped over. Although trapped in an inverted cockpit, the pilot dug his way out.[35]

The folloring day an Air America task force returned to the area to pick up the remaining team members. The team members never made it to the rendezvous point, and all efforts to contact them failed. Since the area was heavily defended, mission planners decided that any rescue attempt inside Sam Neua would be suicidal. Nevertheless teams were told to be on the lookout for downed pilots and prisoners of war. This continued throughout the war. Additionally, planners wanted to establish an underground network of friendly natives in North Vietnam and Laos that would assist pilots as had the French Maquis in World War II. Such an underground never materialized in Southeast Asia.[36]

Other ground-based rescue programs were established, and friendly guerrilla units operating in southern Laos and roadwatch teams were also given a secondary mission of searching for missing and captured airmen.[37]

Air Force and Navy intelligence officers briefed aircrews on team activities and procedures. Flyers were told that team members would wear white arm bands. Furthermore, they would probably have American style uniforms and carry American weapons. Laotian team memebers usually wore snappy red berets.[38]

The roadwatch teams operated until the end of the war as an unconventional complement to regular search and rescue operations. The recovery of downed aircrew members was only a secondary mission for these teams, however, and they rescued only a small number of people. Over the years, the Aerospace Rescue and Recovery Service (as the Air Rescue Service became in January 1966) received new equipment and developed better tactics. Consequently, roadwatch teams were used less. In 1968, for example, there were only seven instances in which roadwatch teams were alerted for possible recovery activity, and in only two cases were teams actually used.[39]

As the war continued, helicopters remained the primary means of recovering downed airmen. On July 6, 1965, two Sikorsky CH-3C turbine-driven helicopters arrived at Nakhon Phanom Royal Thai Air Force Base to initiate a new era for search and rescue in Southeast Asia. The added range, protective armor, and a large carrying capacity made the CH-3C an adequate aircrew rescue vehicle — certainly an improvement over the short-range, unarmed, vulnerable HH-43F. Assigned to the newly established Detachment 1 of the 38th Air Rescue Squadron, the two helicopters were on loan from the Tactical Air Warfare Center at Eglin Air Force Base, Florida.[40] Dubbed the "Jolly Green Giants" because of their green and brown camouflage scheme, these helicopters were hastily converted Tactical Air Command cargo choppers and, as such, were only interim aircraft.

In August 1965, as the temporary duty crews for the CH-3s settled in at Nakhon Phanom, crews for the Sikorsky HH-3Es, the same basic helicopter as the Tactical Air Command models but built for rescue, gathered at Stead Air Force Base, Nevada under the code name "Limelight 36".[41] Maj. Baylor R. Haynes, a rescue veteran of Korea, led these men as they plunged into their orientation and training program. Many were old rescue hands from Korea, who had been in choppers throughout their Air Force careers. Others had recently transferred to helicopters from fixed-wing aircraft. For a few young copilots, helicopters would be their first assignments right out of pilot training. After completing orientation in September they took leave and reported to Udorn in late October. On November 3, a pair of HH-3Es arrived at Bien Hoa Air Base, Vietnam, in a special rush delivery by C-133 transport. Major Haynes and a selected crew tested the choppers over the South China Sea before flying them to Udorn on November 10. One of the CH-3Cs stationed at Nakhon Phanom had been lost to enemy action on November 5, but the remaining CH-3C moved up to Udorn. By the end of December there were six HH-3Es and the CH-3C operating from Udorn. The CH-3C was returned to the Tactical Air Command in Early January 1966.[42]

69

The HH-3E was much more capable than the CH-3C or the HH-43F in the aircrew recovery role. Powered by two 1,250 horsepower turbine engines, the HH-3E had a top speed of over 160 mph at 7,000 feet and a ceiling of 12,000 feet. It could cruise at 100 mph at 10,000 feet, well out of range of small arms and deadly 23-mm or 37-mm antiaircraft guns.[43]

Increased power meant an increase in fuel consumption and consequently a decrease in range. Sikorsky engineers installed a 650-gallon fuel tank, increasing its capacity nearly thirty percent over that of the CH-3C. By using two jettisonable 200-gallon external tanks like those used on the F-100 jet fighter, the HH-3E could attain a combat range of 500 miles, depending on loiter time and other operational considerations.[44] An aerial refueling capability, however, was visualized as the means for making the HH-3E an even more effective aircrew recovery helicopter. On August 7, 1964, the Air Rescue Service submitted a Qualified Operational Requirement for an air-to-air refueling system for the CH-3C. On May 19, 1966, the Aeronautical Systems Division at Wright-Patterson Air Force Base, Ohio, completed a series of flight tests using a modified CH-3 and a C-130. Nevertheless, it would be more than a year before the first air-refuelable choppers joined the rescue forces in Southeast Asia.[45]

To protect the crew and passengers, Sikorsky distributed 1,000 pounds of half-inch titanium armor plating throughout each HH-3E. Other features included a shatter-proof acrylic glass canopy, an engine ice and foreign object damage shield, and a 600-pound capacity, 240-foot hoist cable with jungle penetrator.[46]

The summer of 1965 was a watershed period for search and rescue in Southeast Asia. Trained air rescue crews, flying HH-43Fs and CH-3Cs provided a viable aircrew recovery capability. In addition to the arrival of CH-3Cs, HC-54s replaced HU-16s in the airborne mission control role. The HU-16s were moved from Udorn to Da Nang. Furthermore, an organizational change restructured Air Rescue Service units in Southeast Asia. The temporary duty helicopter rescue detachments on duty in Vietnam and Thailand from the Pacific Air Rescue Center and parent rescue squadrons in the Pacific area, were consolidated organizationally as permanent change of station detachments of the activated 38th Air Rescue Squadron with headquarters at Tan Son Nhut. Locations and designations were: Det 1, Nakhon Phanom RTAFB, Thailand; Det 2, Takhli RTAFB, Thailand; Det 3, Ubon RTAFB, Thailand; Det 4, Korat RTAFB, Thailand; Det 5, Udorn RTAFB, Thailand; Det 6, Bien Hoa AB, Vietnam; Det 7, Da Nang AB, Vietnam. The HC-54 unit at Korat and the HU-16s at Da Nang continued on temporary duty from their parent PACAF organizations.[47] On September 15, 1965, two more detachments were designated and organized: Det 9, Pleiku AB, Vietnam; Det 10, Binh Thuy AB, Vietnam. This structure sufficed until the next big reorganization that occurred at the beginning of 1966.[48] Throughout the war in Indochina, organizational changes met the requirements of an expanding and contracting conflict. Improved rescue aircraft and equipment enhanced aircrew recovery capabilities, as doctrine and tactics evolved to meet the changing demands imposed by ever-improving enemy defenses.

Most of the time, planning, skill, tactics, and equipment, combined with raw courage of the men, pulled rescue forces through the most precarious situations. Death or captivity, however, were always possibilities. All these elements were present during a rescue effort that began on November 5, 1965, when Oak 01, an F-105 returning from a mission near Hanoi, flew into a cloud and disappeared. The wingman reported Oak 01's last known position, but noticed no antiaircraft fire, missile firings, or explosion. Because of the rapidly deteriorating weather and approaching darkness no rescue attempt was made.

At dawn, under clearing skies, Sandy 11 and Sandy 12, a pair of A-1s, flew over North Vietnam to where Oak 01 had disappeared. Antiaircraft fire hit Sandy 12, and the pilot ejected. Sandy 11 circled and soon spotted the downed pilot. Jolly Green 85, a CH-3C commanded by Capt. Warren R. Lilly, was enroute to the survivor as two more A-1Es scrambled from Udorn to form a search and rescue task force. Enemy small arms fire cut into Jolly 85 as it neared the survivor. Lilly managed to raise his badly damaged helicopter to an altitude sufficient for bailing out. As the Sandys circled, Lilly punched in the automatic pilot and made his way to the door. Pilots in the A-1s reported that four chutes had opened and soon made voice and beeper contact with the downed crewmen. Normally, since rescue helicopters usually flew in pairs to meet emergencies like this, the second chopper — the high bird — would have swooped in for the recovery. But, because of mechanical problems, only Jolly Green 85 was available for this particular mission.

Help, however, was on the way. A U.S. Navy Sikorsky SH-3 Sea Knight helicopter, Nimble 62, reported it was flying toward the crash scene from the carrier *Independence*. Two A-1Es, Sandys 13 and 14, flew to intercept the Sea Knight and escort it into the rescue area. They rendezvoused with Nimble 62 just east of the Vietnamese coast and flew alongside it over the beach and westward toward the jungled mountains of North Vietnam. When the pilot of Sandy 14 spotted 37-mm tracers he peeled off into a cloud in an evasive maneuver. Like Oak 01, Sandy 14 disappeared forever. Sandy 13 and Nimble 62 searched the area but found no sign of wreckage or a survivor. When their fuel ran low the A-1s returned to Udorn and Nimble 62 flew back to its carrier. After refueling, Nimble 62, with an escort of Navy A-1Es, returned to search for Sandy 14, but after an hour without contact with the missing pilot they flew on to the wreckage of Jolly Green 85. At dusk, just before abandoning the search until dawn, a Navy A-1 pilot monitored a beeper's signal. As darkness engulfed the circling task force, Nimble 62 dipped down for a tree-top level visual search. The copilot spotted a tiny light and ordered the penetrator down to pick up the parajumper from Jolly Green 85. The A-1Es and the helicopter, with an Air Force sergeant — who would be forever grateful to the U.S. Navy and his Zippo cigarette lighter — safely aboard, returned to the *Independence*.[49]

The early rays of the morning sun reflected off the Gulf of Tonkin as Nimble 62 and its A-1 escort took off from the carrier's deck and set a course for the Jolly Green 85 wreckage. As the green coast of North Vietnam came into view, an orbiting U.S. Air Force radar picket plane issued a Mig alert. Enemy jets were airborne for an intercept attempt. Fishermen on sampans were clearly visible as the helicopter and its escort flew just above the waves then skimmed over the beaches to the jungle where they encountered intense small arms fire. Nimble 62 shuddered as bullets tore through its skin to slash at fuel lines and control cables. Unable to turn back because of rapid fuel loss, the helicopter pilot made a controlled crash-landing inside North Vietnam. As the downed aircrew broke out M-16s and prepared to fight for their lives, the A-1s blasted enemy troops moving toward the wreckage. Meanwhile, a second Sea Knight scrambled from the *Independence* as a CH-3C left its forward operating base in Laos. The North Vietnamese moved an antiaircraft gun into the area and the A-1 pilots suddenly realized they were involved in a shoot-out. Heavily damaged, the two Skyraiders limped southward to make gear-up belly landings at Da Nang. Meanwhile, the Sea Knight raced to the crash site and rescued all the survivors. Additional A-1s from the carrier then demolished the downed chopper to keep it from falling into enemy hands.[50]

Meanwhile, encouraged by the rescue of the parajumper, the search for other survivors of Jolly Green 85 continued. Late on the afternoon of November 7, an Air Force Sandy pilot heard a beeper signal, but darkness precluded pinpointing the source. Throughout the night, in operations rooms at Udorn and Nakhon Phanom, at the Joint Search and Rescue Center in Saigon and Rescue Control Center at Da Nang, and aboard the *Independence,* intelligence officers, operations officers, and pilots planned the next day's efforts. On flight lines and in hangars throughout South Vietnam and Thailand, as well as in the bowels of the *Independence,* mechanics and munitions loaders prepared their planes and helicopters. In the jungles of North Vietnam the enemy cleaned their weapons and rested before the inevitable fight. An aerial task force of A-1s, CH-3Cs, and SH-3s rose with the sun and converged on the Jolly Green crash. Air Force F-100s from Da Nang and Navy F-8 Crusaders from the *Independence* flew toward their assigned anti-Mig combat air patrol orbit.

A-1s flew low over the helicopter wreckage and finally picked up the sound of a beeper. Two Air Force Skyraider pilots were concentrating on the signal when enemy gunfire ripped, almost simultaneously, into both airplanes. While the two damaged A-1s returned to Udorn, their comrades strafed the enemy gunners who answered with 23-mm, 37-mm, and small arms fire. Meanwhle, rescue controllers in Saigon and at the rescue control centers at Udorn and Da Nang decided that further efforts would only result in additional casualties. Grudgingly they called off the rescue operations. Their decision, though a painful one, was correct. Capt. Warren Lilly, Lt. Jerry Singleton, and SSgt Arthur Cromier, captured soon after parachuting into the jungle, were already miles away, on their way to prison camps in Hanoi.[51]

Rescue was indeed a risky business, and A-1 pilots shared the danger with the chopper crews. By 1967 the A-1E had the highest overall loss rate of any airplane in Southeast Asia. Skyraider loss rates per 1,000 sorties ranged from 1.0 in South Vietnam to 2.3 over Laos and up to 6.2 for missions over North Vietnam. The high loss rate over North Vietnam was directly attributable to the A-1s rescue escort role. Of the twenty-five A-1s shot down over North Vietnam between June 1966 and June 1967, seven were lost on rescue missions.[52]

Korean War vintage, propeller-driven A-1 Skyraiders, like the helicopters they escorted, were slow and faced extreme danger when flying into an area where enemy defenses could shoot down a modern jet fighter. Careful mission planning followed by controlled execution took some edge off the danger. The task of controlling rescue missions evolved with the increasing commitment of American forces.

Before June 1964, the covert nature of operations buried the rescue task in secrecy as search and rescue controllers worked in a liaison capacity within the air operations center at Tan Son Nhut. With the rapid increase in air activity, starting in August 1964 and gaining momentum thereafter, the cloak of secrecy lifted and rescue personnel began functioning overtly. On July 1, 1965, when Detachment 3, Pacific Air Rescue Center, became the 38th Air Rescue Squadron, manning the Joint Search and Rescue Center, functioning in Tan Son Nhut's Air Operations Center since 1962, became part of their mission.[53]

The Joint Search and Rescue Center was responsible for rescue operations in the Bangkok-Saigon Flight Information Regions. It had overall control for coordination of rescue activities in the Republic of Vietnam, Cambodia, Laos, Thailand, and most of North Vietnam, with the Seventh Fleet having control of search and rescue in the waters adjacent to North Vietnam. The rescue control centers at Da Nang and Udorn had regional responsibilities and acted in a liaison capacity.[54] Search and rescue in South Vietnam was necessarily a coordinated effort involving the Air Force, U.S. Army, Marines, and the Vietnamese Air Force. Coordination was accomplished through the Joint Search and Rescue Center, the Tactical Air Control Center at Tan Son Nhut, corps direct air support centers — responsible for coordinated air activity within each of the four corps areas — and other agencies like the rescue coordination centers at Da Nang and Udorn. While the Vietnamese Air Force was responsible for its own rescue function, its limited search and rescue capability failed to meet its needs, so the Air Force assumed that burden. In the Gulf of Tonkin the Air Force and the Navy shared the rescue missions.[55]

The Rescue Control Center at Udorn was responsible for coordinating rescue operations in northern Thailand, North Vietnam, and, when requested and authorized by the ambassador, in Laos. Because of the increasing need in Laos, problems posed by political considerations were solved so that a reliable rescue capability became a reality. Negotiations between the Royal Laotian Government, the U.S. Ambassador, the Deputy Commander, 2d Air Division/13th Air Force at Udorn, Central Intelligence Agency representatives, and the Commander, 2d Air Division, established guidelines. These negotiations were conducted at conferences held throughout the long war. In December 1965, a search and rescue conference in Honolulu, attended by representatives of CINCPAC and CINCPACAF, recommended the assigning of a naval representative to the Joint Search and Rescue Center.[56] When the Navy officer began working in the rescue center in Saigon, it became truly a joint operation.

As demonstrated in the rescue efforts of November 5-8, 1965, the Navy too had a search and rescue capability. Navy air units, operating from carriers in the Gulf of Tonkin, flew Sikorsky SH-3 helicopters with A-1 Skyraiders for rescue escort. Additionally, ships could be called upon to pick up water-logged survivors. Although the Seventh Fleet task force commander was designated the search and rescue coordinator for the Gulf of Tonkin area north of the demilitarized zone, the Joint Search and Rescue Center at Tan Son Nhut exercised overall direction for search and rescue.[57]

Located in the Air Operations Center at Tan Son Nhut, an officer controller, enlisted assistant, and radio operator manned the joint center twenty-four hours a day, seven days a week. Late every afternoon the center received the tactical operations plan for the next day's Air Force and Navy sorties. The officer controller analyzed the strike plan and issued a rescue fragmentary order (frag). Usually the Rescue Control Center at Udorn was tasked to position choppers in Laos at Lima Site 98/30 (often called 20 alternate) at Long Tieng, Meo guerrilla leader Maj. Gen. Vang Pao's headquarters and site of a Central Intelligence Agency complex, and Lima Site 36 at Na Khang, closer to the border of North Vietnam. Likewise, two HH-3Es from Da Nang were flown to the forward operating location at Quang Tri. Through careful planning and efficient use of resources, search and rescue became more effective and less dangerous.[58]

As 1965 drew to a close the air war over Southeast Asia intensified. Losses to enemy defenses rose faster than the growth in aircrew recovery capability. Official figures show that from 1962 through June 1965 a total of 71 U.S. Air Force aircraft were lost to enemy action. From July 1, 1965, to January 1, 1966, the number increased by 112.[59] Likewise, the Air Rescue Service was credited with 29 combat saves between January 1, 1965, and June 30. From July 1, 1965, to January 1, 1966, the rescue service made 93 combat rescues.[60]

Enemy defenses intensified as a Soviet-installed air defense system provided North Vietnam with SA-2 surface-to-air missiles, Mig interceptors, and radar-controlled antiaircraft guns. Air Rescue Service units in mid 1965 were still under-equipped, depending on a score of HH-43B/Fs, a pair of CH-3Cs, five HU-16s, and two HC-54s.[61] New equipment and more modern aircraft were programmed into the rescue service inventory but the natural lag time in research and development, testing, and procurement meant that these improvements were not immediate.

On October 28, 1965, Gen. Howell M. Estes, Jr., Commander of the Military Airlift Command, briefed Gen. John P. McConnell, Air Force Chief of Staff, on the urgent requirements of the Air Rescue Service in Southeast Asia. General Estes told the chief that Air Rescue Service was getting along on "lash up and inadequate" equipment. He recommended an acceleration in HH-3E deliveries, ultimate procurement of thirty-two HH-3Es and eleven HC-130 airborne command post aircraft for use in Southeast Asia, development of a new survivor radio, and increased suppressive armament on the HH-3E. General McConnell, impressed, asked General Estes for a written outline of Air Rescue Service's needs.[62]

At about the same time, Col. Allison C. Brooks, commander of the Air Rescue Service, accepted the first HH-3C helicopter from the Sikorsky Aircraft Division of the United Aircraft Corporation at Stratford, Connecticut. The designation HH-3C was changed to HH-3E in subsequent models when the General Electric T-58-5 engine was incorporated for increased power.[63] As discussed earlier, a C-133 had rushed the first two HH-3Es to Bien Hoa on November 3, 1965. Within a month there were six HH-3Es operating with Detachment 5, 38th Air Rescue Squadron at Udorn. At the end of the year the Air Rescue Service inventory in Southeast Asia included: six HH-3Es; one CH-3C (on loan from TAC); twenty-five HH-43B/Fs; five HU-16s; and two HC-54s. All aircraft and personnel were assigned or attached to the 38th Air Rescue Squadron. The expanding rescue mission was, at the end of 1965, beginning to receive the aircraft it required.[64]

In a major change, the Air Rescue Service, on January 8, 1966, became the Aerospace Rescue and Recovery Service. To meet the expanded mission in Southeast Asia, units there were reorganized. The 3d Aerospace Recovery Group was activated at Tan Son Nhut, Vietnam. The Joint Search and Rescue Center was incorporated into this group and the rescue control centers at Da Nang and Udorn were designated Detachments 1 and 2 respectively. Concurrently, the 37th Aerospace Rescue and Recovery Squadron was activated at Da Nang with one detachment at Udorn. Aircrew recovery in North Vietnam, Laos, and the Gulf of Tonkin was the primary mission of this squadron with its HH-3E helicopters. From its headquarters at Tan Son Nhut, the 38th Aerospace Rescue and Recovery

Squadron ran detachments at most Air Force bases in Vietnam and Thailand. Local base rescue would be this squadron's primary mission with aircrew recovery being performed in South Vietnam.[65]

Among the changes that took place in 1965 and 1966, was the introduction of the HC-130 to replace the HC-54 in the airborne mission control function. Colonel Brooks officially accepted the first HC-130H aircraft from the Lockheed-Georgia Company on July 26, 1965. In August an accelerated transition and rescue training program began at the 48th Air Rescue Squadron, Eglin AFB, Florida.[66] In December 1965, two HC-130Hs, one from the 79th Air Rescue Squadron on Guam and one from the 36th Air Rescue Squadron in Japan, arrived at Udorn as replacements for the HC-54s.[67]

These first HC-130s were configured for long-range, over-water search and were equipped with Cook Aerial Trackers (ARD-17). Initially installed at the request of the National Aeronautics and Space Administration to be used in locating space capsules during reentry, the ARD-17 proved very useful in locating downed airmen through the use of their locator beacons.[68]

Three more HC-130s reached Udorn in late June 1966 and became Detachment 1, 37th Aerospace Rescue and Recovery Squadron on July 4. Although attached to the Da Nang-based squadron, this detachment reported directly to the Commander, 3d Aerospace Rescue and Recovery Group. This initial complement of five HC-130s comprised the skeleton force that, on January 16, 1967, became the 39th Aerospace Rescue and Recovery Squadron.[69]

Air action in Southeast Asia through 1966 showed that combat search and rescue was indispensable to tactical air operations. Even the most complicated and expensive jet aircraft were vulnerable to relatively unsophisticated enemy weapons, and losses increased as the air war intensified against the North Vietnamese heartland.

Initially hobbled by a doctrine which conceived of wartime search and rescue as an extension of peacetime procedures, air-sea rescue had by late 1966 established itself as a necessary and viable part of the Air Force operations in Southeast Asia. From January 1964 through December 31, 1966, official figures indicated that rescue forces saved 647 lives. Of these, 222 were combat aircrew recoveries and 55 noncombat aircrew rescues. The remainder varied from a critically ill German seaman airlifted from a merchant ship off Vietnam and taken to the hospital at Da Nang, to evacuation of battlefield casualties. In aircrew rescues, the Air Force effort accounted for 37 fliers saved from inside North Vietnam, 39 rescued in South Vietnam, and 51 carried out of Laos. Additionally, the Air Force picked up 26 men in the Gulf of Tonkin, and 8 men who bailed out over Thailand, sometimes within sight of their bases. Navy rescue forces picked up 11 men in North Vietnam, 19 in the South, 11 in Laos, one in Thailand, and 19 from the Gulf of Tonkin. United States Army helicopters were credited with rescuing 238 people in South Vietnam and 2 from Laos. Most of these saves occurred when one helicopter moved in to save the crew of a nearby downed chopper.[70]

By 1966, the dismal days that saw air operations conducted without effective rescue forces had passed. A downed aircrew, depending on where it was located, could look forward to at least a one in three chance of rescue. Much had been demanded of the men in Aerospace Rescue and Recovery Service, but much more would be required.

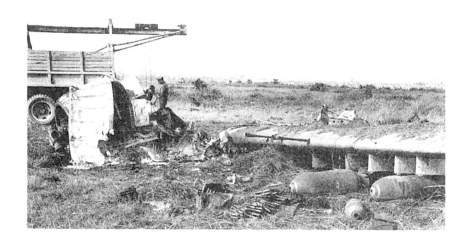

P. 78 top: Lt. Col. Baylor R Haynes (l.) and Maj. Donald A. Vavra (r.) in front of detachment headquarters; center: demolition team cleans up after Viet Cong attack on Nov. 1, 1964; bottom: alert crew races for a CH–3C to take part in rescue; p. 79: top left: pilot uses smoke marker for help; top right: Capt. Harold A. Solberg, 38th ARRS, on a rescue mission; below: U.S. Navy H–3 preparing to land on the USS *Bennington*.

Top: A Jolly Green Giant
rescue in Vietnam waters:
center left: Capt. James R.
Mitchell, F–105 pilot,
immediately after his rescue
on July 27, 1966; center right:
Capt. Lewis E. Lundy samples
plant life in the jungle; left:
A2C George C. Preston
checks survival equipment for
life raft.

4 *Coming of Age:*
1967-1970

By 1967 the war over Indochina comprised the Rolling Thunder campaign against North Vietnam, the Barrel Roll operation in Laos, interdiction of the Ho Chi Minh Trail in southern Laos, and tactical support missions in South Vietnam. As the war dragged on, the cost in aircraft and aircrews rose and the rescue of aircrew members became even more crucial. To meet the rescue needs of airmen fighting in Southeast Asia, the Aerospace Rescue and Recovery Service developed new rescue systems, tactics, and procedures. Although the air war leveled off in this period, new rescue aircraft were introduced and new rescue units were formed in South Vietnam and Thailand.

On January 1, 1967, there were fifty Aerospace Rescue and Recovery Service rescue aircraft in southeast Asia. Five HU-16Bs at Da Nang provided search and rescue cover for the Gulf of Tonkin. The local base rescue force for South Vietnam and Thailand totaled nineteen HU-43Bs and ten HH-43Fs, the latter capable of aircrew recovery operations in a limited small arms environment. Ten HH-3Es were available for rescue missions in northern South Vietnam, Laos, and North Vietnam while six HC-130s performed the airborne rescue mission controller function.[1]

On January 16, 1967, the six HC-130s at Udorn, formerly Detachment 1 of the 37th Air Rescue Squadron at Da Nang, became the 39th Aerospace Rescue and Recovery Squadron. Concurrently, Detachment 2, 37th Aerospace Rescue and Recovery Squadron, was designated and organized at Udorn to perform recovery missions in Laos and North Vietnam. In March 1968, Detachment 2 became the 40th Aerospace Rescue and Recovery Squadron.[2]

In spite of the growing inventory, an atmosphere of concern prevailed at the Aerospace Rescue and Recovery Service headquarters at Scott Air Force Base, Illinois, and at 3d Aerospace Rescue and Recovery Group headquarters at Tan Son Nhut. The primary aircrew rescue helicopters, the HH-43F and HH-3E were "off-the-shelf" vehicles modified to satisfy the immediate rescue requirements. Each aircraft had its peculiar deficiencies.[3] Neither had the speed nor the range to rapidly reach airmen downed deep inside North Vietnam or northern Laos. Primarily restricted to aircrew rescue missions in South Vietnam, the HH-43F was unable to hover over the higher mountains and karst formations. The HH-3E lacked sufficient speed and range to cover North Vietnam without staging from forward operating locations in Laos.[4]

Senior officers and planners at rescue headquarters recognized the limitations inherent in these helicopters. They decided to petition U.S. Air Force headquarters for requirements for an improved search and rescue aircraft. In May 1966, Headquarters, Military Airlift Command, the parent command of the Aerospace Rescue and Recovery Service, submitted a Qualified Operational Requirement for a Combat Aircrew Recovery Aircraft.[5]

The requirements for this advanced recovery vehicle were based on 3d Aerospace Rescue and Recovery Group analysis of Southeast Asia combat rescue experiences. They found that forty-seven percent of all unsuccessful rescue attempts resulted from the slow speed of the helicopters. For the downed airman this meant capture or death. The analysts concluded that if a rescue helicopter could reach a survivor within fifteen minutes, the chances of rescue were good. If the rescue force took more than thirty minutes to reach the downed airman his chances of being successfully rescued diminished rapidly. Considering the 150-nautical-mile distance from the northernmost forward operating location, Lima Site 36, to Hanoi, the advanced rescue vehicle would need a top speed of nearly 300 knots to get there in half an hour. To reach Hanoi in 15 minutes would require a speed of 600 knots. Such speeds were beyond the state-of-the-art in rotary wing technology. The envisioned aircraft would require a combination of a near-supersonic jet and helicopter.[7] Following a thorough evaluation of proposals from companies like Sikorsky and Boeing, it was decided that such an aircraft, if it could be built, would be far too expensive to risk in a combat situation.[8] For the present, existing rescue aircraft would have to suffice. A significant improvement in aircrew rescue was not to be realized until the introduction of the Sikorsky HH-53 in late 1967.

Ingenuity became commonplace, as rescue personnel coped with technological limitations and faced improving enemy defenses. Although the Air Rescue Service had submitted a requirement for an air-to-air refueling system in 1964, the first combat use of the system did not occur until late June 1967. Until then the HH-3Es had no alternative but to use the forward operating locations at Quang Tri in northern South Vietnam and Lima Sites in northern Laos. Even after June 1967, when aerial refueling of helicopters became standard practice, HH-3Es and HH-53s continued to use Lima Site 98 (20 alternate) at Long Tieng and Lima Site 36 at Na Khang to the north of the Plain of Jars.

But there were political risks involved in using the Lima Sites. Washington and Vientiane risked adverse political ramifications by having a U.S. Air Force helicopter and an American military aircrew situated near Vang Pao's headquarters at Long Tieng. To minimize these risks, rescue crews flew to Long Tieng at dawn and left at dusk when the last strikes over

North Vietnam and northern Laos ended. Lima Site 36 at Na Khang, which was sometimes surrounded by the Pathet Lao, was not a headquarters. However, the enemy regularly shelled this base and often threatened to overrun it. It would have been embarrassing for the U.S. Government if an American aircrew had been captured while involved in such an obvious violation of the 1962 Geneva Accords on Laos.[9]

Staging from the Lima Sites made for a long day. Usually the crews at Udorn climbed out of their bunks at 3:30 in the morning. After breakfast at the officers' or noncommissioned officers' clubs they rode a van to the flight line. There they picked up their helmets, checked out survival gear, flak vests, and parachutes, and signed for pistols and M-16 rifles. After attending briefings on the weather, operations, and intelligence, the crew gave their helicopter its preflight check. By dawn they were airborne and headed north. The choppers headed for either Long Tieng or Na Khang. Neither place looked like much from the air, nor for that matter from the ground, with Lima Site 36 being somewhat more primitive than Long Tieng. Na Khang was a strong point perched on the top of a mountain. It included a short dirt runway, a few sand-bagged shacks, and trenchworks. Laotian troops defended it from the Pathet Lao and from the North Vietnamese who often held the surrounding countryside.

After landing at Na Khang the rescue crew passed the time sleeping in or under their choppers, reading, or joking with native troops. If they did not receive a call for help before the strike aircraft reached their targets in North Vietnam, their mornings passed quietly. During the heaviest air strikes, however, the crew would fly the Jolly Green Giant to its orbit 10,000 feet above the North Vietnam-Laos border area. The chopper orbited there until needed or, before inflight refueling became a reality, for about two or two-and-a-half hours before returning to Na Khang for fuel. After June 1967, when the air-refuelable HH-3E became operational, the choppers could refuel in flight and double their time on orbit.[10]

Aerial refueling revolutionized search and rescue operations. However, the first inflight transfer of fuel between an HC-130P and an HH-3E did not occur until December 14, 1966. Before 1964 aerial refueling was not thought feasible for helicopters. Innovative thinking and bold action by a handful of Air Force and civilian engineers in the H-3 Systems Project Office at Wright-Patterson Air Force Base, Ohio, made it a reality.[11]

Running against the tide of contemporary thought, Mr. James Eastman, Mr. Richard Wright, and Maj. Harry P. Dunn, an experienced helicopter pilot who had spent his entire Air Force career in choppers, thought that aerial refueling of the H-3 might be a distinct possibility. Working under an Air Rescue Service operational requirement for inflight refueling, Dunn jury-rigged a fuel probe to the front of a CH-3 in December 1965. After flying to Andrews Air Force Base, Maryland, he contacted a U.S. Marine Corps aviation unit at Cherry Point, North Carolina, and persuaded its commander to join him in a refueling experiment. The Marines agreed to contribute a KC-130 tanker with a drogue refueling apparatus. Dunn then flew the Air Force CH-3 to Cherry Point to perform the tests.

Dunn, Eastman, and Wright disagreed with most of the engineers in the H-3 Systems Project Office who thought that for aerial refueling to be feasible at all, the helicopter would have to precede the refueling aircraft or risk being torn apart in the wind blast from the propeller wash of the larger airplane. These engineers proposed having the helicopter reel out a hose to the refueler and then pump the fuel aboard. Dunn, Wright, and Eastman objected because they thought that it would be inadvisable to have the lower-performance helicopter in front of the higher performance C-130. Major Dunn believed that the CH-3 could fly on the slip-stream of the four-engine turbo-prop without being ripped apart. He thought the hull-like design of the CH-3's fuselage could be used to give it buoyancy on top of the slip stream. The helicopter would then float along on this blast of air like a boat on water.

On December 17, 1965, Eastman and Wright took off from Cherry Point. Dunn and a Marine crew took to the air in a KC-130. They rendez-voused over the ocean and Eastman pulled the helicopter in behind the transport and settled on top of its prop wash. His theories proved correct as the chopper floated along on this slip stream. He nosed the probe into the KC-130's drogue and air rescue was revolutionized.

Although the first actual transfer of fuel was a year away, Dunn had proven aerial refueling was a valid concept for helicopters. He returned to Wright-Patterson Air Force Base to first win over doubters in the systems project office and then convince his superiors in the Air Rescue Service.[12] He succeeded in both endeavors and in the spring of 1966 the Air Force began a series of tests using a modified CH-3 and a C-130. Satisfied with the feasibility of inflight refueling, the Air Force approved an initial rescue service order for eleven HC-130Hs converted for the aerial refueling role. The modifications were made at the Lockheed plant in Marietta, Georgia, near Atlanta. Lockheed installed fuel tanks with a 48,500 pound capacity, pumps, and drogues. Each of the HC-130Hs had previously served as rescue control ships and contained the latest search and rescue avionics including the AN/ARD-17 aerial tracking system, AN/APX-65 IFF interrogator, the AN/ARA-25 UHF/VHF homer, and rescue kits containing life rafts, flares, and first aid equipment.[13]

Lockheed delivered the first modified aircraft, redesignated the HC-130P, to the Aerospace Rescue and Recovery Service on November 18, 1966. Five more HC-130Ps were available by the end of the year with three additional airframes delivered in January 1967 and two more that spring. Beginning on November 7, 1966, rescue crews reported to the 48th Aerospace Rescue and Recovery Squadron at Eglin Air Force Base, Florida, to be trained in refueling techniques. It was there, on December 14, 1966, that the first inflight transfer of fuel between an HC-130P and an HH-3E occurred.[14] Even as crews trained at Eglin, HC-130Ps were being flown to Southeast Asia to replace HC-130Hs in the 39th Aerospace Rescue and Recovery Squadron which had been relocated from Udorn to Tuy Hoa Air Base, South Vietnam on June 8, 1967.[15]

Meanwhile, the innovative nature of inflight refueling of helicopters began to draw accolades in America and abroad. On May 12, 1967, the American Helicopter Society awarded the Grover E. Bell Award to the Aerospace Rescue and Recovery Service for its contribution to helicopter technology.[16] Less than a month later, on June 1, Majs. Herbert R. Zehnder and Donald B. Burass piloted two HH-3Es from Brooklyn Naval Air Station, New York across the Atlantic Ocean to the Paris Air Show. They were accompanied by five HC-130Ps from Eglin Air Force Base. One HC-130P flew with the choppers throughout the entire journey. This aircraft, the command tanker, flew "high cover" checking the weather ahead of the flight all the way. In the last stages of the journey it flew ahead of the choppers, landed at the Royal Air Force base at Mildenhall, England, refueled, and rejoined the choppers over the English Channel. During this leg of the flight it refueled one of the choppers. The eight other refuelings also were performed by HC-130Ps: one at Loring Air Force Base, Maine, two at Goose Air Base, Canada, and one at Keflavik Air Base, Iceland.[17] The mission, which covered 4,157 miles, set several helicopter world records, including the longest rotary-winged flight, endurance, and even a speed record as the two HH-3Es averaged 131 mph throughout the trip.[18]

While world records and accolades from aviation societies delighted the people in public relations, the reason for the development of aerial refueling was to save lives in Southeast Asia. On June 21, 1967, 3d Aerospace Rescue and Recovery Group crews carried out the first operational test of aerial refueling between an HC-130P and an HH-3E. By September this technique had become routine throughout Southeast Asia.[19]

In-flight refueling offered rescue forces new flexibility by extending the range of the helicopters and allowing them to orbit, thereby cutting down the time it took to reach airmen down in North Vietnam and Laos. On a typical rescue sortie, the choppers topped off their fuel prior to heading for the assigned orbit. Reaching the orbit area at least thirty minutes before the first attack aircraft reached its target, the rescue choppers could remain in orbit until the last fighter-bomber unloaded its ordnance and returned to safer skies, or until they were called upon to make a recovery. The HC-130P Crown (later King) airborne rescue command post orbited in the same pattern and refueled the Jolly Greens when needed. If the choppers received a rescue call that required hovering at higher altitudes, above mountains and karst formations, it was often necessary to dump fuel. Before aerial refueling became a reality, this was impossible in many cases because the choppers could not make it back to friendly territory on the remaining fuel.

After June 1967, however, the refuelable choppers dumped fuel when the situation demanded and refueled from the airborne command post on the way back.[20]

There were four orbit areas in 1967: two orbits along the border between Laos and North Vietnam, one of them in northern Laos parallel to Hanoi, the other in central Laos due west of Vinh; another orbit was near the demilitarized zone; and, at least one HH-3E flew the fourth orbit over the Gulf of Tonkin during the peak strike periods.[21]

With the HH-3E and the HC-130P team in operation, air rescue in Southeast Asia reached a new level. The HC-130Hs had already replaced the venerable HU-16B Albatrosses as rescue communications aircraft. As a logical extension of the Gulf of Tonkin orbit, the HH-3E had supplemented the aging HU-16 in the water-borne rescue role with the Albatross flying its last Southeast Asia sortie on September 30, 1967.[22]

In the spring of 1967, 3d Aerospace Rescue and Recovery Group planners began working with the U.S. Navy to make the HH-3E a viable replacement for the HU-16 in rescue operations over the Gulf of Tonkin. Together they devised a system for helicopters to take on fuel from Navy ships if, for some reason, it was impossible for the HH-3E to get to a tanker. Known as "Operation High Drink", the HH-3Es, and later the HH-53s, could take on fuel from virtually any vessel carrying a supply of fuel, a hose, and a suitable nozzle for the transfer. Fuel was transferred while the helicopters hovered alongside the vessels or landed on the decks of larger destroyers, cruisers, and aircraft carriers.[23]

Operation High Drink and aerial refueling made it possible for the HH-3E, which was capable of landing on water, to replace the aging HU-16B. When the Albatross completed its last Gulf of Tonkin rescue sortie on September 30, 1967, it ended five years of service as an airborne command post and amphibious recovery aircraft in Southeast Asia. During their amphibious recoveries HU-16 crews performed some of the most dangerous rescue missions of the war. In the final tally, Albatrosses picked up twenty-six U.S. Air Force and twenty-one Navy aircrew members. Enemy gunfire and weather combined to destroy four Albatrosses and took the lives of nine HU-16 crew members.[24]

These nine men died in two separate incidents. On March 18, 1966, North Vietnamese shore-based artillery blasted an HU-16 out of the water killing two crewmen. On October 18, 1966, an HU-16 commanded by Maj. Ralph H. Angstat took off in marginal weather to fly a normal patrol over the Gulf of Tonkin. The weather deteriorated and Angstat failed to report in on a routine radio check. When conditions cleared, a second HU-16 scrambled to search for the missing aircraft but found nothing. Navy planes and ships joined the search to no avail. Neither wreckage, bodies, nor survivors were ever found. Angstat and six crewmen disappeared.[25]

Because HU-16 operations occurred over the Gulf, the U.S. Navy often became involved. The Joint Search and Rescue Center in Saigon and the Rescue Control Center at Da Nang coordinated rescue forces from both the Navy and the Air Force. Usually these forces included not only the Air Force HU-16 on precautionary orbit but also Navy patrol planes, helicopters, and A-1 rescue escort aircraft. On one occasion, on February 12, 1967, an Air Force HU-16 flown by Lt. Col. Alan R. Vette, Commander of the 37th Aerospace Rescue and Recovery Squadron worked with a Navy E-2A patrol plane, two SH-3 helicopters, four F-4B Phantom jets, four A-1Hs, and a destroyer to save the crew of a Navy RA-5 reconnaissance jet down in the surf just off the shore of North Vietnam. Colonel Vette acted as on-scene commander controlling the Navy SH-3s. When enemy gunfire and mechanical difficulties prevented the helicopters from making a successful recovery, Vette landed the Albatross in the rough surf and quickly picked up the survivors. During this effort Navy A-1s and the destroyer bombarded enemy gun emplacements firing at the rescue aircraft.[26]

Later Colonel Vette gave credit to his parajumper for making the mission a success. As usual the pararescueman had several problems to solve. The downed pilot had a broken arm which kept him from freeing his tiny one-man life raft from his parachute shrouds. Additionally, a Navy helicopter crewman had leaped into the water to attempt to cut the injured pilot and raft free and had himself become entangled in the shrouds. The parajumper had to get the two men out of what had become a floating mass of men, rubber raft, rope, and parachute. According to Vette, his parajumper dove beneath the raft, grabbed all the shrouds in one hand and sliced through them with his survival knife. The pilot and Navy helicopter crewmen were free of the shrouds in less than ten seconds and thirty seconds later were aboard the HU-16.[27]

William B. Karstetter, former historian for the Aerospace Rescue and Recovery Service, once described the pararescuemen (known as parajumpers or PJs) as "the cutting edge of the rescue tool". These men were a product of their specialized training which was varied and intense. Every pararescueman was a scuba diver, trained and certified by the U.S. Navy. Expertise in first aid qualified the parajumper as a medical technician. The Army gave them jump training which Air Force specialists improved upon to make each parajumper an expert parachutist. They were adept at survival in the desert, jungle, swamps, and the arctic. Finally, each parajumper was an expert with small arms and qualified in hand-to-hand combat.[28]

Pararescuemen were a special breed. The military produced several elites during the Vietnam conflict, mostly men dedicated to taking human lives in any number of ways. Air Force parajumpers were an elite committed to saving human lives. Their tradition began in World War II and continued through the Korean conflict. It received new vitality in the late fifties and early sixties as the Air Rescue Service became involved in recovering satellites and manned space vehicles.

SEARCH AND RESCUE

During the war in Indochina, pararescue jumpers became the most admired men on the rescue team. The parajumper was always the first friendly face seen by a flier downed in enemy territory. It was the parajumper who stood at the helicopter door to lower the jungle penetrator and, if the survivor was injured, it was the parajumper who went down to help him. On several occasions, when only one man could get out, it was the parajumper who stayed behind.

On March 7, 1966, A1C William H. Pitsenbarger, a parajumper with the 38th Aerospace Rescue and Recovery Squadron, grabbed the hoist cable, wrapped his legs around the jungle penetrator, and began riding it to the ground to help evacuate American army troops from a Viet Cong ambush. As he passed through the trees an AK-47 bullet ripped into his back. Pitsenbarger held on, and when he reached the ground he worked under enemy fire to aid the soldiers. The hoist operator on the HH-43F hauled up as many wounded GIs as the little chopper would hold. Pitsenbarger chose to stay behind to help the remaining soldiers, all of whom were wounded, fight off the Viet Cong. Soon another HH-43F showed up and the second helicopter's parajumper surveyed the now quiet battle scene below. He went down and found that the enemy had killed Pitsenbarger and massacred the wounded soldiers. For his bravery, Airman Pitsenbarger was posthumously awarded the Air Force Cross. He was the first enlisted man to receive this award.[29]

A1C Duane D. Hackney, a parajumper with the 37th Aerospace Rescue and Recovery Squadron, appeared in numerous after action reports as he established a record that made him legendary in the world of rescue. On February 16, 1967 Hackney was searching for a downed pilot in the underbrush of a North Vietnamese jungle. He found the injured pilot and strapped him into a Stokes litter, the standard metal frame litter used by rescue forces since the Korean War, and both of them rode up to the safety of the helicopter. As the men reached the door, North Vietnamese Army troops began firing at the chopper. The pilot pulled the HH-3E up, but an enemy gunner found his mark and the Jolly Green Giant began to burn. Hackney put a parachute on the injured man and then climbed into one himself. Suddenly the helicopter exploded throwing Hackney out. His parachute opened just above the trees. The second HH-3E, the "high bird", rushed in and its parajumper went down to search for survivors. He found only Hackney, dazed but not seriously injured, and brought him up to safety.[30]

Less than a month later, on March 13, Hackney was one of two parajumpers aboard an HH-3E Jolly Green flying deep into Viet Cong territory just south of the demilitarized zone. A Marine H-34 troop transport helicopter was down and the survivors reported enemy soldiers closing in for the kill. A second Marine helicopter crew overheard the radio transmissions calling for help and turned their larger H-46 troop and cargo helicopter toward their beleaguered comrades. Hackney's Jolly Green arrived in time to see the H-46 chopper stall, roll over on its side and fall on top of the first downed helicopter.

On the ground the Marines gathered their injured and set their defenses against the enemy forces closing in from all sides. Above, in the door of the HH-3E, Duane Hackney watched as Air Force A-1s darted in to blast at the Viet Cong. When the Skyraiders had laid down a smoke screen, Maj. Adrian D. Youngblood cautiously moved the Jolly Green over the embattled Marines. As soon as the giant chopper came to a hover, Hackney was on the Stokes litter and on his way to the ground. He loaded as many injured men as he could on the litter and rode up with them, exposing himself to enemy snipers on each trip. On one foray up the hoist, just as Hackney and a wounded Marine got to the door, Major Youngblood saw warning lights flash on indicating the hydraulics were out. With bullets smashing into the fuselage, the pilot pulled the chopper up and headed for Da Nang. Meanwhile Hackney, working in the cabin tending the wounded, suddenly slumped to the floor. An enemy bullet had grazed his helmet knocking him out, but he soon regained consciousness and continued setting fractures, tending head wounds, and applying tourniquets.[31] For his efforts, Airman Hackney received the Air Force Cross from General Estes on September 9, 1967.[32] Duane Hackney was the most decorated parajumper to serve in Southeast Asia. That in itself was quite an accomplishment because parajumpers won more decorations than any other group of men in the Air Force serving in Indochina.[33]

The pararescuemen were a part of the Aerospace Rescue and Recovery Service that extended beyond the confines of machinery to adapt themselves to the physical conditions surrounding the survivor. They were the link between the rescue helicopter and the downed flyer. Crucial as parajumpers were to the rescue mission, they depended on the rescue helicopter to get them to the individuals in need, hover during the recovery, and then return them and the survivors to safety. Through the years of the Vietnam conflict, helicopters improved from the HH-43 through the HH-3E to the Sikorsky HH-53.

In 1966 the Aerospace Rescue and Recovery Service decided that a combat aircrew recovery aircraft would be too sophisticated, too expensive, and possibly too late to use in Southeast Asia. The only viable alternative was to take another "off-the-shelf" helicopter and modify it for the aircrew recovery mission. Although the HH-3E represented a milestone in rescue technology and greatly increased the capabilities of search and rescue forces, it had certain limitations. These shortcomings necessitated the acquisition of a newer, more capable aircrew rescue helicopter.

Some of the deficiencies were a lack of sufficient armor, limited firepower, and marginal hover capabilities. Although the HH-3E had enough armor plate in its vital areas to endure limited small arms fire, it was not able to survive the increasingly intense antiaircraft fire in North Vietnam, parts of Laos, and even South Vietnam. Furthermore, its engines were not sufficiently powerful to maintain a hover above the tree tops of the higher mountains. Finally, with only one 7.62-mm machine gun, roughly equal to a .30 caliber gun, the HH-3E did not have the firepower to "shoot its way out" of many situations.[34]

In August 1962, the U.S. Marine Corps placed a contract for a heavy lift helicopter with Sikorsky.[35] Air Force officials thought the Sikorsky CH-53A, which first flew in October 1964, had the necessary power, speed, range, and physical size to meet the needs of rescue units in Southeast Asia.[36]

Combat requirements in Indochina were not the only factors influencing the decision to procure the Sikorsky helicopters. In addition to the combat aircrew rescue mission, the Aerospace Rescue and Recovery Service was charged with recovering space hardware for the National Aeronautics and Space Administration. With the advent of the three-man Apollo spacecraft, a helicopter with tremendous lift capabilities was needed to haul it out of the ocean after its space trips. The CH-53 was capable of performing that mission, and could be modified to fill the aircrew recovery requirements in Southeast Asia.[37]

On November 28, 1966, Sikorsky delivered a CH-53A to the 48th Aerospace Rescue and Recovery Squadron, at Eglin Air Force Base, Florida. It was the first of two Marine CH-53As on temporary loan to the Aerospace Rescue and Recovery Service. The second helicopter reached Eglin in December, and crew training began shortly thereafter.[38] On June 19, 1967, the rescue service took delivery of the first HH-53Bs specifically designed and built for aircrew rescue in Southeast Asia.[39]

Lt. Col. James M. Dixon, Commander of Detachment 2, 37th Aerospace Rescue and Recovery Squadron, and Majs. Garland A. York, Frederick M. Donohue, and William F. Williams went to the Sikorsky plant to pick up the helicopter. They spent a few days familiarizing themselves with the HH-53B. On June 21 they flew the giant helicopter to Washington, D.C. to demonstrate its capabilities to the Secretary of Defense, the Secretary of the Air Force, and the Joint Chiefs of Staff.[40]

In August 1967, after a number of crews had been trained at Eglin, two HH-53Bs were loaded aboard the USS *Card,* an old aircraft carrier converted to an aircraft ferry, and shipped to Vietnam. On September 14, the choppers reached Vung Tau where Air Force specialists and Sikorsky representatives received them.[41]

Detachment 2, 37th Aerospace Rescue and Recovery Squadron at Udorn received the first two HH-53Bs. However, it was impossible to use them fully. For instance, they could not be used in continuous orbits as originally planned. At least part of the problem resulted from deficiencies in training the crew members received at Eglin. Copilots arriving from the

48th Aerospace Rescue and Recovery Training Squadron at Eglin were, in many cases, unqualified in aerial refueling techniques. Pilots had to spend time training these men before they were fully prepared for combat missions. Additionally there were, as with any new aircraft, mechanical problems. The hydraulic seals on the spindle of the rotor head leaked. Engine starters were not reliable, and Sikorsky representatives had to add a booster motor. And, fins on the oil cooler often collapsed at high speed, impeding the air flow through the cooler, a problem remedied by using stiffer fins.[42]

The HH-53B represented almost as much of an improvement over the HH-3E as that helicopter had been over the HH-43F. Aircrews called it "BUFF", short for Big Ugly Fat Fellow. The Aerospace Rescue and Recovery Service designated it the Super Jolly Green Giant, primarily because crews often substituted an obscenity for the word "fellow". In any event, its names connoted its size, which was almost twice that of the HH-3E.[43]

The Super Jolly Greens had all the avionics of the HH-3Es. Their biggest improvements were in lift power and defensive armament. Two GE-T64-3 turboshaft engines produced 3,080 horsepower to increase lift power. On one occasion an HH-53B lifted an A-1E weighing 12,000 pounds and carried it fifty-six miles from the central Laotian panhandle to Nakhon Phanom. This added lift power increased its hover capability by forty percent to make aircrew recoveries from the higher mountain regions less hazardous.[44] The increased performance of the HH-53C, the ultimate rescue chopper used in Southeast Asia, compared to that of the HH-3E is shown in the following table:

CHARACTERISTIC	HH-3E	HH-53C
Normal gross weight (pounds) with crew and ammo	18,000	36,000
Useful Load Capacity (pounds)	3,000	13,000
Engines: Number/Type	(1) T-58-GE-5	(2) T-64-GE-7
Horsepower	1,250	3,925
Speed (Knots):		
Cruise	120	140
Maximum	143	170-190+
Altitude (feet)	12,000	16,000
Hover Limit (feet)	4,000	6,500
Crew Complement	4	4-6
Armament:		
Number / Type	(2) M-60 .30 cal. machineguns	(3) GAU-2B/A[45] miniguns 7.62-mm

As a result of its larger size and increased capacity the HH-53B/C usually carried two pararescuemen rather than the one carried on HH-3Es.

On some missions a combat photographer was carried as a sixth crewmember. Although it was only rarely used as a transport, up to forty fully-equipped soldiers could be carried on the HH-53C.[46] (During the evacuation of Saigon on April 1, 1975, up to ninety Vietnamese men, women, and children crowded into each chopper on every sortie.)

Improvements in defensive armament included the installation of three General Electric 7.62-mm gatling type miniguns, each capable of firing up to 4,000 rounds per minute.[47] The use of titanium armor in vital engine and hydraulic areas improved the HH-53B/Cs chances for survival when it encountered small arms or light antiaircraft fire (.50 caliber, 14.5-mm and 23-mm). These improvements made the BUFF less vulnerable if it were moving at its top speed of over 170 knots. However, in a hover over a survivor it was still quite assailable.[48]

Six additional HH-53Bs reached Southeast Asia before the first HH-53Cs arrived in September 1969. In the HH-53B/C choppers the rescue service had an aircraft that, with inflight refueling, had excellent range and an improved defensive system. It had its limitations, but the most serious performance restrictions were not due to deficiencies in aircraft design but to darkness and poor weather. Missions in foul weather were hazardous, and night efforts were rarely attempted and virtually always unsuccessful.

The need for a night recovery capability was illustrated on Christmas Day, 1968. On the night before Christmas an F-105 crashed in Laos. The wingman made radio contact with the downed pilot who reported he was injured. The wingman told the injured pilot to take cover for the night and that help would arrive at first light.

A search and rescue task force arrived at dawn on Christmas. One of the pilots spotted the survivor's parachute and the A-1s began trolling for fire. Enemy troops, hiding in wait, did not shoot at the A-1s, so the HH-53 moved to a hover position over the parachute. The aircraft commander ordered the parajumper down to find the wounded flyer. When he reached the ground, the parajumper discovered the pilot and reported that he had been killed. He strapped the corpse to the jungle penetrator, grabbed on and began to ascend through the trees. When he reached the foliage the enemy opened fire, knocking the parajumper off the penetrator before turning their weapons on the hovering chopper. Badly wounded and injured from the fall, the pararescueman used his survival radio to contact the helicopter pilot and told him to get out of the area because enemy troops were nearly on top of him. If the rescue could have been attempted the night before, the rescue task force might have reached the downed pilot before the Pathet Lao. The enemy would certainly not have had time to set up a trap, and both the pilot and parajumper might have survived.[49]

There was indeed an urgent need for a night recovery system. Southeast Asia Operational Requirement 114, dated April 3, 1967, stated that with state-of-the-art technology, combat aircrew recoveries at night or in foul weather were almost impossible. SAOR 114 made several proposals to remedy this situation, with infrared detection as the most promising. This detection system worked by comparing body heat with the heat generated by objects in the background. The limiting factors included not being able to differentiate between body heat of a downed aircrew and that of enemy soldiers.[50]

In March 1968, the Aerospace Rescue and Recovery Service issued a modified program directive to Aeronautic Systems Division at Wright-Patterson Air Force Base, Ohio, providing for a limited night recovery system using low-light-level television. The resulting system incorporated a viewing device that had to be mounted in the starboard door under the hoist and in front of the minigun. Rescue crewmen did not like this arrangement, because it restricted the usefulness of the minigun and limited their defensive capabilities. Nevertheless, after testing at Eglin, the low-light-level television and the viewing device were installed in a Udorn-based HH-53B in November 1969. The system was so unreliable that rescue headquarters decided against installing this limited night recovery system in favor of a full night recovery system that would, supposedly, be much improved. However, it would not be ready until 1972.[51] Even then the full night recovery system was not adequate. The only night recovery credited to the system occurred on December 21, 1972. The survivor was picked up from an isolated area in southern Laos. The recovery chopper met no enemy opposition, and the pilot was able to concentrate on using the system.

The HH-53B/C represented the best in rescue technology, yet there were some limitations in the system. Too large to be an ideal rescue helicopter, its size kept it from maneuvering in tight areas like karst valleys. Its large size and relatively slow speed made it an easy target for enemy gunners. At its top speed of 170-190 knots, the HH-53C was vulnerable to 14.5-mm heavy machinegun fire for more than half a minute. It remained within range of a 23-mm antiaircraft gun for almost a full minute while a 57-mm gunner could fire on it for nearly two and a half minutes.[53]

Pilots complained about the limited field of view. The position of the rotor mast forced the pilot to maintain a five degree nose-up attitude during the hover, thus further restricting his view forward and down. Crew commanders were also concerned that during a hover the starboard side was not covered by the minigun because if one parajumper was on the jungle penetrator or helping the survivor aboard, and the other was working the winch, there was no one available to fire the minigun.[54]

In spite of those shortcomings, the HH-53s were the finest rescue helicopters in the world. With subsequent modifications, and within the framework of the entire rescue effort, the HH-53s contributed to making successful aircrew rescue the norm rather than the exception for aircrews shot down in Southeast Asia.

The HH-53s, with increased speed and defensive armament, formed the heart of the search and rescue task force. Basic rescue tactics, developed through the mid-sixties, although constantly evaluated, remained fundamentally unchanged. In October 1970, Col. Frederick V. Sohle, Jr., Commander of the 3d Aerospace Rescue and Recovery Group said, "Our development . . . has been a history of relearning lessons already learned by someone else, but who unfortunately could not or did not document it for others to profit by." [55]

A-1 Sandys , retaining their rescue mission, worked under controllers in HC-130P Crown control planes and patrolled crash areas looking for antiaircraft positions while they pinpointed downed airmen's exact locations. Normally, four A-1s in two flights of two were used in rescue escort. The flights were referred to as "Sandy High" and "Sandy Low" and flew either individually or with the helicopters. One of the pilots in the Sandy Low flight acted as the on-scene commander. Unless Crown specifically decided otherwise, it was Sandy Low who cleared the helicopter to make the final pickup.

The two-plane flight called Sandy High escorted the helicopters to the crash site. Sandy High lead, the first plane, navigated and controlled the formation up to the initial point, the point at which the actual recovery operation began. He then directed the helicopters to an orbit at a given altitude and location chosen with regard to geographic formation, weather, and disposition of enemy forces.

Simultaneously, Sandy Low at the rescue area determined the condition of the downed aircrew, its location and the exact disposition of enemy defenses with relation to terrain, and other factors. If he encountered enemy resistance, Sandy Low had to decide if he would attack the guns or call in other attack aircraft. Ultimately, Sandy Low lead, as on-scene commander, determined exactly when the pickup attempt would be made. In some cases he called in air strikes for several days before finally directing the Jolly Greens in for the actual recovery.

Forward air controllers were usually part of the search and rescue task force, much more so in the early stages of the recovery mission than in the latter part. The forward air controller was often the first aircraft in the area and assumed the role of on-scene commander until Sandy Low arrived. Often it was the forward air controller, flying in a small, single-engine O-1, a twin-engine O-2, or a larger twin-engine OV-10, who first spotted the survivor. Because these controllers generally worked in the same area, they had intimate knowledge of its geography and generally knew enemy force dispositions and capabilities. After Sandy Low reached the initial point, the forward air controller assisted by directing jet strike fighters if they were needed.

If Sandy Low wanted additional support from better-suited A-1s, he asked Crown to send aircraft equipped with special ordnance used in search and rescue missions. This ordnance included smoke rockets and bombs, riot control chemicals, and cluster bombs. Normally, these aircraft remained on the ground, fueled and fully armed, until requested by Sandy Low lead.[56]

When Sandy Low determined that it was safe for the Jolly Greens, recovery attempt, he called Sandy High down for a detailed briefing on the survivor's location, enemy force dispositions, and any other factors deemed important. Sandy High then joined the two choppers in their orbit area and escorted the helicopter designated as "low bird" down for the pickup. The other helicopter, the "high bird", remained in its orbit, ready to rush in if the need arose.[57] This constituted the classic search and rescue task force, virtually unchanged from the mid-sixties through the end of the war, and very much like the rescue patterns flown by the Germans in World War II. In reality, rescue situations always differed, with terrain, enemy resistance, and the condition of the survivor determining specific tactics.

As the war continued, the North Vietnamese, Viet Cong, and Pathet Lao used increasingly sophisticated weapons and tactics to frustrate rescue efforts. Rescue forces reacted to these challenges by developing new weapons and changing tactics. Tear gas bombs and riot control chemicals were some of the most controversial weapons used to support rescue operations. These weapons included Cluster Bomb Unit (CBU)-19A/B and CBU-30A antipersonnel area denial bombs, which were essentially tear gas bombs. Also used was the Bomb Live Unit (BLU)-52A/B, a weapon concocted by mixing bulk tear gas with the ingredients in the BLU-1C fire bomb.[58]

Since November 3, 1965, the Commander, U.S. Military Assistance Command, Vietnam had the authority to authorize use of riot control agents. Command policy for the use of these munitions, as stated in MACV Directive 525-11, considered riot control agents as normal components of combat power. Tear gas was used by American as well as South Vietnamese forces in operations that included forcing the Viet Cong out of their tunnel hideaways.[59]

On February 2, 1968, the Joint Chiefs of Staff authorized the use of riot control munitions during search and rescue operations in Laos.[50] The use of weapons with chemical and biological overtones was politically sensitive, and their use was even more of a problem in Laos where all military operations were hypersensitive. Although the on-scene commander was authorized to use riot control munitions if he felt the rescue operation was in jeopardy, he had to relay his decision immediately to Headquarters, Seventh Air Force, and to the 3d Aerospace Rescue and Recovery Group in Saigon.[61] Consequently, betweeen February 1968 and June 1971, riot control munitions were used only a score of times in Laos.[62]

A February 15, 1969, mission on which CBU-19 tear gas bombs were used demonstrated the power of these weapons. A rescue effort for the pilot of an F-4, down in the enemy-infested A Shau Valley area near the Laos-South Vietnam border, dragged into its second day. Enemy 37-mm and

57-mm antiaircraft gunners shot down and killed the on-scene commander, Sandy Low lead. The whole effort to rescue the F-4 pilot seemed in jeopardy. Any attempt to use the Jolly Greens would have been suicidal. The only hope of success seemed to be with the use of riot control munitions. A-1s, loaded with CBU-19, took off from Pleiku Air Base, Vietnam, and reached the A Shau Valley half an hour later. Braving the constant hail of antiaircraft fire, the Skyraiders made the required mile-long run at 300 feet and 220 knots to hit all their targets — enemy antiaircraft gun positions. While the gunners choked, coughed, cried, and retched uncontrollably, a Jolly Green, with its crew wearing gas masks swooped in and saved the pilot.[63]

Though classic recovery tactics such as those described earlier remained basically the same, each mission required innovation and the application of varying amounts of aerial firepower. Rescue efforts generally took precedence over normal strike missions and aircraft were often diverted from their assigned targets to support the A-1s and rescue choppers. On one mission in December 1969, 336 sorties were flown over a three-day period to help rescue forces recover a navigator evading capture near Ban Phanop, Laos, just outside Tchepone. In addition to the A-1 and Jolly Green sorties, the Air Force used fifty F-105, forty-three F-4, four F-100, plus assorted O-1 and O-2 sorties. The Navy contributed a number of A-6 and A-7 sorties.[64]

Any friendly airplane in the sky might be diverted to drop bombs in support of a search and rescue mission. Col. William M. Harris, IV, commander of the 37th Aerospace Rescue and Recovery Squadron in 1971 and 1972, noted, "During my tour rescue efforts have called upon every conceivable military resource as well as . . . Air America, special ground teams, clandestine operations, frogmen, aircraft carriers, tanks, and so on. There is no limitation on tactics or concepts to be employed to effect a rescue."[65]

In the summer of 1969 the Aerospace Rescue and Recovery Service's strength in Southeast Asia peaked with a high of seventy-one rescue aircraft operating in four squadrons under the 3d Aerospace Rescue and Recovery Group. The 37th and 40th Aerospace Rescue and Recovery Squadrons, at Da Nang and Udorn respectively, were responsible for aircrew recoveries over North and South Vietnam as well as Laos. The 38th Aerospace Rescue and Recovery Squadron had its headquarters at Tan Son Nhut. With detachments at fourteen bases throughout South Vietnam and Thailand, they were responsible for local base rescue with aircrew recovery as a secondary mission. Finally, the 39th Aerospace Rescue and Recovery Squadron operated eleven HC-130Ps from its base at Tuy Hoa.[66]

Force levels remained steady into 1970 when withdrawals began as politicians sought a negotiated end to the conflict. There were technological improvements to be made, as the Aerospace Rescue and Recovery Service strived to achieve a truly workable night recovery system. Nevertheless, in the period between 1966 and 1970 Aerospace Rescue and Recovery Service units saved 980 aircrew members from captivity, suffering and death in Laos, North Vietnam, and South Vietnam. In other rescue efforts, ranging from the evacuation of the Citadel at Hue during the Tet offensive of 1968 to picking up battlefield casualties, an additional 1,059 lives were saved. It added up to a grand total of 2,039 human lives.[67]

Maj. Joseph Hutto, rescued pilot

3 ARRGp COMBAT SAVES

	1966		1967		1968		1969		1970		TOTALS		
	ACR	NAC	ACR	NAC	ACR	NAC	ACR	NAC	ACR	NAC	ACR	NAC	ALL
HH-3	92	38	122	68	163	138	72	1	47	14	496	259	755
HH-43	65	186	68	147	79	92	94	102	37	18	343	545	888
HH-53	0	0	1	0	21	79	48	164	46	12	116	255	371
HU-16	22	0	1	0	0	0	0	0	0	0	23	0	23
HC-130	0	0	0	0	0	0	0	0	0	0	0	0	0
OTHER¹	0	0	0	0	0	0	0	0	2	0	2	0	2
TOTALS	179	224	192	215	263	309	214	267	132	44	980	1059	2039

¹Credit of 2 combat saves to parajumpers remaining overnight on ground with survivors.

	1966		1967		1968		1969		1970		TOTALS		
	ACR	NAC	ACR	NAC	ACR	NAC	ACR	NAC	ACR	NAC	ACR	NAC	ALL
USAF	117	1	99	43	129	12	138	6	87	3	570	65	635
USA	27	169	45	66	80	47	46	32	17	21	215	335	550
USN	29	3	42	55	47	69	26	45	6	0	150	172	322
FWMF	6	23	2	43	6	45	4	181	0	7	18	299	317
CIVIL	0	10	4	4	1	136	0	2	0	0	5	152	157
OTHER	0	18	0	4	0	0	0	1	22	13	22	36	58
TOTALS	179	224	192	215	263	309	214	267	132	44	980	1059	2039

ACR – Aircrew Rescue; NAC – Non-Aircrew Rescue; FWMF – Free World Military Forces

Upper left: 1st Lt. Terry O. Larimore and SSgt. Robert E. Miller coordinate directions for a rescue; upper right: SSgt. Little E. Ross drops a smoke flare to mark position for rescue; left: Col. Albert P. Lovelady, Commander of 3d ARRS; lower left: SSgt. Robert Riley lowers a jungle penetrator from a Jolly Green Giant; below: SSgt. William O. Johnson, a flight engineer of the 38th ARRS, aboard an HH–43 helicopter.

A2C Allen R. Stanek rides a jungle penetrator up to a hovering H-43 during a rescue training operation.

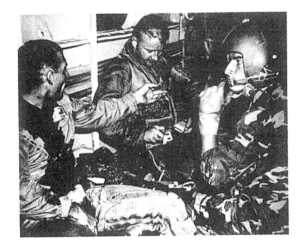

Left: Maj. Michael Muskrat (center) and Capt. Kyle Stouder (l.) discuss with a pararescue man the first night rescue made in SEA by an HH–53B helicopter.

Right: pilot hoisted into an HH–3E.

Left: Sgt. Thomas R. Pope, wounded amputee, prepares for his last flight in an HH–53E.

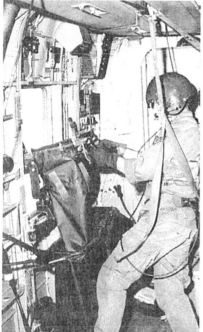

Upper left: Lt. Col. Chester R. Ratcliffe, commander of the 40th ARRS; above: a pararescue man at the machine gun of an HH–53 during a search and rescue mission over the Gulf of Tonkin.

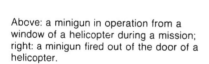

Above: a minigun in operation from a window of a helicopter during a mission; right: a minigun fired out of the door of a helicopter.

5 *Son Tay to Cease-fire: 1970-1973*

Late November nights in Udorn, Thailand, are crisp and cool. The night of November 20, 1970, was cooler than usual because a cold front was moving into the area, a prelude to Typhoon Patsy building over the Gulf of Tonkin. Besides providing a break from the 100-degree heat of the tropical day, the weather acutely affected a group of men gathered at Udorn to fly an unusual and risky mission.

For several days people assigned to Udorn had wondered why tents had been put up beside the dispensary. No one seemed to know (or no one would say) who the "civilian" men and women were who lived in the tents, stayed together, and talked to none other than their own. The briefers at 432d Tactical Reconnaissance Wing enjoyed the respite from duties that these and other "civilians" brought. For several days the intelligence officers (especially the intelligence officers with their ceaseless questions) had been isolated from the aircrews. And, to preclude any chance of accidental drunken disclosures of information, fighter pilots were banned from the officers club bar. The base nestled in a tight blanket of security.

One hour before midnight pilots, navigators, pararescuemen, radio operators, flight mechanics and engineers, and a small group of assault troops boarded two C-130E transports, an HH-3E, and five HH-53 helicopters. Within ten minutes this armada was airborne and enroute to Son Tay prison, twenty-eight miles northwest of Hanoi. This contingent became the center of a task force that included five A-1Es, five F-105s and ten F-4 Phantoms hurtling northeastward toward the enemy's heartland. From the Gulf of Tonkin a diversionary Navy force of F-4s, A-6s, and A-4s flew toward Haiphong and the eastern coastal cities. The purpose of this mission was to rescue up to a hundred prisoners of war from the suffering and despair they had experienced at Son Tay prison. It was an operation unique in concept and bold in planning.[1]

Plans for the Son Tay raid began on June 5, 1970, when Brig. Gen. Donald D. Blackburn, Special Assistant for Counterinsurgency and Special Activity, received permission from the Joint Chiefs of Staff to undertake a study concerning the problem of rescuing up to fifty prisoners of war from Son Tay prison. After discussing the concept with Brig. Gen. James A. Hill, Deputy Chief of Staff for Operations at Headquarters, Military Airlift Command, and Brig. Gen. Frank K. Everest, commander of the Aerospace

Rescue and Recovery Service, General Blackburn gathered representatives from all the services, the Central Intelligence Agency, and the Defense Intelligence Agency to form a study group. Lt. Col. Warner A. Britton, Chief of Flying Training at the Aerospace Rescue and Recovery Training Center, Eglin Air Force Base, Florida, represented the Air Force. The group met for the first time at the Pentagon on June 10 in a session chaired by Col. Norman H. Frisbie of the Joint Chiefs of Staff's office. After a month of study, Colonel Frisbie told the Joint Chiefs that a rescue raid to Son Tay was possible. The Joint Chiefs sanctioned this concept, and directed that detailed planning begin immediately.[2]

An unusually heavy rainy season in northern Laos and North Vietnam caused the stream that ran by Son Tay prison to spill over its banks. Consequently, the wells that served the camp were filled with turbid, unhealthy water. Lately, too, the prisoners had insisted on holding religious services: Protestant services and separate Catholic masses. Following the death of Ho Chi Minh in 1969, the North Vietnamese had started treating the POWs better. And even though the prisoners at Son Tay seemed to be more recalcitrant than those held in Hanoi, this policy apparently also was applied to them. Because the water at Son Tay was fouled and because they wanted to separate the Protestants from the Catholics in a misconception that it would make practicing their respective religions easier and thus bring praise from the international community, Hanoi ironically, decided to close the Son Tay camp. On July 14 the last prisoner was taken from Son Tay to Dan Hoi prison seven and one half miles away. The POWs immediately named this prison Camp Faith.[3]

Nevertheless, activity at Son Tay continued. Some guards remained. Other people, possibly convalescing North Vietnamese soldiers, moved into the old guard quarters. Additionally, because the North Vietnamese ran a sapper school only a quarter of a mile from the Son Tay compound, the extra room might have been used to house additional students. In any event, there were enough people around the camp to plant a garden, keep the grass trampled, and leave enough signs of life so that overhead photography would indicate that the facility was, indeed, occupied.[4]

On August 8, at the direction of General Blackburn, the Joint Contingency Task Group was formed. The following day Brig. Gen. Leroy J. Manor, commander of the Special Operations Force at Eglin Air Force Base, Florida, was called to Washington. On its way to the capital, General Manor's plane stopped off at Pope Air Force Base, North Carolina, to pick up Col. Arthur "Bull" Simons, a fifty-two-year-old Army Ranger assigned to nearby Ft. Bragg. Colonel Simons, General Blackburn's choice to lead the raiders, had extensive experience in covert operations and clandestine warfare that began in the Philippines in World War II and, more recently, included tours in Laos as well as Vietnam.[5] During the invasion of the Philippines, Captain Simons led a Ranger company in an assault on a

Japanese prison camp. The Rangers took the camp to prevent the Japanese from killing the American prisoners of war before the main invasion force could liberate them.[6]

Other members of the task group of twenty-five people included representatives from the Defense Intelligence Agency, the Central Intelligence Agency, and the National Security Agency. Under the code name "Ivory Coast" they labored for nearly three weeks on details of intelligence and mission planning. Security was tight as evidenced by the code name which was deliberately chosen to conjure up images of Africa, a continent and a half away from the objective.[7]

While planning continued at the Pentagon, Manor and Simons selected people for the mission. Manor wanted men with Southeast Asia experience. Some, like Air Force Lt. Col. Royal A. Brown, were ordered to report to Eglin from combat assignments in Vietnam. Others came from Europe and bases across the United States. Almost half of the forty-six Air Force people selected for the raid were on the faculty of the rescue training school at Eglin.[8]

Meanwhile, planners in Washington decided on the composition of the task force. They determined that it would consist of two C-130E Combat Talon unconventional warfare aircraft, five A-1Es, five HH-53s, one HH-3E, and two UH-1s. During the training it was decided that the UH-1s were unsuitable for the mission, but they were still included in case they were needed as backup aircraft.[9]

As the plan emerged, it called for crashing a helicopter loaded with shock troops directly into the small compound to achieve surprise. Because of the trees in the compound this helicopter would be damaged and would have to be left behind. An older chopper, like the UH-1, was more expendable. Unfortunately the UH-1 could only carry a handful of combat-equipped troops. Furthermore, its limited range would make it necessary to preposition the chopper at Lima Site 32, Na Khang, in northern Laos. The Joint Contingency Task Group decided to use the HH-3, a larger chopper with sufficient range but nevertheless expendable. If the mission had to be aborted halfway to Son Tay, the HH-3 could, with refueling, return to Udorn. The UH-1, on the other hand, would have to land in Laos. Finally, the HH-3 could carry enough troops to keep the guards busy while other Rangers blasted a hole in the prison's outside wall so that the assault forces landing around the compound could get in to search the cells. The only possible flaw in the plan was that the HH-3s were due to be phased out of the Southeast Asia theater in December. Rather than risk a security leak by insisting that an HH-3 be kept on hand, General Manor decided to practice with both helicopters.[10]

Training for the flight portion of the mission began on August 20. The crews concentrated on night formation flying. By early September the ninety-two assault troops joined with the Air Force to begin their part of the training. This included attacks on a mockup structure made of wood and cloth which was put up every night and taken down before dawn to keep Soviet photo reconnaissance satellites from spotting it.[11]

Aircrews for the C-130Es and A-1Es worked out their portion of the mission. The C-130s were to provide navigational assistance to and from the camp. Also, when these aircraft reached Son Tay, the plan called for dropping a pallet loaded with napalm canisters which would form a flaming pool to act as a reference point for the other aircraft. The A-1Es also carried specially configured napalm canisters which, upon bursting, would also form flaming pools — just in case the C-130s did not have a chance to drop their napalm. Also, the A-1Es were to bomb a bridge near the camp to slow down any enemy force that might try to intervene. If this failed they were to use their cannons to strafe the enemy troops.

The task force expected considerable enemy opposition. In addition to the guards at the prison there was the sapper school up the road. Son Tay also lay at the outer perimenter of Hanoi's northern defenses, accounting for the eight missile sites which would threaten the task force. And, as if that were not enough, there was a battery of 85-mm radar-controlled antiaircraft guns located only two miles from Son Tay. However, because of geographical features and the way these guns were built, they could only be depressed to an angle that made them effective down to 3,000 feet in the vicinity of the camp. Likewise, the missile threat would force the task force down to 500 feet on their way to Son Tay, but because of the missiles' slant range and other factors bearing on their capabilities, the missile threat over the compound was above 3,000 feet.[12]

While tactics were refined at Eglin, the Joint Contingency Task Group put the final touches to the mission plan. A weather expert on the planning staff estimated there would be a ninety-seven percent chance of clear weather over Son Tay on any given day in October and November. Other planners, considering light conditions, decided lunar phases would have to be just right to provide enough light for Army night viewing devices to work, but not silhouette the choppers or the assault troops when they unloaded. With this advice, the planners determined the dates had to be between October 21 and 25 or November 21 and 25.[13]

On September 16 the Joint Contingency Task Group presented the plan to the Joint Chiefs of Staff. They told the Joint Chiefs the force would be ready to go by October 8. Briefings to Melvin R. Laird, Secretary of Defense, Richard M. Helms, Director of the CIA, and Adm. John S. McCain, Jr., Commander in Chief, Pacific, who was in Washington for a conference, followed. Secretary Laird agreed with the recommended target date of October 21 to 25, but defferred approval until "higher authority" could be consulted.

On October 8, the task group briefed Dr. Henry Kissinger, Special Assistant to the President for National Security Affairs. Kissinger was enthusiastic but ordered the operation delayed until November. Although he did not say so at the time, this was probably done for political reasons. On that very day Ambassador David Bruce, in Paris, handed North Vietnamese negotiator Xuan Thuy a new American peace proposal that promised the United States would never invade North Vietnam and offered a total withdrawal of American troops from South Vietnam. Kissinger probably wanted to get an answer from Hanoi before he authorized any operation that would put up to 150 Americans on the ground so close to the enemy's capital.[14]

Training at Eglin continued through October. In early November General Manor called all the participants to a mess hall, where he unveiled a model of the POW camp, complete to the last detail including a forty-foot palm tree in the courtyard and clothes on a clothesline. They called it "Barbara", and from the model it was apparent to those who did not know where the mission was headed, that it would be in the tropics. Some theorized that they were going to Cuba to kidnap Fidel Castro. Others, more correctly, thought the raid would free political prisoners held in some tropical dictatorship. For security reasons, only a handful had been told that the suburbs of Hanoi was their destination.[15]

On October 27 the Chairman of the Joint Chiefs of Staff, Adm. Thomas H. Moorer, gave his approval for a November 21-25 raid. To maintain security no messages had been transmitted concerning the operation. In keeping with this policy, General Manor flew to Scott Air Force Base, Illinois, to brief Gen. P.K. Carlton, commander in chief of the Military Airlift Command. General Carlton personally authorized the C-141 jet transports and C-130s needed to airlift the force to Southeast Asia. General Manor and Colonel Simons flew on to Pacific Command headquarters at Hawaii, where they briefed Admiral McCain who, incidentally, had a son in a Hanoi POW camp. Finally they flew to Saigon to brief Gen. Creighton Abrams, commander of MACV, and Gen. Lucius Clay, commander of the Seventh Air Force.[16]

After General Abrams and General Clay had been briefed, the staff that had accompanied Manor and Simons went to work in Southeast Asia securing seven HH-53s and two HH-3Es as primary and backup helicopters for the mission. The seven HH-53s were obtained from the 40th Aerospace Rescue and Recovery Squadron at Udorn and the two HH-3Es were contributed by the 37th Aerospace Rescue and Recovery Squadron at Da Nang. The squadron commanders, although close friends with most of the rescue crews on the raid, were not told how these choppers would be used, just that it was important.[17]

On November 10, the task force began to move from Eglin to Takhli Royal Thai Air Force Base. Just in case the HH-3Es could not make the flight from Da Nang to Udorn, a dangerous undertaking in itself because it entailed flying across the highly-defended Ho Chi Minh Trail at relatively low altitude, the raiders took along one of the UH-1s. Security was tight during the trip to Takhli. Most of the men still did not know their exact destination, but to further confuse anyone they met along the way they were told to make cryptic references to a special operation in the Middle East.[18] On November 18, the last rescue elements reached Takhli.

Meanwhile, in-theatre coordination had begun. At Udorn some of the newly arrived "civilian" men and women were Air Force doctors and nurses brought in from bases throughout the Pacific to attend any sick or wounded prisoners or raiders who might be brought back from Son Tay. Across the base, special "civilian" briefers detailed the Mig combat air patrol role to those F-4 crews scheduled for the mission. At Takhli other briefers filled in crews slated to fly the F-105 Wild Weasel surface-to-air-missile suppression sorties.

Weather stepped in to determine the final hour for the raid. Typhoon Patsy was bearing down on North Vietnam. By November 21, the original target date, the Gulf of Tonkin would be too rough for aircraft carrier operations, and the Navy would not be able to make the diversionary flights needed to confuse the North Vietnamese. Late on the morning of November 20, General Manor decided the raid must go one day early — that night.[19]

At 1600, Manor gathered the aircrews and assault troops at the Takhli base theater. There he told those who did not already know, the name of the target and its location. The men cheered when they heard they were going to Son Tay. Many of the Aerospace Rescue and Recovery Service crewmen knew Tom Curtis, an HH-43 pilot who had been a prisoner of war since 1965. They were delighted to see him on a roster of POWs thought to be in Son Tay. At dusk the task force members boarded C-130 transports for the flight to Udorn where the choppers and C-130Es waited. After a briefing specifying routes, times, and altitudes, the raiders reviewed the actions they would be taking when they reached Son Tay.[20]

When the two C-130s, the HH-3E, and five HH-53s were airborne, about 2310 Udorn time, they set course for North Vietnam. At the first ridge of mountains north of Vientiane, Laos, they flew into clouds. The choppers spread out, giving each other room. The single HH-3E, flown by Maj. Herbert R. Zehnder and Maj. Herbert D. Kalen, stayed behind the lead C-130, riding the crest of its propwash like a racing car drafting in the slipstream of a preceding vehicle. Otherwise, the HH-3 would have been too slow to keep pace with the C-130s and HH-53s.[21]

As the choppers crossed northern Laos and approached North Vietnamese radar coverage, a vast force of 116 mission support aircraft took off from seven bases in Thailand and three carriers in the Gulf of Tonkin.[22] Five F-105 Wild Weasels passed the task force to reach the Son Tay area early in order to keep the SAM sites from acquiring fixes or radar locks on the approaching aircraft. Ten F-4Ds from Udorn held in a Mig combat or-bit over northeastern Laos. Eight KC-135 tankers orbited near the F-4s ready to fuel the gas gulping jets. Four more KC-135s were standing by over the Gulf of Tonkin to provide the same service to Navy jets. Two Lockheed EC-121Ds, four-engine Constellation transports used by the Air Force as Early Warning/Ground Control Intercept and Mig warning aircraft, flew along the Laos/North Vietnam border gathering intelligence on enemy fighter reactions. Three RC-135 Combat Apple Electronic Intelligence collection aircraft from the Strategic Air Command provided communications support which included relaying messages to the National Military Command Center in the Pentagon.[23]

Twenty minutes before the raiders reached Son Tay, fifty-nine Navy aircraft started confusing North Vietnamese radar defenses in the east. Flights of A-7s flew across North Vietnam, just far enough north of the Hanoi-Haiphong area to activate Chinese radar, thus drawing more elements into the problem and saturating the Chinese/North Vietnamese cross border defense system. Meanwhile, other A-7s raced along the coast off Haiphong dropping flares while A-6s flew low toward the harbor, making the enemy think that Air Force B-52s were heading for their cities. Farther out to sea, F-8 Crusaders and F-4s patrolled for Migs.[24]

The raiders entered the objective area below 500 feet. The C-130s led the six choppers until Son Tay lay only three and one half miles ahead. At that point the leading C-130 climbed to 1,500 feet followed by two HH-53 choppers: Apple 4, piloted by Lt. Col. Royal H. Brown and Maj. Ryland R. Dreibelbis, and Apple 5 with Maj. Kenneth D. Murphy and Capt. William M. McGeorge at the controls. Brown's Apple 4 was the primary flare chopper and one of those designated to haul back the released prisoners. Apple 5 was the secondary flare helicopter. Over the Son Tay compound the flares worked perfectly, so the two choppers flew to a planned orbit area nearby while the C-130 circled to drop a fire-fight simulator (firecrackers with timed fuses) on the sapper school. It then released its pallet of napalm before flying off to its designated orbit. The second C-130, only a minute behind the first, came in leading the five A-1s. After the A-1s pulled away, this C-130 dropped a napalm marker and then joined the other C-130 in its orbit while the Skyraiders bombed a nearby bridge before taking up their orbit over the flaming pool of napalm.[25]

In most operations something goes wrong. The Son Tay raid was to be no different in that respect. In the third helicopter, Apple 3, flown by Maj. Frederick M. Donohue and Capt. Thomas R. Waldron, an instrument panel light marked "transmission" flickered on. Captain Waldron jabbed excitedly at the instrument panel. Both men knew the transmission is the most vital piece of machinery in any helicopter. Transmissions can disintegrate in a matter of seconds. If that happens the chopper crashes. Instrument panel lights, however, often short causing them to flicker on when nothing, in fact, is wrong. Donohue weighed the factors. Normally he would declare an emergency and land the chopper in the first available safe spot until he could determine if anything was, indeed, amiss in the transmission. These were not normal circumstances, and if he declared an emergency and pulled out of the operation the entire mission might be jeopardized. Donohue coolly told his copilot, "Ignore the sonofabitch."[26] In those few seconds of confusion, Donohue let Apple 3 drift slightly off course.

Apple 3 was directly on course for the sapper school instead of the Son Tay prison, some 400 yards beyond. Just before his gunners opened up on the guard towers, Donohue realized his mistake and wheeled his chopper north toward the camp. In Banana 1, the HH-3E just behind Apple 3, Colonel Zehnder and Major Kalen did not realize they were over the wrong compound until they had settled down inside the walls and the gunner had blasted the guard towers. When Zehnder and Kalen realized their mistake they poured on the power, lifted their chopper over the school's walls and headed for the camp. In Apple 1, Lt. Col. Warner A. Britton and Maj. Alfred C. Montrem were too busy concentrating on landing and getting a stuck rear ramp down to hear the radio warnings from Donohue and Zehnder. As their parajumpers blasted the buildings and guard towers with the chopper's gatling-like miniguns, assault troops rushed out the back and fanned out across the landing zone. After a few minutes Col. Bull Simons realized he and his men were in the wrong compound. By this time Simons' troops had breached the wall and were inside the courtyard encountering very heavy opposition. Nevertheless, Simons gathered his troops and beat a hasty retreat back to the landing zone. Meanwhile, Britton and Montrem had relaxed enough to hear the frantic calls of their comrades warning them that they had assaulted the wrong target. Britton spun the chopper around and rushed back to the landing zone just as Simons and his troops arrived. Within three minutes they were loaded up and off to the Son Tay compound. Behind them they left many dead enemy troops.[27]

In his book, *The Raid,* author Benjamin F. Schemmer claims the raiders killed a number of Chinese or Russian advisors at this school. While intelligence sources do not confirm this allegation, some of the raiders say that the men they fought at the school were larger than the normal Vietnamese and were wearing jockey shorts and white T-shirts rather than black pajamas. Nevertheless, it should be noted the North Vietnamese Army wore western-style fatigue uniforms while black pajamas, traditional Vietnamese peasant garb, were sometimes (though not always) worn by the Viet Cong. In any event, the mistake that caused the attack on the sapper school may have been a fortuitous one. It probably caused considerable confusion and may have been responsible for keeping the troops, whoever they were, at the school and prevented them from interfering with the raiders at Son Tay Prison.

Four hundred yards from the sapper school the battle raged. First, Donohue flew Apple 3 across the prison blasting the guard towers with its miniguns. Zehnder brought Banana 1 in fast on Apple 3's heels. Herb Kalen, copilot in Banana 1, cut the engines at precisely the right second and the HH-3E dropped into the compound, swinging around on its rotors as the blades sliced into the forty foot tree, just as expected. When it hit the ground, troops rushed out the rear ramp, each running to his assigned objective. Above the roar of battle a bullhorn sounded, "Keep down! We're Americans."[28]

Inside the cell houses two-man teams began a systematic clearing of each cell block. One team broke in on the camp commandant and shot him in his bed where he lay. Every North Vietnamese they caught, they killed. Nine minutes after landing the first assault team reported, "negative items" no POWs. Three minutes later all teams had reported the same "negative items". Three more minutes passed while the choppers returned from their holding area. While the bulk of the assault force loaded aboard the helicopters outside the compound, a team rigged explosives on Banana 1, the crippled HH-3 inside the prison walls. Twenty-seven minutes after the first C-130 flew over Son Tay these men rushed up the ramp of the last chopper out of Son Tay. Seconds later Banana 1 blew up.[29]

People in Son Tay village heard the fire-fight simulators and the aircraft overhead. They watched as sixteen SAMs arched across the sky. For half an hour they saw the napalm burning and the planes circling above. One man home on leave from the army, when subsequently captured in South Vietnam, told U.S. Air Force interrogators that he saw tanks moving toward the camp just as the last chopper pulled away.[30]

Above and to the west, on the receiving end of those sixteen SAMs, two F-105s were damaged. One of them limped back to Udorn to make an emergency landing. The other flew toward Udorn but, over northern Laos, the crew ejected.[31]

In the darkness over western North Vietnam, a Mig sought the remnants of the task force heading back toward Thailand. His air intercept radar found Apple 4 piloted by Lt. Col. Royal H. Brown. When Brown realized his chopper was under attack he put it into a violent turning dive. The Mig pilot fired a heat seeking missile, but it streaked by the twisting helicopter to hit a hill. With the HH-53 turning and maneuvering low to the ground, the hunter soon realized he would not be able to find his prey. The Mig turned for home.[32]

It was almost 0300 when Apple 4 found Apple 5, flown by Maj. Kenneth D. Murphy. Together they continued toward Udorn. Suddenly they received a mayday call from the F-105 in trouble over Laos. These two choppers, slated to carry back the prisoners, were empty, so they rendezvoused with Lime 01, an HC-130P tanker, refueled, and flew toward the downed crewmen. An Air America C-123 showed up and began dropping flares. The rescue choppers searched, but could not spot the survivors. When they started picking up small arms fire, the HC-130P, acting as airborne mission control, ordered them to orbit with him until dawn. About three hours passed before the sunrise brought four A-1s from Nakhon Phanom. Sandy Low, the lead, soon located both men, ordered his three wingmen to strafe the area, and then told the choppers to make their pickups. Apple 4 got the backseater and Apple 5 picked up the pilot. Both choppers refueled and headed for Udorn.[33]

Success cannot always be measured in unqualified triumphs. The Son Tay raid was a tactical success in that the plan worked. Had there been prisoners at the compound, and had the raiders met with a similar level of enemy resistance, they probably would have been rescued. Additionally, the raid showed the Hanoi leadership that their country was still quite vulnerable to attack. It also focused the attention of the world on the plight of American prisoners of war in North Vietnam. Moreover, it served to bolster the morale of the prisoners who knew they had not been abandoned. Finally, the North Vietnamese, fearing the Americans might attempt another raid, moved all of their American POWs to two or three central complexes. This afforded individual prisoners more contact with each other and boosted their morale.[34]

Meanwhile, the war continued. Rescue operations in the period from 1970 to the ceasefire in 1973 were distinguished by three things: withdrawal from Vietnam of rescue units, relocation to Thailand, and the introduction of new equipment to make existing search and rescue forces more effective. Most of the HH-53s withdrawn from Southeast Asia were reassigned to rescue units throughout the world. Some of the HH-43s reached local base rescue units in the United States, others became part of a military assistance package for the Royal Thai Air Force. New electronic gadgets, including an improved night recovery system, were placed aboard some of the HH-53s before the ceasefire.

In March 1968 President Lyndon B. Johnson committed the United States to a policy of eventual withdrawal from Vietnam. During his 1968 run for the Presidency, Richard M. Nixon promised ". . . policies which will end the war and win the peace as quickly as possible."[35] Following his election, President Nixon announced a program to "Vietnamize" the war, which meant reducing American forces while increasing aid and training to the Vietnamese so their forces could shoulder the major burden in fighting the war. As Air Force tactical units withdrew from Southeast Asia, the need for a search and rescue force correspondingly decreased.

In late 1969 and early 1970, the U.S. Air Force began reducing its forces in Vietnam by transferring or inactivating units at the smaller bases. Accordingly, Aerospace and Recovery Service reductions and realignments were confined to local base rescue units through 1970. Some bases were turned over to the Vietnamese, while the U.S. Army took charge of others. Responsibility for local base rescue devolved on whatever organization ran the base.[36]

The first reduction of Aerospace Rescue and Recovery Service forces in Southeast Asia occurred on December 20, 1969, when the local base rescue unit at Binh Thuy Air Base, Vietnam, Detachment 10, 38th Aerospace Rescue and Recovery Squadron was disbanded. Local base rescue unit transfers and inactivations continued throughout 1970. Detachment 9 was relocated from Pleiku to Nakhon Phanom Royal Thai Air Force Base on February 16. Detachment 8, 38th Aerospace Rescue and Recovery Squadron at Cam Ranh Air Base ceased to exist on September 15 with the dissolution of the 12th Tactical Fighter Wing. U.S. Air Force units left Tuy Hoa in September; accordingly, Detachment 11, 38th Aerospace Rescue and Recovery Squadron was inactivated on October 15. After the transfer of all strike F-105s from Takhli to the United States in November 1970, Detachment 2 became inactive on November 15, 1970.[37]

On September 16, 1970, the 39th Aerospace Rescue and Recovery Squadron's eleven HC-130Ps moved from Tuy Hoa to Cam Ranh Air Base, Vietnam. The relatively short distance of the move (only 70 miles down the coast) had no effect on the airborne mission control and refueling functions of the HC-130Ps. This squadron continued to keep three aircraft on alert (one airborne alert from dawn to midday, replaced by a second aircraft from midday to dusk, with a third HC-130P on ground alert twenty-four hours a day) at Cam Ranh and three on alert at Udorn as well.[38] The movement of the 39th Aerospace Rescue and Recovery Squadron was the only relocation of a major rescue unit in Southeast Asia during 1970. On January 1, 1971, the following rescue units were in Vietnam and Thailand: Headquarters, 3 ARRGp, Tan Son Nhut Afld, RVN; Joint Rescue Control Center, Tan Son Nhut Afld, RVN; Operating Location A, Son Tra AB, RVN; Operating Location B, Udorn RTAFB, Thailand; Headquarters, 37th ARRSq, Da Nang AB, RVN; Headquarters, 38th ARRSq, Tan Son Nhut Afld, RVN; Det 1, 38th ARRSq, Phan Rang AB, RVN; Det 3, 38th ARRSq, Ubon RTAFB, Thailand; Det 4, 38th ARRSq, Korat RTAFB, Thailand; Det 5, 38th ARRSq, Udorn RTAFB, Thailand; Det 6, 38th ARR-Sq, Bien Hoa AB, RVN; Det 7, 38th ARRSq, Da Nang AB, RVN; Det 9, 38th ARRSq, Nakhon Phanom RTAFB, Thailand; Det 12, 38th ARRSq, Utapao Royal Thai Naval Air Base, Thailand; Det 13, 38th ARRSq, Phu Cat AB, RVN; Det 14, 38th ARRSq, Tan Son Nhut Afld, RVN; Headquarters, 39th ARRSq, Cam Ranh AB, RVN; Headquarters, 40th ARRSq, Udorn RTAFB, Thailand; Det 1, 40th ARRSq, Nakhon Phanom RTAFB, Thailand.[39]

More sweeping changes occurred when, on July 1, 1971, the entire 38th Aerospace Rescue and Recovery Squadron, the unit that managed HH-43s in Southeast Asia, was inactivated. Staff positions were transferred to Headquarters, 3d Aerospace Rescue and Recovery Group at Tan Son Nhut. The local base rescue choppers and their crews then became detachments under the 3d Aerospace Rescue and Recovery Group.[40]

SEARCH AND RESCUE

On July 21, the 40th Aerospace Rescue and Recovery Squadron moved from Udorn to Nakhon Phanom. This move reflected a shift in the air war. From the time of President Johnson's 1968 bombing halt above 20° latitude in North Vietnam, air strikes had concentrated on the Ho Chi Minh Trail and southern North Vietnam. Nixon's Vietnamization plans also implied increased air support for the South Vietnamese Army. The move to Nakhon Phanom put the 40th Aerospace Rescue and Recovery Squadron closer to this action. Additionally, at that base rescue people were co-located with crews flying the A-1 escorts and the 21st Special Operations Squadron's CH-53As. The latter performed clandestine missions throughout Southeast Asia.[41]

As part of the Vietnamization effort, between September 13 and 16, 1971, the 37th Aerospace Rescue and Recovery Squadron moved across Da Nang to new facilities. The Vietnamese Air Force then inherited its old hangars and administrative buildings. Responsible for search and rescue in the southern panhandle of North Vietnam, Military Region I and II in South Vietnam, and central Laos, planners at the 37th worked out the move so well that they avoided any loss of effectiveness while trucking 1600 items of equipment across the base.[42]

In November 1971, when American air activity at Phu Cat Air Base, north of Qui Nhon on South Vietnam's central coast, ceased, Detachment 13, 3d Aerospace Rescue and Recovery Group, the local base rescue unit, was subsequently inactivated. Instead of dispatching its two HH-43s to a stateside unit or relegating them to mothballs, they reinforced Detachment 14 at Tan Son Nhut.[43] However, these HH-43s were not to remain at Tan Son Nhut for long. In mid-December the Air Force reduced its operations at Bien Hoa, the sprawling air base north of Saigon. The rescue service lost a forward operating location for HH-53s flying in support of air strikes in the southern part of the country and in eastern Cambodia. Furthermore, it appeared that the Air Force A-37 unit at Bien Hoa would be without local base rescue coverage. To remedy that situation, the two HH-43s that had become part of Detachment 14 at Tan Son Nhut only a month before, began rotating to Bien Hoa on a daily basis to provide local base rescue.[44]

In early 1972 communist forces kept up a steady if low level of combat activity as they positioned for the April thrust. A dry season offensive battered at friendly forces in northern Laos, but until the North Vietnamese spring offensive began in late March there was no reason to slow the American withdrawal. Accordingly, Detachment 1, 3d Aerospace Rescue and Recovery Group, a local base rescue unit, closed down on January 31, 1972.[45] One of its helicopters was placed on a C-5A and flown to McChord Air Force Base, Washington. The other became part of the Royal Thai Air Force.[46]

The new year began with a drawdown in aircrew rescue helicopters. One HH-53 from the 40th Aerospace Rescue and Recovery Squadron and one from the 37th were disassembled and loaded aboard a C-5A for a flight to Woodbridge Royal Air Force Base, England, on January 20.[47] On February 9, Air Force headquarters reduced the HH-53 authorization for Southeast Asia from twenty to thirteen machines.[48]

In March the 39th Aerospace Rescue and Recovery Squadron moved from Cam Ranh Air Base, Vietnam, to Korat Royal Thai Air Base, Thailand. During the move all HC-130P missions were flown from their operating location at Udorn. After that operating location closed on March 17, all King missions were flown out of Korat.[49] On April 1 the 39th Aerospace Rescue and Recovery Squadron was dissolved and the aircraft and men with the King mission became, temporarily, part of local base rescue Detachment 4, 3d Aerospace Rescue and Recovery Group at Korat.[50] Detachment 4 was the largest local base rescue unit in the world until July 8 when the unit was redesignated the 56th Aerospace Rescue and Recovery Squadron. Subsequently the HH-43s at Korat became part of that squadron and Detachment 4 was disbanded. On April 1, 1972, the Aerospace Rescue and Recovery Squadron had the following units in Southeast Asia: Hq 3d Aerospace Rescue and Recovery Group, Tan Son Nhut AB, RVN; Rescue Coordination Center (OL-A), Son Tra AB, RVN; Rescue Coordination Center (OL-B), Udorn RTAFB, Thailand; 37th ARRSq, Da Nang AB, RVN; 40th ARRSq, Nakhon Phanon RTAFB, Thailand; 3d ARRGp, Det 3, Ubon RTAFB, Thailand; Det 4, Korat RTAFB, Thailand; Det 5, Udorn RTAFB, Thailand; Det 12, Utapao RTNAB, Thailand; Det 14, Tan Son Nhut AB, RVN.

The enemy offensive that opened in the early morning hours of March 31 slowed the reduction of search and rescue forces. Air Force headquarters suspended its order to reduce the number of HH-53s from twenty to thirteen. (Through combat attrition the number stood at seventeen by September.) In mid-April the 3d Group reinforced its aircrew recovery forces by obtaining four HH-3Es from a rescue squadron in the Philippines. The choppers were sent to Tan Son Nhut where they became part of Detachment 14 and provided search and rescue services for the southern part of South Vietnam until they were removed on September 15, 1972.[51]

As the North Vietnamese Army rolled into South Vietnam, it was primarily opposed by the Army of the Republic of Vietnam. Because of the Vietnamization program, most American combat troops had already been withdrawn. American air and naval forces, however, gave the Vietnamese Army heavy support.

Since President Nixon's July 25, 1969, speech at Guam announcing the "Vietnamization" of the war, American forces had been steadily leaving South Vietnam. As provided in the President's plan, the Vietnamese were given massive amounts of military hardware, and they gradually assumed an increasing responsibility for the conduct of the war. Vietnamization, however, was not a success in search and rescue.[52]

SEARCH AND RESCUE

From the early 1960s, the Vietnamese armed forces had been receiving a large number of helicopters. Hard pressed by the day-to-day requirements of warfare, they increased the combat effectiveness of their army by using these choppers as troop transports and gunships. Search and rescue was a luxury that the Vietnamese could not afford.

The development of search and rescue operations in Southeast Asia was a phenomenon peculiar to America's involvement. Few other nations, faced with similar conditions of warfare, would have developed such an extensive rescue capability. Even fewer nations could have afforded it. The cost of rescue operations was high because they required a task force composed of large HH-3 and HH-53 helicopters, enormous amounts of tactical air support, and a sophisticated command, control, and coordination system. The heart of the search and rescue task force was the giant Sikorsky helicopters and the expensive HC-130P tanker/command aircraft. These items were not made available to the Vietnamese Air Force under the Vietnamization program.

Also, the humanitarian aspects of American rescue operations involved concepts which were much less meaningful to the Vietnamese. Western philosophies stress the cohesive nature of society, and the American tradition, reflecting its Judeo-Christian background, emphasizes the worth of the individual as a part of that society. Each member, therefore, perceives a responsibility to society as a whole, thus leading to the "team effort" concept. The Vietnamese socio-cultural patterns are much more limited. Brought up in the close confines of family living in an isolated village, Vietnamese do not readily identify with their nation or even their race. Furthermore, Buddhism instilled a sense of fatalism that does not inspire a keen desire to influence the results of events, especially those resulting from combat operations. Therefore, because they did not have the expensive military resources to expend and because they did not have the commitment to the individual that Americans felt, the Vietnamese did not pursue the development of their own rescue forces.[53]

Nevertheless, from 1962 onward, the U.S. Air Force encouraged the Vietnamese to develop their rescue capability. As mentioned earlier, when the first Air Rescue Service coordinators reached Saigon in 1962, they often relied on Vietnamese choppers to carry them to a crash site or to recover a survivor. And, as early as November 15, 1962, Vietnam and the United States had signed a joint rescue agreement which designated the Vietnamese Air Force as the agency responsible for all civil and military search and rescue in the Republic of Vietnam. Over the years the Americans wrote regulations for the Vietnamese on the subject of rescue operations. Published in 1967, Vietnamese Air Force Regulation 64-1 established an organization to provide rescue zones, a search and rescue mobilization center in the Vietnamese Tactical Air Control Center communications complex, where air operations were planned and controlled, and search and rescue mobilization offices in the Vietnamese Direct Air Support Centers at corps level. Other regulations called for a search and rescue training program as well as instructions to aircrews on rescue procedures.[54]

In reality, the Vietnamese Air Force did not translate regulations into combat capability. For instance, when American local base rescue detachments at Binh Thuy and Pleiku were inactivated, the Vietnamese did not take over the mission. Whereas the 38th Aerospace Rescue and Recovery Squadron had previously maintained two HH-43s at each of these bases, the Vietnamese Air Force occasionally kept one UH-1 at Binh Thuy for general usage, and its crew was untrained in rescue operations and procedures. Vietnam's search and rescue capability remained unfulfilled. Rescue operations were conducted haphazardly, generally with no planning or coordination. After the last Aerospace Rescue and Recovery Service units left Vietnam in early 1973, downed Vietnamese aircrew members had to hope that a Vietnamese troop transport, cargo, or gunship helicopter would be able to pick them up. Otherwise they had to depend on their own ingenuity at evasion to get them safely back to friendly territory.[55]

Fortunately for the Vietnamese and American aircrews, the Aerospace Rescue and Recovery Service still had units stationed in South Vietnam during the hard fighting in the spring and summer of 1972. Indeed, during this period rescue service units participated in some of the largest and most difficult rescue operations of the war. On April 2, three days after the North Vietnamese began pouring into the South, Bat 21 and Bat 22, a pair of Douglas EB-66 twin-engine jet electronic warfare planes, were escorting three B-52s on a mission near the demilitarized zone. A missile site launched three SA-2s at Bat 21. One hit it broadside. The force of the explosion blew Lt. Col. Iceal E. Hambleton, an electronics warfare officer, out of the aircraft. All others presumably perished. Unhurt, except for a minor singeing, Hambleton used his survival radio to contact an OV-10 pilot circling nearby. The OV-10 pilot remembered hearing that an effort to evacuate U.S. Army advisors from Quang Tri had been canceled. He contacted the rescue force assembled for this operation, and soon its A-1s located Hambleton hiding in the underbrush near the Cam Lo River. Intense enemy fire convinced the A-1 pilots that the area was too dangerous for the Jolly Greens, so while the choppers hovered a safe distance away, the A-1s spent three hours blasting enemy positions and strafing anyone who got too close to the survivor.

Meanwhile, four U.S. Army UH-1 choppers heard the radio chatter from the rescue task force and decided to make their own unauthorized pickup attempt. As the four helicopters approached the downed airman, enemy gunners shot one of the choppers out of the sky, killing all aboard. Another damaged UH-1 limped toward the sea to make a crash landing on the beach south of Quang Tri.[56]

Operations officers at Seventh Air Force, realizing that the rescue activity was located in the middle of a major enemy troop concentration, established a no-fire zone, an area in which artillery fire was tightly controlled, seventeen miles in radius around the downed officer. This no-fire zone encompassed most of the area of operation of the Army of the Republic of Vietnam's 3d Division, struggling to blunt the communist invasion drive.[57]

Dawn brought poor weather that grounded the rescue forces. Nevertheless, two OV-10s from Nakhon Phanom obtained loran navigation fixes on the beleagured flyer's position. The OV-10 pilots relayed the information back to the targeting center at Nakhon Phanom Royal Thai Air Force Base for analysis and collation with recent photography of the area. Computers then printed out targets for bombers to pound through the clouds and haze. From April 2 through April 13 up to ninety strike sorties a day were used to keep enemy troops away. Enemy missiles shot down two OV-10s with the loss of two crewmen. The only HH-53 attempt to recover the man ended when enemy gunners brought it down killing its entire crew.[58]

In spite of the air strikes, there were still too many troops, too many guns, and too much danger for the HH-53s to be used. Finally, the Marines volunteered to send a squad up the Cam Lo river to meet the officer if he would swim downstream out of the main enemy force concentration. The forward air controllers relayed the instructions, and he made his way to the nearby river. He spent the next three nights floating downstream. On the third day he sighted a sampan with Americans in it. Using a pre-arranged signal he called out his rank and a color. The Marines scooped him out of the water and took him to an armored personnel carrier that carried him to a safe helicopter landing zone for evacuation to Da Nang.[59]

These eleven days raised serious questions about search and rescue. Operational questions concerned the capabilities of the rescue task force. Giant HH-53 choppers, the finest aircrew recovery helicopters in the world, had been unable to operate in a concentration of enemy troops backed by radar-guided antiaircraft guns and surface-to-air missiles. The only Jolly Green that dared to go in for a recovery attempt was shot down. Col. Jack Allison, a helicopter pilot since 1951 and a veteran of numerous combat rescue missions, said that against opposition like that encountered in the Bat 21 mission, the traditional search and rescue task force was useless.[60]

Large questions of suffering and morality were also raised. How much was one man's life worth? Was it worth more than the lives of those members of the Vietnamese Army's 3d Division, jeopardized when American air strikes were used to keep the North Vietnamese away from one downed flyer rather than used to support their efforts to halt the enemy offensive? Was one man's life worth more than the lives of two OV-10 crewmembers, five crewmen in the HH-53, and the crew of the Army Huey chopper that were lost during the rescue operation?

In the eleven day operation, thousands of enemy troops backed by tanks and artillery rushed into Military Region I. Maj. David A. Brookbank, a U.S. Air Force air liaison officer with the South Vietnamese 3d Division reported, "With three enemy divisions plus heavy artillery striking . . . the 3d ARVN was unable to return fire or request TACAIR [tactical air strikes] in the area . . . This operation cost the 3d ARVN dearly." Brookbank added, "After the zones were terminated, the enemy was already south of the Cua Viet and Mieu Cay rivers in strength."[61]

With the Vietnamese unable to call for air support and restricted from firing their own artillery into this no-fire zone, "The SAR restriction" as Brookbank said, "gave the enemy an opportunity unprecedented in the annals of warfare to advance at will."[62] For eleven days any damage inflicted on the North Vietnamese Army in this part of their invasion corridor was coincidental to the rescue operation. On one occasion, however, that damage was considerable. A forward air controller spotted a column of tanks on Route 1. Task Force Alpha targeteers called for a B-52 strike and six of the giants rippled the road destroying thirty-five tanks and, as was later discovered through intelligence sources, an enemy command center.[63]

How did the Aerospace Rescue and Recovery Service units in Southeast Asia determine how much rescue effort was enough? At what point did someone in authority decide that a downed airman could not be rescued because the cost was too high? There were, in fact, no guidelines. No regulations existed which defined when anyone had to be abandoned because the danger was too great or the cost in lives and aircraft might be too great.

During the Korean War, the commander of the Air Rescue Service Brig. Gen. Richard T. Kight, coined the motto, "That others may live."[64] True to those words, rescuemen have tried never to stop short of giving each rescue attempt every possible effort. On occasion, rescue operations diverted hundreds of Air Force and Navy sorties to support recovery forces. In the December 1969 attempt to pick up Lt. Woodrow Bergeron, Jr., the navigator in Boxer 22, an F-4 shot down near Tchepone, Laos, one pararescueman died and several others were wounded. Five of the ten helicopters that were damaged never flew again. Additionally, five A-1s were heavily damaged. A total of 336 sorties were flown in that operation.[65] Yet no one asked if the life of one man was worth all the effort. To people in the Aerospace Rescue and Recovery Service such a question has always seemed unnecessary. Nevertheless, the Bat 21 rescue operation brought the question of how much was one man's life worth back into focus. U.S. Air Force Brig. Gen. R.G. Cross, Jr., Deputy Director of Air Operations at MACV commented, "As airmen or soldiers or sailors we should expect that there are times when as one person, we must be sacrificed for the overall."[66]

The difficult question of how much rescue effort was too much, was never adequately addressed and never answered. Diversion of sorties to a search and rescue mission meant that targets that were supposed to have been struck in support of ground troops might not have been hit at all. Given the value of airpower in ground operations, one must assume that reducing the number of sorties supporting ground forces in order to divert these aircraft to a rescue operation must have caused these troops to suffer increased casualties. In the case of the Bat 21 rescue operation, it seems certain that large numbers of enemy troops moved through a vital part of South Vietnam's Military Region I without being molested by air or artillery strikes. It also seems logical to assume that many South Vietnamese troops died because air and artillery support was not available. It could, therefore, be argued that the Americans were vastly more concerned with saving the life of one of their own and, conversely, held the lives of their Asian allies in lower regard.

Meanwhile, the killing and dying continued as the North Vietnamese offensive rolled on through April. Among the rescue efforts during that offensive, the evacuation of 132 American and Vietnamese troops from the citadel at Quang Tri stands out as one of the largest rescue operations of the war. At the height of the invasion, four North Vietnamese divisions surrounded Quang Tri City cutting off the American advisors and South Vietnamese troops in the old citadel.[67]

On May 1 four HH-53s from the 37th Aerospace Rescue and Recovery Squadron at Da Nang took off for Quang Tri. They planned to have three Jolly Green Giants pick up all the survivors while the fourth chopper hovered outside the city, ready to dash in if needed. The North Vietnamese had moved SA-2 surface-to-air missiles south and their area of coverage encompassed Quang Tri City. Consequently the helicopters had to approach the city at tree-top level. At that low altitude they ran the risk of automatic weapons fire which they usually avoided by flying above 3,000 feet.[68]

Over the nearly-demolished outskirts of the city, three Jolly Greens moved into a single file to proceed up a corridor blasted by the A-1s to the walls of the fortress. As the first chopper settled into the citadel, enemy small arms fire increased to an intensity that caused so much confusion that only thirty-seven men managed to climb aboard before the pilot pulled away. Staff Sergeant Robert LaPinte, pararescueman on Jolly 71, remained behind to organize the remaining survivors. With order restored, the next chopper loaded forty-five people and quickly took off.[69]

The third Jolly Green into the fortress loaded fifty people just as quickly as the second helicopter. Its pilot pulled up and headed for safety. When it seemed that the rescue effort had ended, Capt. Donald A. Sutton, commander of the backup helicopter, received a frantic radio message, "Hey, we've got more people down here!" Sutton rushed to the citadel, landed, and lowered his ramp. No one ran to the waiting chopper. Suddenly North Vietnamese troops leaped from the wrecked buildings and opened fire on the sitting Jolly Green. Sutton realized he had been suckered into a trap. As his parajumper blasted everyone in sight with the minigun, the last

120

Jolly rose from the fallen fortress and headed for Da Nang. Minutes later the North Vietnamese flag flew over the citadel's ruins.[70]

Because of the enemy's big offensive, air action and air losses in 1972 increased significantly over those of the previous year. In 1971, the U.S. Air Force suffered 88 combat and operational losses in Southeast Asia. In 1972, the figure more than doubled to 194.[71] Over South Vietnam, total allied combat losses for fixed-wing aircraft rose from 29 in 1971 to 63 in 1972. Air Force, Navy, and Marine Corps combat losses over North Vietnam went from 6 in 1971 to 149 a year later. The focus of the air war had shifted back to the Vietnams. As a result, losses over Laos dropped from 42 in 1971 to 25 in 1972. Finally, in 1971 in Cambodia 12 planes were shot down, but only 2 went down the following year.[72] HH-53 losses totaled 4 in 1971 and 4 the next year. One Jolly Green went down on March 27, just before the North Vietnamese offensive. During the Bat 21 effort heavy small arms fire destroyed an HH-53, killing all hands. One HH-53 was lost during a rocket attack on Da Nang in August and the last Jolly Green Giant loss occurred during Linebacker II, the massive bombing in the Hanoi and Haiphong area in December 1972 .[73]

The number of saves in 1972 reflected the nature of the war. In March 1972, the Aerospace Rescue and Recovery Service rescued 18 people with 17 being picked up by HH-53s. In April, 12 people were saved, 10 by the Jolly Greens and two by HH-43s. May saw more people rescued than any other one month during the 1961-73 conflict with 138 saves credited to the rescue service. The daring operation at the citadel in Quang Tri accounted for 132 people. Only one flier was picked up in North Vietnam during May. Throughout the summer the main focus of action continued to be in the South with 24 Aerospace Rescue and Recovery Service pickups there and only 6 in North Vietnam. Even during the Linebacker II bombing of North Vietnam, no one was rescued from that country because the targets were in densely populated, highly defended areas. The Aerospace Rescue and Recovery Service, however, did make 25 aircrew rescues in Laos and 7 in Thailand. These people were saved because they managed to fly their damaged aircraft out of the highly defended areas of North Vietnam.[74]

By contrast, in 1967, at the height of Rolling Thunder, the Air Force lost 189 aircraft in combat over North Vietnam. Throughout Southeast Asia, the Air Force lost 327 fixed-wing aircraft to hostile forces. The Navy and Marine Corps lost 171 fixed-wing aircraft and the Army fixed-wing losses totaled 16. The Aerospace Rescue and Recovery Service made 192 aircrew rescues and picked up 34 men in North Vietnam in 1967.[75]

When the communist offensive stalled in late summer, the reduction of rescue forces resumed. Reduced rescue resources prompted a streamlining of the organization. On August 20, 1972, the entire 3d Aerospace Rescue and Recovery Group became part of the 41st Aerospace Rescue and Recovery Wing at Hickam Air Force Base, Hawaii, with the 37th, 40th, and

56th Aerospace Rescue and Recovery Squadrons, the 3d Aerospace Rescue and Recovery Group and its local base rescue detachments (including Detachment 14 with the temporarily assigned HH-3Es) coming under the command of the wing. The local base rescue units were detached from the 3d Aerospace Rescue and Recovery Group and placed under the 40th Aerospace Rescue and Recovery Squadron. In spite of the reorganization, operational control remained with Headquarters, 3d Aerospace Rescue and Recovery Group at Tan Son Nhut.[76]

Force reductions and realignments brought changes and improvements in equipment as the Aerospace Rescue and Recovery Service continued to search for ways to improve its search and rescue capabilities. For instance enemy defenses had long since grown too sophisticated and strong for the HH-3. This had been graphically illustrated during the rescue of Lt. Bergeron from the highly defended area around Tchepone in December 1969. During that operation the intensity of fire was such that, after five sorties with the HH-3s, the 37th Aerospace Rescue and Recovery Squadron had to stop trying to pick up the survivor.[77]

Before the spring offensive of 1972, the appearance of SA-2 missiles and radar-guided antiaircraft guns in the southwestern part of North Vietnam and along the Ho Chi Minh Trail constituted an alarming threat to slower-moving aircraft like the HC-130P and the HH-53 helicopters. Aware of the threat posed by SAMs and radar-guided guns, the Seventh Air Force had asked in November 1971 that twenty HH-53s be equipped with radar homing and warning equipment called "RHAW gear".[78] This electronic gear detected enemy radar emissions and then translated the impulses into visual and auditory warnings that could be used to determine the direction and intensity of the threat.

HC-130Ps and HH-53s were slow, relatively unmaneuverable, and therefore vulnerable to radar-guided missiles and antiaircraft guns. Once the crew of a helicopter or an HC-130 knew that they were being tracked by a Fan Song radar associated with the SA-2s or a Whiff or Firecan radar associated with antiaircraft guns, they had to rely on electronic countermeasures rather than speed and maneuverability to counter the threat. In May 1972, the Seventh Air Force began seeking jamming systems for these aircraft.[79] Problems in acquiring this equipment were serious and remained unsolved through the end of hostilities. One of the big problems was weight. Available electronic countermeasures pods, which were relatively light, could not be placed under the belly of the helicopter because of low ground clearance. Systems that could be installed inside the chopper weighed 1,200 pounds. This much weight was unacceptable for the HH-53, because on some rescue missions it was necesary to jettison as much weight as possible to improve hover capability. The countermeasures gear would be too expensive and too susceptible to technological compromise to be thrown overboard.[80]

In March 1972 Air Force Logistics Command began working on an electronic countermeasures jammer for the HC-130P. Existing pods were found to be incompatible with the wing because of the refueling drogues. The war ended before the JC-130P got a RHAW system and it never got an electronic countermeasures jamming capability.[81]

Because these developments in equipment were underway at a time of force reductions in Southeast Asia, Air Force headquarters assigned them low priorities in study and funding. Consequently, when the North Vietnamese began their offensive on March 31, 1972, most proposals were unfulfilled. For instance, the installation of an electronic location finder on the HH-53s, a proposal under consideration since February 1970, did not become a reality in Southeast Asia until May 1972. On May 12 an HH-53 used an electronic location finder on a combat checkout flight. On June 2 an HH-53 equipped with this gadget recovered a crewmember down inside North Vietnam. Consequently, the Aerospace Rescue and Recovery Service began installing electronic location finders on all HH-53s, but this process was not completed before April 1973.[82]

It took the enemy's spring offensive of 1972 to get qualitative improvements in equipment that were needed to keep the rescue forces competitive with improved enemy defenses. The enemy forces that attacked South Vietnam in the spring of 1972 were more heavily armed with sophisticated weapons than any previously encountered below the demilitarized zone. Rescue crews were unprepared for the intensity of opposition which rivaled that found in the most highly defended areas of North Vietnam. The enemy's new SA-7 hand-held, infrared antiaircraft missile proved to be especially disconcerting. Although it accounted for no HH-53 losses, the rescue crews were forced to be more cautious. One tactic to counter this missile was to fly very low, but this was only partially successful because then the choppers attracted more small arms fire. However, a readily available, low-technology remedy sufficed to counter the threat. When a missile was sighted a crewman fired a flare to decoy its infrared homer.[83]

In May 1972, after the SA-2 missile appeared in Laos and South Vietnam, radar homing and warning gear was placed aboard five Jolly Green Giant helicopters. By September all the HH-53s in Southeast Asia had this warning system.[84] Also in May, laboratories at Wright-Patterson AFB, Ohio, began fitting a modified version of a 160-pound electronic countermeasures pod for use inside the HH-53.[85] By that time the North Vietnamese offensive had been ripping through South Vietnam for more than a month and rescue crews were hard-pressed to overcome the array of missiles and antiaircraft guns they brought with them.

In the autumn of 1972, as massive airpower and a revitalized Army of the Republic of Vietnam with the latest U.S. equipment slowed and then stopped the spring offensive, Vietnamization gathered momentum. This meant not only reductions, realignments, and relocations but also changes in aircraft. For the rescue forces these changes revolved around replacing the A-1 Skyraider with the Vought A-7 single-engine jet in the Sandy role. Also, other aircraft, like the OV-10, were integrated into the search and rescue task force.[86]

Proposed ceasefire agreements included arms limitations on weapons supplied to the Republic of Vietnam. The U.S. Government quickened the transfer of weapons, including aircraft, to the Vietnamese. This meant that rescue forces would be without the services of the A-1 sooner than had been anticipated. The Skyraider had been a magnificent rescue escort aircraft. But, by 1971, age, enemy action, and the Vietnamization program had depleted the A-1 inventory to the point that it was evident the aircraft would have to be replaced in the rescue escort role. Most chopper pilots felt that only another A-1 could replace the A-1. But, the cost of reopening the production lines for the Skyraider, closed since the late 1950s, would have been prohibitive.[87]

Rescue escort was only one of several missions assigned the Skyraiders of the 1st Special Operations Squadron of the 56th Special Operations Wing at Nakhon Phanom. Additionally, A-1s provided close air support for the Royal Laotian Army and the Central Intelligence Agency's Meo guerillas. A-1s from the 1st Special Operations Squadron also escorted CH-53 helicopters of the 21st Special Operations Squadron on clandestine missions throughout Southeast Asia.[88]

As part of the rescue escort mission, two A-1s were on alert at Da Nang for missions in northern South Vietnam and North Vietnam, two at Nakhon Phanom for operations over Laos and North Vietnam, and two at Ubon Royal Thai Air Force Base in southeast Thailand for missions into southern Laos and Cambodia.[89] With the reduction in aircraft, the 1st Special Operations Squadron was the only U.S. Air Force combat squadron flying the A-1. With eight of its twenty planes designated for rescue alert, wear on the remaining aircraft began to show by 1972. Flying hours fell from 4,589 in the first quarter of 1971 to 2,995 in the same period the following year. The operationally ready rate dropped from 81.7 percent to 69.7 percent as the percentage of aircraft in maintenance rose from an average of 16.6 to 25.5 on any given day.[90]

In early 1972, the 56th Special Operations Wing was told it would lose six A-1s to the Vietnamese Air Force by the end of March. Since such a reduction would have seriously degraded the effectiveness of the 1st Special Operations Squadron,[91] the American Ambassador to Laos, G. McMurtrie Godley, asked the State Department to delay this plan.[92]

A reprieve was granted, but the 3d Aerospace Rescue and Recovery Group and the 56th Special Operations Wing knew the Skyraider's days were numbered. In August 1971 the Tactical Air Command had conducted flight tests of various aircraft to determine their suitability for the rescue escort mission. A year later, in August 1972, after reviewing the test results, the Seventh Air Force decided the A-7D could perform the rescue escort role. A plan was prepared to replace the A-1 with the A-7 over a six months period. The announcement by Dr. Henry Kissinger on October 28 that "peace is at hand" accelerated the pace of Vietnamization. All A-1s were to be turned over to the Vietnamese Air Force by the end of the year, and the 1st Special Operations Squadron transferred to Kadena Air Base, Okinawa.[93]

On October 31, 1972, representatives from the 56th Special Operations Wing, 1st Special Operations Squadron, 40th Aerospace Rescue and Recovery Squadron, 3d Aerospace Rescue and Recovery Group, and the Seventh Air Force met with representatives from the 3d Tactical Fighter Squadron, an A-7 unit based at Korat, in a rescue conference at Nakhon Phanom. They reviewed the A-1 mission to consider possible problems that might be encountered in replacing the A-1 with the A-7. On November 2, the Seventh Air Force began designating twelve A-7s for daily search and rescue training missions.[94]

The A-1s flew their last rescue escort mission on November 7. An Army UH-1 helicopter, with seven persons aboard, had crashed west of Quang Ngai, South Vietnam. With a typhoon closing in, the A-1s took off into heavy rain, wind, and low clouds to fly below 200 feet in an effort to locate the survivors. After finding the men, they strafed the nearby enemy troops, then called in the Jolly Green to make the recovery. Even as this last mission was being flown, the inactivation of the 1st Special Operations Squadron had begun. On November 3 four A-1s were turned over to the Vietnamese Air Force at Bien Hoa. Twelve days later the final delivery was made.[95]

Early in November A-7s began working with the Jolly Greens in practice missions. As part of the training, an A-1 pilot rode in a helicopter to comment on the A-7s performance. This tactic helped to smooth the transition from the slow Skyraiders to the faster A-7s.[96]

A-7s flew their first combat rescue mission on November 16, when an F-105G on a surface-to-air missile suppression mission over North Vietnam was shot down. The search and rescue effort took three days during which the search and rescue task force coped with many problems. Because of their greater speed, the A-7s could not fly alongside the helicopters. In flying large "race track" or oval patterns around the choppers, the A-7 pilots often lost sight of their charges. Additionally, because the rescue task force operated at low altitudes, the A-7 jets burned fuel rapidly and were forced to make many more trips to the KC-135 tanker than was usual with the A-1s. With F-4s flying on Mig combat air patrol and F-105s flying the SAM suppression mission needing fuel also, the tankers were hard pressed to provide service to all their customers. Finally, on November 18, after both downed crewmen were picked up, the members of the rescue task force got together at Nakhon Phanom to discuss their problems.[97] They decided to call another rescue conference.

The search and rescue conference was held on November 25 at the Seventh/Thirteenth Air Force's headquarters at Udorn. The conferees decided the A-7s problems were its speed and fuel consumption. Their high speed made keeping the helicopters in sight difficult if not impossible. It was suggested that helicopter rotor blades be painted with a luminescent paint or that there be a strobe light affixed to the top of the chopper's fuselage. These suggestions would have to be worked out in the laboratories at the Aerospace Systems Division at Wright-Patterson Air Force Base, Ohio, and at the new Aerospace Rescue and Recovery Service Training Center which had recently moved from Eglin Air Force Base, Florida, to Hill Air Force Base, Utah. To alleviate the problem of providing escort while A-7s went to refuel, the number of aircraft assigned for a helicopter escort mission was raised from four to six. This meant that at least two airplanes would be with the chopper at all times.[98]

In spite of these weaknesses, the A-7 brought some unique features to the rescue task force. Its higher speed, while a disadvantage in some ways enabled the A-7s to reach survivors more rapidly thus providing the supportive fire they might need quickly, a factor often crucial in avoiding capture. Furthermore, its computerized navigation system improved the capability of the search and rescue task force. The A-7 computers could mark and store the exact coordinates of a downed airman's location. Its radar altimeter, forward looking radar with terrain avoidance features, and direction-finding homing devices increased the rescue task force's capabilities in foul weather.[99]

The bomb load of the A-7 was theoretically twice that of the Skyraider. However, this was irrelevant in the rescue escort mission because the ordnance load typically included special munitions rather than a large load of 500-pound bombs. In the rescue configuration the first three rescue escort aircraft, Sandys 1, 2, and 3, usually carried two CBU-38 cluster bombs, two LAU-3 launcher pods packed with high explosive rockets, and two additional LAU-3 pods filled with white phosphorus rockets. The fourth plane in the rescue escort flight, Sandy 4, carried two CBU-38s and a pair of CBU-12 cluster smoke bombs. All aircraft carried two external fuel tanks.[100]

Beginning in 1970, twin-engine OV-10 "Broncos" began working with the search and rescue task force as forward air controllers. Because of their fast speed, armament that included four 7.62 machine guns as well as a rocket or gun pod, and great visibility, the Jolly Green pilots preferred the OV-10 to the slower, unarmed O-1s and O-2s. As the number of A-1s was reduced, the role of the OV-10 in the search and rescue task force expanded.[101]

OV-10s were equipped with the Pave Nail night observation system that enabled their crews to find, track, and designate targets for laser-guided weapons in daylight or at night provided there was some moonlight. Applied to the search and rescue mission, Pave Nail OV-10s could locate survivors in bad weather or at night.[102] During a rescue effort any Pave Nail aircraft in the vicinity were often diverted to help find the survivors.[103] Pave Nail OV-10s were equipped with a night observation device that included a bore-sighted laser range designator called Pave Spot, which also provided an asset to the rescue task force. Using Pave Spot, the operator in an OV-10 beamed a laser to mark the slant range and heading of targets, thus pinpointing their location.[104] The Pave Nail/Pave Spot OV-10s helped the search and rescue task force develop away from the A-1/Jolly Green Giant combination which relied on firepower, tactics, and courage to the A-7/Jolly Green team which relied more on advanced technology.[105]

As the A-1 faded and the rescue task force accommodated to its A-7 replacement, the war in Indochina erupted into Linebacker II. After B-52s hammered at the Hanoi-Haiphong area, North Vietnam's leadership decided to resume peace negotiations in Paris. The bombing of North Vietnam stopped on January 15, 1973, and on January 23, Dr. Henry Kissinger and Le Duc Tho completed the final ceasefire agreement.[106]

Planning for the ceasefire had resulted in the near total withdrawal of rescue forces from Vietnam prior to December 1972. On November 30, the 37th Aerospace Rescue and Recovery Squadron at Da Nang was inactivated. Five of its HH-53s were transferred to the 40th Aerospace Rescue and Recovery Squadron at Nakhon Phanom Royal Thai Air Force Base, while its two HH-43s remained at Da Nang to provide local base rescue during Linebacker II as Detachment 7, 40th Aerospace Rescue and Recovery Squadron. This augmentation put the 40th over its authorized number of eleven helicopters, and on December 15 two HH-53s were airlifted to Hickam. The 40th Aerospace Rescue and Recovery Squadron retained three of the helicopters that remained; two served as replacements and one was kept in reserve as an excess over the authorized number. When, in mid-December, an HH-53 was lost, this reserve chopper became part of the regular force.[107]

In accordance with the ceasefire agreement of January 1973, Aerospace Rescue and Recovery Group, 3d headquarters moved with the Seventh Air Force from Tan Son Nhut to Nakhon Phanom. It became active on February 15, 1973, as part of the United States Support Activities Group/7AF (USSAG/7AF). The Commander, 3d Aerospace Rescue and Recovery Group was redesignated Director of Air Rescue and placed under the Assistant Chief of Staff, USSAG J-3/7AF, Director for Search and Rescue.[108] The manning at USSAG/7AF included seven spaces in the 3d Aerospace Rescue and Recovery Group and ten in the Joint Rescue Coordination Center. With the transfer of the rescue control function of the coordination center from Saigon to Nakhon Phanom, the 40th Aerospace

Rescue and Recovery Squadron Rescue Coordination Center became superfluous and was inactivated.[109]

The force level of rescue aircraft stood at eleven HH-53s and fourteen HH-43s. Two HH-43s were assigned to each of the local base rescue detachments at Ubon, Udorn, Takhli, Korat, and Utapao, and two additional HH-43s were kept at Nakhon Phanom as overages awaiting disposition. Additionally, there were six HC-130P rescue control aircraft in the 56th Aerospace Rescue and Recovery Squadron at Korat.[110]

The ceasefire in Vietnam did not mean the end of all hostilities in Southeast Asia, although it did mean an end to rescue missions in Vietnam. Bombing and reconnaissance flights continued in Laos and Cambodia. Ironically, the war had come full circle for the men in rescue. Nine years before, in 1964, when the first rescue helicopters were sent to Southeast Asia, they were sent to Nakhon Phanom. Then they were a vanguard of the expanding American commitment. In 1973, the rescue helicopters were back at Nakhon Phanom, on the way out of Southeast Asia as a rear guard during force reduction and eventual disengagement from America's long involvement in Indochina. Still, more action and heartbreak lay ahead.

Top left: pararescue man reeled into a hovering helicopter; left: Capt. Ben Smith hoisted out of Laotian jungle; above: TSgt Charles F. Salome bandages Capt. Paul J. Fairbanks' head following the latter's rescue; bottom: the first HH–43B unloaded at Utapao Airfield, Thailand, Feb. 29, 1969.

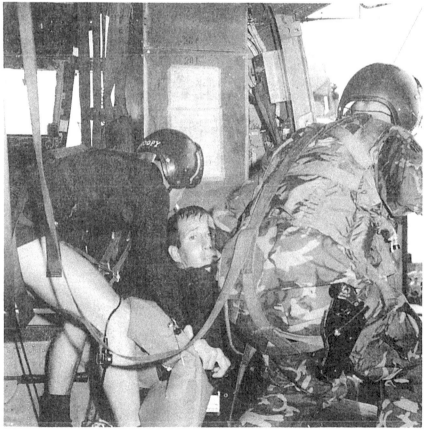

Top: Vigil of a Jolly Green Giant at Da Nang; bottom: anguished pilot pulled aboard a helicopter, March 17, 1968.

130

Top left: Jolly Green Giant on a rescue mission; top right: A1C George T. Schmitt, 40th ARRS, installs radio equipment in helicopter; bottom: interior of an HH–3E helicopter.

Helicopter sent to the rescue

6 Cease-fire to Mayaguez

Following implementation of the Paris agreements, units of the Aerospace Rescue and Recovery Service remained in Thailand. In 1973, as fighting continued in Laos and Cambodia, rescue forces flew combat aircrew recovery missions. After Congress halted the bombing of Cambodia in August, the 3d Aerospace Rescue and Recovery Group kept a helicopter on alert. However, most activities entailed sharpening their combat aircrew recovery skills while practicing their roles in the developing plans for the evacuations of Laos, Cambodia, and South Vietnam.

With the signing of the agreements in January, a short-lived, quasi-peace began in South Vietnam. Fighting continued in Laos until the Royal Laotian Government and the Pathet Lao signed a ceasefire in February, then flared again briefly in April. The bombing of Cambodia went on until August 15, 1973. As long as American aircrews were involved in combat, the Aerospace Rescue and Recovery Service provided rescue support.

The final aircrew recoveries in Laos were made in early January 1973 when rescue choppers picked up three aircrewmen after their aircraft were damaged in strikes over North Vietnam. Even though the Air Force flew 386 attack sorties in Laos in January and 1,449 in February, there were no losses. Pathet Lao air defenses were considerably less than those of the North Vietnamese who manned the antiaircraft systems along the Ho Chi Minh Trail.[1]

In Cambodia, the communist Khmer Rouge remained a force without sophisticated weapons up to the day they took power in April 1975. Throughout the war they rarely, if ever, employed the larger caliber antiaircraft guns used by the North Vietnamese and, to a lesser extent, by the enemy forces in South Vietnam. Consequently, rescue activities in Cambodia never assumed the scope that they did elsewhere in Indochina.

With the overthrow of Prince Norodom Sihanouk in March 1970, the U.S. and Vietnamese Air Forces began tactical air operations in Cambodia in support of the Cambodian Army which was almost immediately caught up in an expanding war with Khmer Rouge insurgents. The level of activity soared from 20 Air Force and 20 Vietnamese Air Force tactical sorties in 1969 to 14,663 Air Force and 9,855 Vietnamese sorties in 1970.[2] Even before the ouster of Sihanouk, in February 1970, the Air Force flew two A-37 and two F-100 sorties in Cambodia. In March, following the coup in Phnom Penh, the Americans and Vietnamese stopped their air operations while the political climate calmed. Meanwhile, the Khmer Air Force, flying

133

Soviet-and Chinese-supplied Mig-17s, attacked North Vietnamese and Khmer Rouge positions. Responding to the unfavorable turn of events in Phnom Penh, the Russians and Chinese suspended aid to Cambodia and by the end of April the Migs were grounded for lack of spare parts. The only U.S. Air Force support of the Khmer Air Force came with two A-37 strikes in April. Then, on May 1, the U.S. Army and the Army of the Republic of Vietnam invaded Cambodia. American air support accelerated to 7,104 sorties for the month. In May the Air Force lost three F-4s and one OV-10.[3]

With the end of the American invasion on June 29, 1970, American air support diminished. There were 3,397 attack sorties in June and only 754 in support of Khmer forces in July. In August the Air Force flew 1,400 attack missions in Cambodia. By the end of the summer, the Air Force had lost nine aircraft. Five aircrew members were rescued, six were killed and two more were listed as missing. During the Cambodian invasion, the U.S. Army lost eighty-two people in helicopter crashes. Many others, aircrew members and passengers, were picked up by other Army choppers after being shot down. Because of the informal nature of search and rescue activities, no accurate record exists.[4]

Rescue operations in Cambodia were an extension of operations in southern Laos and South Vietnam. An HC-130P King aircraft normally flew a dawn to dusk orbit between Nakhon Phanom and Paksane, Laos.[5] This aircraft responded to search and rescue requests in Cambodia. After February 1973, an HC-130P flew an airborne orbit over Thailand near the Cambodian and Laotian border in anticipation of possible rescue operations. Additionally, another HC-130P remained on thirty-minute alert during daylight hours and forty-five-minute alert at night at Korat Royal Thai Air Force Base.[6] To cover aircrew recovery, two HH-53s were available at Bien Hoa until that forward operating location closed on December 5, 1971. Thereafter, two HH-53s, rotated from Nakhon Phanom, were on fifteen-minute alert at Ubon.[7]

Losses in air action over Cambodia were light in comparison to the rest of Indochina. From 1970 to the bombing halt in August 1973, the Air Force suffered only thirty-two aircraft losses in combat with three lost for "operational" reasons.[8] Sixty-one Air Force personnel went down in these aircraft. Twenty-seven were rescued while twenty-two were listed as missing as of November 1973. No Air Force personnel were known to have been captured by the Khmer Rouge.[9]

One of the Air Forces operational losses in Cambodia was that of an HH-53 from the 40th Aerospace Rescue and Recovery Squadron. On June 14, 1973, Jolly Green 64 went out of control immediately after refueling. It crashed upside-down into the Tonle Sap, the giant lake in the middle of Cambodia. Two pararescuemen bailed out and were rescued by another HH-53. Seven other crewmen perished in the crash.[10]

America's part in the air war over Cambodia ended on August 15,

1973. At this time the airborne orbit was discontinued, although an HC-130P remained on half-hour alert at Korat during the day and forty-five-minute alert during the night. At Nakhon Phanom two HH-53s were on fifteen-minute alert during daylight and forty-five-minute alert at night. The A-7s at Korat designated for rescue escort had to be ready to be airborne within a quarter of an hour during the day with no alert at night. Local base rescue units, as usual, maintained a constant around-the-clock alert.[11] In mid-February 1974, just over a year after the signing of the Paris agreements, the A-7 rescue escort alert slipped to twenty-minutes.[12]

In addition to keeping a portion of their forces on alert, Aerospace Rescue and Recovery Service units participated in a series of exercises to keep up their proficiency should they ever be ordered back into action over Southeast Asia. These exercises, which included virtually all Air Force units in Thailand, were known as "Commando Scrimmage" and they took place at practice bombing ranges south of Udorn, outside Ubon, and near Nakhon Phanom.[13] Between September 1973 and April 1975, there were eleven such exercises. Rescue forces, including HH-53s as well as HC-130Ps, and A-7s along with OV-10s and AC-130 gunships participated. In addition to their rescue escort role, A-7s acted the part of Mig interceptors to provide opposition.[14]

To sharpen their skills further, rescue forces began, on February 15, 1974, to conduct their own training exercises. These events usually took place at an abandoned airport at Loeng Nok Tha, seventy miles south of Nakhon Phanom.[15] Other elements of the search and rescue task force joined the HH-53s from the 40th Aerospace Rescue and Recovery Squadron. These included 3d Tactical Fighter Squadron A-7s, and OV-10s from the 23d Tactical Air Support Squadron, HC-130Ps from the 56th Special Operations Squadron, and, to determine their usefulness in search and rescue missions, AC-130 gunships from the 16th Special Operations Squadron.[16] Exercises, conducted weekly, involved rescue attempts in various situations. To add realism, "survivors" were placed on the grounds of the Loeng Nok Tha airport to evade, be spotted, and eventually picked up by an HH-53.[17]

These exercises benefited all participants in the search and rescue task force. Pilots new to rescue gained valuable experience from the realistic situations. Rescue crews became more familiar with the capabilities and limitations of the A-7 in the Sandy rescue escort role. Likewise, Sandy pilots learned new and better ways to use their A-7s in search and rescue missions. Finally, a very important aspect of these experiences was to explore and develop ways of using the AC-130 "Spectre" gunships in the search and rescue force.

The idea of using AC-130s in rescue work can be traced to an incident in late 1972.[18] In December 1972, an AC-130 was diverted from its patrol along the Ho Chi Minh Trail to help an HH-53 search for the crew of another Specter gunship shot down over Laos. Using its night vision devices, the AC-130 pinpointed two survivors. Following the ceasefire, the 40th Aerospace Rescue and Recovery Squadron began working with the 16th Special Operations Squadron to integrate the AC-130 into the rescue task force.

Indeed, the AC-130s demonstrated numerous capabilities in these exercises. Its long loiter time, abundance of sophisticated electronic gear, including low-light-level television and infrared sensors, and awesome firepower which included 20-mm and 40-mm cannons and a 105-mm howitzer, made it a contender for a spot on the rescue team. Additionally, AC-130 pilots learned to act as forward air controllers to call in A-7 strikes thus assuming a role usually performed by Sandy low lead. So successful was the Specter gunship at this mission that, in early April 1975, the Thirteenth Air Force tasked the 16th Special Operations Squadron with preparing a search and rescue integration training program.[19]

Meanwhile, as rescue and tactical crews trained for contingencies that seemed less likely, reductions in forces in Thailand continued. Local base rescue units Detachment 10 at Takhli and Detachment 3 at Ubon were inactivated in July and August 1974 respectively. On February 20 Detachment 1 at Nakhon Phanom disbanded.[20]

As Air Force units withdrew from Thailand, the number of aircraft in rescue service units there decreased. By January 1975, there were eight HH-53Cs (eleven authorized), four HH-43Fs, and five HC-130Ps (six authorized) in Southeast Asia. Additionally, the 3d Aerospace Rescue and Recovery Group exercised operational control for search and rescue missions over six AC-130s, twenty-four A-7Ds, and twenty OV-10s.[21]

As rescue forces in Thailand shrank, training exercises continued and were, for the most part, concerned with combat aircrew recovery. There was no practice for evacuation of Americans from Phnom Penh, Saigon, or Vientiane in either the Commando Scrimmage exercises or at the sessions at the Loeng Nok Tha airport.[22] However, beginning in the summer of 1973, command and control exercises were conducted using plans for the evacuation of Phnom Penh.[23] The focus of this training was a simulator that had been used by HC-130P detachments since 1970. A simple machine, it included five interphone jack boxes connected to an instructor in an adjacent room. A pilot, copilot, navigator, radio operator, and rescue controller sat at each of the boxes. The instructors played the role of HH-53 pilots, forward air controllers, or Sandy pilots.[24] Because rescue controllers provided the key to these plans, their rehearsal was particularly important.[25] The part that might be played by other members of the search and rescue task force was not as complicated. Depending on which option of the rescue plans was used, some elements, such as the HH-53s, might not have a role.[26]

Following the American withdrawal from South Vietnam, the winding down of the war in Laos, and the cessation of bombing in Cambodia, Air Force planners began working on contingency plans for the evacuation of Americans and selected foreigners from those countries. On June 27, 1973, the United States Support Activities Group/Seventh Air Force published Contingency Plan 5060C, "Eagle Pull", concerning the evacuation of Phnom Penh. Even while the bombing of Cambodia continued, in the spring of 1973, Phnom Penh seemed in danger of falling to the Khmer Rouge. They surrounded the city in April and pushed the troops of the Forces Armées National Khmer back into the suburbs. Unlike Vietnam, the American bombing ended in Cambodia with no reciprocal "ceasefire" from the enemy. To many it seemed that Cambodia would fall after the last American bomb fell.

Rescue units received the first edition of CONPLAN 5060C in late June. The immediate response was to put an HC-130P on three-hour alert twenty-four hours a day.[27] Operations officers in all the rescue units became familiar with the plan and its options. King crews began working in the simulator.

CONPLAN 5060C had three options. Under Option I, American embassy personnel and their families, U.S. Government workers, and all other American citizens as well as certain designated Cambodian nationals would use scheduled airlines or chartered flights from Phnom Penh's Pochentong airport to fly to whatever country the State Department designated. Of course, any Cambodian who could afford the price of an airline ticket also could flee, so under Option I, the number of people to be evacuated was indefinite.

According to Option II, if enemy action caused the cancellation of regularly scheduled airline flights into Pochentong, American military planes were to be used for evacuation. Tactical air support would be available if needed. Air Force C-130 turboprops and C-141 jet transports would be used to evacuate most of the designated people, with HH-53 and CH-53 helicopters available if needed. Air Force Security Police from the 56th Security Police Squadron at Nakhon Phanom, Thailand, would be flown in on two CH-53s to provide security around the airport. About 600 people would be evacuated under Option II, mostly Americans and their families along with a limited number of Cambodians.

Option III was the most complicated of the three alternatives. It was to be used if enemy forces closed Pochentong. This option provided for the use of helicopters to evacuate people from designated landing zones in Phnom Penh as well as in Battambang, Kompong Som and other major towns as needed. As in Option II, tactical air support was to be available. Aerospace Rescue and Recovery Service HC-130Ps were designated as controllers for the 21st Special Operations Squadron CH-53s and the HH-53s of the 40th Aerospace Rescue and Recovery Squadron. A ground security force of security police would protect the landing zones. The plan called for

the use of fourteen CH/HH-53s to evacuate up to 600 people and still provide four helicopters in reserve.[28] The 3d Aerospace Rescue and Recovery
Group was specifically tasked to provide the HH-53s, the rescue control aircraft (HC-130Ps), and the four backup helicopters.[29]

When the bombing stopped on August 15, 1973, the fate of the Khmer
Republic rested with its army, a force officially estimated at 200,000 men
but which may have contained up to 150,000 payroll-padding phantom
troops and part-time, fair-weather soldiers. The Khmer Air Force consisted
of about forty T-28s and a few Fairchild AU-23 single-engine and twin-
engine AC-47 gunships.[30] On a good day, if the Khmer Air Force got every
T-28 into the air, they could deliver the bomb load of two B-52s. And Cambodia's airmen had very few good days.

Unexpectedly, Cambodian government forces held outside Phnom
Penh and defended their major cities. The Khmer Rouge withdrew to the
countryside in the autumn of 1973 and spent 1974 extending their control
throughout rural Cambodia. By late 1974, as the Khmer Rouge consolidated their gains in the countryside and isolated the forces of the
republic in their larger towns and cities, the inevitable became discernible.
Accordingly, USSAG/7AF changed Eagle Pull to meet the evolving circumstances. A change issued on November 1, 1974, updated Option III of
the basic plan by establishing a complicated priority system to classify non-
combatant evacuees according to citizenship, sex, age, and physical condition. For instance, a priority code of "I" was assigned an American citizen
with documents, "II" was given to an alien member of an American family,
"III" to alien employees of the embassy, and "IV" to other aliens. Minor
categories of A to E were assigned, with nine-month pregnant American-
born wives getting an "A" priority and able-bodied 18-year-old Cambodian
males an "E".[31]

A further change to Eagle Pull was circulated on February 24, 1975.
This change to Option III, provided for U.S. Marine Corps helicopters to
be used along with Air Force choppers. Also a 234-man ground security
force of Marines replaced the security police in the plan. Additionally,
because the Khmer Rouge either threatened or had isolated many of the
provincial towns previously designated as alternative evacuation sites, all
helicopter landing zones were to be near the American Embassy in Phnom
Penh.[32]

By the first of March 1975, Eagle Pull was ready. Rescue forces in
Thailand stood at their authorized strength of eleven HH-53s and six HC-
130Ps. On March 1 all Air Force Eagle Pull forces were ordered to be ready
to respond within twenty-four hours.[33] As the battlefield situation in Cambodia deteriorated, on March 27 USSAG/7AF issued a detailed, twenty-
five section special instruction. It was based on the third option, helicopter
evacuation, and directed the 3d Aerospace Rescue and Recovery Group to
prepare eight HH-53s for the transfer to Ubon when so ordered. Two HC-

130Ps, call signs King 21 and King 22, were designated as rescue controllers.[34]

The C-130 airborne command and control center from the 7th Air Command and Control Squadron at Udorn, was designated overall airborne controller for Eagle Pull. It would coordinate the air armada up to the outskirts of Phnom Penh. At that point King 21 became the primary controller to coordinate helicopters coming into and leaving the landing zone. King 22, meanwhile, was tasked to refuel the rescue choppers, and if any aircraft went down would become the rescue mission controller. Another HC-130P, King 23, was to be placed on fifteen-minute alert at Korat ready to perform any or all of these tasks.[35]

The final version of CONPLAN 5060C did not neglect the remainder of the search and rescue task force. Four A-7s were scheduled for search and rescue combat air patrol. The plan included use of the AC-130 gunships and tasked the 16th Special Operations Squadron with providing four AC-130s to fly in orbit ready to bring their array of guns to bear upon any concentration of enemy troops that might oppose the operation, or to act as forward air controllers if the operation occurred at night or in bad weather.[36]

While these plans circulated, the military situation worsened. The Khmer Rouge sealed off all land routes between Phnom Penh and the other cities of Cambodia. Mekong River convoys made their way to and from Phnom Penh at the greatest peril. An emergency American-sponsored airlift brought in food and ammunition, but the Cambodian Army continued to distintegrate. When the Khmer Rouge overran the naval base at Neak-Luong, just south of Phnom Penh, on April 1, President Lon Nol flew into exile.

On April 3, CINCPAC ordered all Eagle Pull forces to assume a six-hour alert. At Korat the 388th Tactical Fighter Wing put twelve A-7s and four AC-130s on alert for the six-hour response.[37] Across the base, three HC-130Ps stood ready. Also, the same day, at the request of American Ambassador to Cambodia John Gunther Dean, an HH-53 flew an eleven-man command element of the Marine ground support force into Phnom Penh to organize the evacuees and make final preparations for the arrival of helicopters. The day after reaching the beleaguered city, the Marines selected a soccer field behind an apartment house only a quarter mile from the embassy. They called it "Landing Zone (LZ) Hotel". [38]

Meanwhile, the number of Americans in Phnom Penh dropped as nonessential personnel at the embassy, businessmen, and some journalists began leaving on the remaining available airline flights and on returning airlift planes.[39] By April 6 all but about fifty members of the ambassador's staff had flown to Thailand. Ambassador Dean then began sending the embassy's 294 Cambodian employees to safety.[40] Events began to move more rapidly and, on April 7, CINCPAC ordered the USS *Hancock,* an assault carrier with sixteen U.S. Marine CH-53 and sixteen CH-46 helicopters aboard, from Subic Bay in the Philippines to the Gulf of Thailand. There it joined the assault ship *Okinawa* carrying the Marine ground security force.[41]

Through the first week of April and into the second the Khmer Rouge tightened its noose around Phnom Penh. By April 10 Ambassador Dean knew the city would soon be in enemy hands. He requested that Eagle Pull, Option III, be executed on April 12. Accordingly, USSAG/7AF issued the execute order on April 11. The first helicopters would reach LZ Hotel by 9:00 the following morning.[42]

When the 40th Aerospace Rescue and Recovery Squadron received the execute message it sent seven HH-53s to Ubon where they were fueled and armed for the next day's work. Before dawn on the 12th, an eighth rescue chopper arrived from Nakhon Phanom. Just at sunrise, according to the plan, an HH-53 left for Phnom Penh with a four-man Air Force combat control team, an elite team of forward air guides trained to direct air operations from the middle of a battlefield. They landed promptly at 8:50 A.M. Three minutes later the first U.S. Marine CH-53 spiraled onto the soccer field to disgorge the first element of the Marine security force. The leathernecks fanned out across the field, bayonet-tipped rifles at the ready, to be greeted by a crowd of curious, laughing, waving Cambodians.[43]

While Marine helicopters carried 276 people, including 82 Americans, 159 Cambodians, and 35 foreign nationals to the assault carriers in the Gulf of Thailand, three HH-53s orbited just north of the city, ready to dash to the aid of any helicopters that might be shot down. Overhead, one HC-130P controlled the rescue forces while another worked with the airborne command and control center coordinating the Marine choppers at Landing Zone Hotel. At 10:00 three more HH-53s arrived from Ubon, refueled and flew to the landing zone. As the last Marine helicopter pulled up with its load of civilians, one Aerospace Rescue and Recovery Service HH-53 swooped onto the soccer field. Khmer Rouge gunners across the Mekong had just found the range on the evacuation site and the friendly crowd scattered as the mortar rounds exploded. The first rescue chopper in picked up the members of the combat control team. Three minutes later, at 11:15, a second helicopter sat down on the field to take out the remaining troops in the ground security force. A rocket hit nearby throwing up a geyser of dirt from the soccer field as the last helicopter from Phnom Penh climbed for safety in the sky. Before it was out of range, a 12.7-mm heavy machine gun round found its tail rotor. Escorted by the backup Jolly Green, the badly vibrating helicopter managed to make it to Ubon.[44]

Later in the day the Marines transferred the people taken to the ships to Utapao Royal Thai Naval Air Base, Thailand. A total of 291 people were brought out of Phnom Penh, including 276 evacuees, the combat control team, and the advance element of the ground security force. There were no casualties. Two rescue service choppers, the last two at Landing Zone Hotel, were hit by small arms fire, including the one that had the 12.7-mm round in its tail.[45]

Before the evacuation began, Cambodian President Sokham Koy, who replaced Lon Nol on April 3, said, "The United States led Cambodia into this war, but when the war became difficult, the United States pulled out."[46] President Sokham Koy came out on a Marine helicopter. The war was over and for the rescue people in Thailand there was nothing left to to do but accept the letters of congratulations for a job well done in Eagle Pull.[47]

Even as Phnom Penh fell, Saigon's days were numbered. Not even the Politburo in Hanoi realized how short the time would be before North Vietnamese tanks would break down the gates of President Nguyen Van Thieu's palace.[48] The North Vietnamese mapped out their 1975 offensive to take the central highlands and, if possible, cut South Vietnam in two. On March 14, when they overran Ban Me Thuot, a key provincial capital in the highlands, President Thieu, realizing his army was spread too thinly, ordered it to draw back to defend the cities, especially Da Nang, Hue, and Saigon.[49] Within two weeks the Army of the Republic of Vietnam had collapsed as a cohesive fighting force. North Vietnamese forces moved east from their sanctuaries near Khe Sanh and south across the demilitarized zone. By the end of March they were poised at the outskirts of Da Nang.

The evacuation of Da Nang brought the dimensions of the debacle into focus. As the North Vietnamese closed in on the city, a number of Americans remained there. These included members of the U.S. consulate, U.S. Agency for International Development, Central Intelligence Agency operatives, journalists, teachers, private citizens working for the United States or South Vietnamese governments under contract, a handful of retired military men, and deserters who chose to live in the city. The U.S. Embassy in Saigon had a basic evacuation plan which included plans for each of the consulates. At Da Nang the plan called for evacuation by sea.[50] When, at the end of March, the Americans started to leave Da Nang, they had to fight their way aboard the ships, planes and helicopters sent to get them out. The American public, watching the horror unfold on the evening television news, saw South Vietnamese soldiers force their way onto the last plane from Da Nang, a World Airways 727, flown into the city to carry out women and children.[51]

The disaster at Da Nang demonstrated the need for more precise planning to get the five thousand or so remaining Americans out of Vietnam. Official U.S. policy was that the Republic of Vietnam would survive. Even when there had been a large number of U.S. troops in South Vietnam, there was no evacuation plan. During the North Vietnamese offensive of 1972, MACV headquarters ordered a planning board to convene to draw up such a plan. The planner soon decided that U.S. forces could not leave the country en masse if the enemy forces proved successful. They thought that if such a case arose, the South Vietnamese, upon whom the Americans depended to run the airports and harbors, would also be fleeing. Furthermore, the planners feared that the Army of the Republic of Vietnam might well turn on the withdrawing Americans. Therefore, a plan to evacuate large numbers of Americans, other than that which existed to get embassy, USAID, and Central Intelligence Agency personnel out, was never formulated.[52]

In accordance with the development of evacuation plans for Phnom Penh and Vientiane, CONPLAN 5060V, "Talon Vise", was published on July 31, 1974. It had four options, three of them relying on fixed-wing aircraft or evacuation by sea under secure conditions. Option IV provided for the use of helicopters and a ground security force in a "worst case" situation.[53]

Revision of CONPLAN 5060V began in January 1975. The Aerospace Rescue and Recovery Service contributed eleven officers to the Joint Planning Force that met at Nakhon Phanom. These included four men from the 3d Aerospace Rescue and Recovery Group, six from the 40th Aerospace Rescue and Recovery Squadron, and one man from the 56th Aerospace Rescue and Recovery Squadron.[54] In early April, planning for any evacuation of Vietnam assumed secondary importance in the face of the more immediate danger in Cambodia. There were not enough heavy lift helicopters, especially not enough rescue service choppers, to cover both contingencies. For example, as the North Vietnamese closed in on Da Nang, the CIA's station chief there reportedly sent an urgent message to USSAG/7AF at Nakhon Phanom requesting the dispatch of rescue helicopters to take his people out. Because these helicopters were standing by for Eagle Pull, none was provided for Da Nang.[55]

After the fall of Da Nang, CINCPAC advised the Joint Chiefs of Staff that, because of the rapidly deteriorating conditions in Vietnam, helicopters would probably play the leading role in any evacuation, especially if the enemy closed Tan Son Nhut.[56] Accordingly, as the North Vietnamese offensive accelerated so did planning for a helicopter evacuation of Saigon. On April 5, headquarters at Nakhon Phanom refined CONPLAN 5060V by designating helicopter landing areas in Saigon. These included the Defense Attaché's Office in the old MACV compound near Tan Son Nhut, the grounds of the American Embassy, and a landing zone on a soccer field in a section of the city called "Newport" near the Saigon River.[57] Ten days later, after the evacuation of Phnom Penh, the code name for the operation was changed from Talon Vise to Frequent Wind. On April 18, USSAG/7AF published CONPLAN 5060V-7-75, a 135-page message detailing a helicopter evacuation. The 3d Aerospace Rescue and Recovery Group was charged with providing search and rescue forces in case an aircraft went down during the operation and with sending four HH-53s to the aircraft carrier *Midway* to participate in the evacuation.[58]

On April 19 the rescue portion of Frequent Wind began with the sending of seven HH-53s to Utapao. There Col. J.J. Anders, Jr., Director of Operations of the 56th Special Operations Wing, took charge of all Air Force helicopters as directed by the plan. The following day Anders sent four HH-53s and six 21st Special Operations Squadron CH-53s to the USS *Midway*. On April 22 two additional CH-53s flew to the *Midway* to replace two of the four HH-53s because the special operations helicopters, which were not filled with rescue equipment, could carry more people. Still, the presence of two HH-53s aboard the *Midway* meant that the evacuation forces would have two rescue choppers available in case they were needed during the operation. On the *Midway* the Air Force had eight CH-53s and two HH-53s. Maj. John F. Guilmartin, Jr. was the ranking Aerospace Rescue and Recovery Service man aboard.[59]

Throughout April, as the final outcome of the Vietnam war became more apparent, many Vietnamese and Americans fled Saigon on regularly scheduled airline flights. Others took ships. By the end of the month, as the outskirts of the city became the battlefield and Tan Son Nhut came under attack, Ambassador Graham Martin gave the order for Frequent Wind, Option IV. Rescue choppers were ready with one Jolly Green on alert at Nakhon Phanom, six at Ubon, and two aboard the *Midway*. The helicopters on alert in Thailand were to provide a rescue force in case any of the F-4s, A-7s, and AC-130s participating in the operation from Thai bases were shot down.[60]

On the afternoon of April 29 the evacuation of Saigon began. U.S. Marine Corps CH-46 helicopters, CH-53s, and Air Force choppers rose from the *Midway* and flew to Saigon. The two rescue service choppers, Jolly 12-1 and Jolly 12-2, were part of a three helicopter flight, the last of a twelve-ship formation.[61] Major Guilmartin, commander of Jolly 12-1, knew that the next hours would be hectic. Already he had problems contacting a U.S. Marine combat control team at the Defense Attaché's office. The combat control team was using an FM field radio with limited range, and every Marine Corps, Air Force, and Air America chopper in the air was descending on downtown Saigon using the same FM frequency.[62]

As the two HH-53s and the CH-53 crossed the coast, they were joined by a pair of Marine Cobra gunships. When the choppers reached the city, Guilmartin switched course and headed for the Defense Attaché's complex near Tan Son Nhut. As the sprawling airfield came into sight, he saw heavy artillery shells tossing up dirt and concrete as they hit the runway. His crewmen noticed muzzle flashes from small arms fire all around the city.[63]

Opposition to the evacuation, if lacking in direction, was nonetheless real. North Vietnamese and Viet Cong units, as well as disgruntled South Vietnamese troops, fired on the choppers with everything from small arms and antiaircraft guns to hand-held missiles. Guilmartin noticed his radar-warning gear picking up SA-2 Fansong indications thirteen minutes after leaving the *Midway*. The audio indications of Fansong tracking, a rattlesnake-like buzz, bothered him so much that he shut off his radar-warning gear. Meanwhile, an F-105, flying a surface-to-air missile suppression mission, locked on to the SA-2's radar and fired an antiradiation homing missile at it. That ended the Fansong activity for a while.[64]

The three-ship formation wheeled in over the Defense Attaché's complex. After the CH-53 loaded up, the two rescue helicopters took on loads of refugees and returned to *Midway*. It was darker when they headed back across the South China Sea for their second trip to the complex. Shadows of buildings in Saigon reached to meet them as the sun settled ahead. It appeared to the crews of the rescue choppers that the entire North Vietnamese Army was firing into the sky. Their perception was no doubt heightened by the visibility of tracers against the darkening sky. The two Jolly Greens loaded up and headed for the *Midway*. As they slid over the rooftops of Saigon, a gunner on Jolly Green 12-1 spotted a number of figures firing at them from the roofs. He opened up with one of the miniguns. As these guns sometimes did, this one jammed. The parajumper cursed, picked up his AR-15 automatic rifle, and fired away at the figures until the chopper passed out of range.[65]

It was dark when the choppers reached the *Midway* to unload their second haul of refugees. After refueling, the two Jolly Greens returned to Saigon. Opposition appeared to be more intense. All three miniguns were busy on the way to the Defense Attaché's complex. Before the action began, Guilmartin and Capt. Vernon L. Sheffield, Jr., commander of Jolly Green 12-2, told their crews to pack in as many Vietnamese as they could. They were not to count children. Above all, the parajumpers and flight mechanics were to maintain order. During loading they were instructed to allow boarding to one side of the ramp minigun only. This procedure was meant to facilitate counting and to help keep the people calm.[66] On this last trip, as soon as Jolly Green 12-1 touched down, Vietnamese refugees rushed up the ramp. The parajumpers and flight mechanics were engulfed in a rising tide of fear-crazed human beings. A young parajumper managed to restore a semblance of order and the flow of people started moving to the left of the minigun as ordered. One frightened woman tried to claw her way pass the parajumper on the opposite side of the gun. He jabbed her back into line with his rifle butt. Again she rushed forward, trying to climb over him. This time he swung the butt of his automatic rifle hard into her abdomen. She stumbled backwards grasping at anything she could grab. Her hands found the barrel of the minigun. It swung toward the crowd. The woman reached again, this time clutching the trigger. To the horror of the parajumper he heard the electric motor that drives the firing mechanism of the 2000-round-per-minute gun engage. He knew that a split second later the gun would begin spewing death into the mass of refugees. The first round chambered; then the gun jammed. Few, if any, of the refugees knew what had almost happened, and the loading continued.[67]

Jolly Green 12-1 took on ninety-seven men, women, and children, twice its normal capacity. Jolly Green 12-2 picked up ninety. The last Aerospace Rescue and Recovery Service choppers then headed out of Saigon. As the helicopters passed over the eastern suburbs a flight mechanic on Jolly Green 12-1 spotted an SA-7 heat seeking surface-to-air missile streaking toward them. He fired a flare pistol. The missile went for the flare, missing the chopper by less than sixty feet.[68]

As the two rescue service helicopters neared the *Midway*, Jolly Green 12-2 developed a fire in its instrument panel. The copilot turned an extinguisher on the fire. In the darkness, Captain Sheffield landed the helicopter on the *Midway*. Because its instrument panel was burned out, Jolly Green 12-2 was out of action for the rest of the operation. Jolly Green 12-1 fared no better. In landing it broke a wheel strut. According to Major Guilmartin, in an emergency situation he could have flown the helicopter. However, the officer controlling the operation aboard the airborne command post ordered him to stay on the *Midway* because he wanted at least one rescue chopper available in case a helicopter or airplane was shot down. With that order, the Aerospace Rescue and Recovery Service had flown its last mission in Vietnam. In all, the Aerospace Rescue and Recovery Service had evacuated about four hundred people from Saigon.[69]

Air Force CH-53s and Marine Corps helicopters continued the evacuation of Saigon. Thousands of Vietnamese surged around the American Embassy. Gunfire from small arms peppered the choppers, but no one knew who was doing the shooting. Earlier in the afternoon the American consul at Vung Tau, heading for the ships in the South China Sea in a commandeered boat, had been strafed by a South Vietnamese Air Force helicopter. The airborne command post, answering his plea for help, ordered an AC-130 gunship to "kill" the chopper. An electrical fire aboard the gunship forced it to break off the chase, but in the meantime the boat made it to safety. The incident confirmed the fear of Americans during the last days of Saigon that the Army of the Republic of Vietnam, at least some of it, was trying to disrupt the evacuation.[70]

At midnight the weather and visibility remained good, so the evacuation continued. At 1:45 in the morning the Joint Rescue Control Center reported that 6,619 people had been carried out. An hour later the control center transmitted a presidential order that Americans only were to be evacuated from that time on. This would include several hundred members of the Marine ground security force.[71]

As the sun came up there was panic among the thousands of Vietnamese swarming around the embassy walls. They climbed the barbed wire fence only to have U.S. Marines force them back with rifle butts.[72] America's withdrawal from Vietnam came down to a rush to the top floors of the embassy. At 7:30 A.M. Marines slammed and barred the building's huge oak doors. One Marine shut off the elevators and then tossed tear gas grenades into the shaft. He then joined the others in a race up the stairs. At the fourth floor they turned to throw tear gas grenades down behind them. As they rushed the last steps to the rooftop helicopter pad, panic-gripped Vietnamese smashed through the doors below and surged through the gas into the embassy and up the stairwell. At the top of the stairs the Marines threw more gas and smoke grenades down the well, then they ran out onto the pad barring the small door behind them. They climbed aboard Swift 22, a waiting Marine CH-53. The turbines whined, the rotor blades moved around, picking up speed with each revolution. The ramp came up and the chopper lifted.[73]

The log of the joint rescue coordination center summed it up:

APR

29/2325	SWIFT-22 AIRBORNE WITH 11 GSF [ground support forces], ALL EVAC [evacuees] EXTRACTED.
29/2357	KING-23 [airborne command aircraft] CLEARED TO RTB [return to base], ETA [estimated time of arrival] 0090.
29/2359	LOG CLOSED. **FREQUENT WIND COMPLETED**.[74]

At dawn the rescue crews aboard the *Midway* repaired their damaged helicopters. Throughout the day they watched as forty-eight South Vietnamese Huey helicopters, three CH-47s and even a small, single-engine O-1 observation plane brought out more Vietnamese refugees. When a Vietnamese Air Force major in the O-1 contacted the carrier's air traffic controller to request landing instructions, the controller told him to ditch. The major agreed but added, "Please have a helo alongside, my wife and five children are with me." The ship's captain, who was in the control room, heard the plea. He told the major to land on deck. The Vietnamese, who had never landed on an aircraft carrier, brought the O-1 down successfully without the use of arresting cables or hooks.[75]

Bad weather delayed the rescue crews departure from the *Midway* until May 2. When they arrived back at Nakhon Phanom the crews went through the usual round of debriefing followed by a party.[76]

America's involvement in Vietnam spanned a generation. Throughout those years, the United States slipped into the conflicts in Southeast Asia. Most Americans thought that withdrawal from Southeast Asia, which began in 1969, ended in the frantic rush to the rooftop of the American Embassy in Saigon. However, the Aerospace Rescue and Recovery Service faced yet another challenge.

During the first week in May 1975 two merchant vessels bound for Thailand were accosted by Cambodian gunboats. A Korean ship was fired on but escaped. On May 7, the Cambodians seized a Panamanian registered vessel, held it for thirty-five hours, then released it.[77]

On May 12, 1975, the American-registered cargo ship *Mayaguez* was taken by Cambodian naval forces. Three hours after the seizure, at 6:15 A.M. in Washington, the watch officer at the State Department's Intelligence and Research Bureau awakened Secretary of State Henry A. Kissinger with news of America's newest crisis in Southeast Asia. Dr. Kissinger briefed President Gerald R. Ford an hour and a half later. The President called a meeting of the National Security Council for noon.[78]

Meanwhile, the master of the *Mayaguez*, Capt. Charles T. Miller, stalled his captors to frustrate their efforts to move the ship to Sihanoukville harbor on the mainland. The ship was riding at anchor near Poulo Wai island when a U.S. Navy P-3 four engine reconnaissance plane spotted it shortly after dawn.[79]

On the morning of May 13, PACAF headquarters ordered the Aerospace Rescue and Recovery Service units in Thailand to prepare a rescue force for the thirty-nine crewmen being held by the Cambodians. Meanwhile, following orders from the President, CINCPAC instructed fighter-bombers and gunships to prevent the ship or its crew from being taken to the mainland. The pilots were told to fire warning shots across the bow of the *Mayaguez* if it moved toward the mainland under its own power. If shots across the bow failed to halt the ship, the pilots were to strafe its aft portion in an effort to disable it. Should the Cambodians try to tow the vessel to the mainland, the towboat was to be first warned, then sunk.[80]

It was late on the afternoon of May 13 when crews in Thailand received these orders. That night AC-130 gunships orbited over the *Mayaguez*. One Khmer gunboat fired at the gunship. The Spectre opened up on the boat forcing it aground.[81]

Rescue forces swung into action that evening when the Joint Chiefs of Staff ordered eight HH-53s from the 3d Aerospace Rescue and Recovery Group and eight CH-53s (Knives) from the 21st Special Operations Squadron to Utapao on the Gulf of Thailand. They were told to carry seventy-five security policemen from Nakhon Phanom to Utapao as a possible recovery force.[82] Tragedy struck when one of the CH-53s crashed in a wooded area thirty-seven miles west of Nakhon Phanom killing all aboard: eighteen security policemen and five helicopter crewmen. An HH-53 a couple of miles back in the formation saw the fire. By the time the chopper landed, the heat was so intense that no one could get closer than seventy-five feet.[83]

On the morning of May 14, at 8:17, two HH-53s took off for a search and rescue mission to assist any survivors of a Cambodian gunboat sunk by strafing A-7s. The chopper crews spotted no one and returned to Utapao. Helicopter crews and air policemen spent the rest of the day waiting for instructions.[84]

Meanwhile, action in the Gulf of Thailand picked up. A few minutes after sinking the gunboat, the same flight of A-7s spotted a wooden fishing boat full of people headed for the mainland. They suspected that the boat contained the crew of the *Mayaguez*. In an effort to turn the boat back to Poulo Wai island, the A-7s fired across the bow and dropped tear gas all around.[85]

On board the fishing boat, the thirty-nine members of the *Mayaguez* crew plus some captured Thai fishermen, along with their Khmer Rouge guards, gasped and vomited as the gas took effect. The crewmen wanted to overpower the guards, but the riot control agent incapacitated them as well as the communists. The Thai boat captain tried to turn back, but at each attempt a Cambodian guard put his AK-47 to the Thai's head. As the boat continued to the mainland the A-7s returned to Thailand. The *Mayaguez* crew, first taken to Sihanoukville, was later transferred to Kaoh Rong Samloem, a nearby island.[86]

Other A-7s, F-4s, and AC-130s resumed the watch over the *Mayaguez*. At mid-morning A-7s destroyed a forty-foot patrol boat towing a barge east of Koh Tang. That night an AC-130 sank another patrol boat as it approached the *Mayaguez*.[87]

As the sun set on May 14, no one knew for sure where the crew of the captured vessel was located. Military preparations continued in Thailand, while in Washington the Ford administration made diplomatic approaches to obtain the release of the crew. When it appeared diplomatic efforts had failed, the President ordered the Joint Chiefs of Staff to take back the ship and recover the crew.[88]

Intelligence estimates indicated that a handful of Khmer Rouge guards and Cambodian civilians were holding the ship's crew on Koh Tang. Accordingly, a plan emerged whereby sixty marines would be landed on the USS *Holt,* a Navy destroyer. These men would then board the *Mayaguez,* thus fulfilling the first part of the President's order by taking back the ship. Meanwhile, Air Force helicopters would shuttle up to six hundred marines from Utapao to Koh Tang to recover the crew. The plan called for a U.S. Army interpreter, in the first helicopter load, to tell the Khmer Rouge that the U.S. Marines had landed and that the only way to avoid certain destruction lay in immediately handing over the crew of the *Mayaguez*. It was not going to work out like that.[89]

The attack on Koh Tang began early on the morning of May 15. Eight helicopters, five CH-53s and three HH-53s, approached their designated landing zones on the north end of the island in two waves. Their objective was to land marines on the western and eastern sides of the north peninsula. The first chopper to the island, Knife 21, met no resistance until most of the marines had rushed down the ramp and fanned out across the beach. Then the Khmers opened fire knocking out one engine of the chopper as it lifted off the beach. Knife 21 skipped over the waves until it was a mile out to sea, there it settled into the water.[90]

Two Jolly Greens, having just unloaded marines on the USS *Holt,* moved in to pick up the crew of Knife 21. They recovered the pilot, copilot, and one of the flight mechanics. SSgt. Elwood E. Rumbaugh, after saving the life of his copilot by diving under water to pull him from the wreckage, disappeared beneath the surf. He was never seen again and later declared dead.[91]

Back on the island, Knife 22 tried to land its load of marines, but enemy fire damaged it too severely. The chopper limped toward the Thai coast escorted by a pair of Jolly Greens. There Knife 22 ran out of fuel and made a forced landing.[92]

Meanwhile, in action at the island, Knife 23 and Knife 31 headed for the eastern landing zone. As they approached the beach, the enemy blasted them with small arms, heavy machine guns, rockets, and mortars. One chopper antirotated making a controlled crash landing in the surf and snapping its tail boom as it hit. Its crew and twenty marines ran ashore to fight for their lives on the beach. The other chopper burst into flame as it fell into shallow water just off shore. Eight people died in the wreckage. Five more died in the surf as the Khmer Rouge fired at the survivors trying to swim out to sea. Those who made it were picked up by a launch from a U.S. Navy destroyer.[93]

During this initial assault, a simultaneous effort to recapture the *Mayaguez* was underway. The USS *Holt*, with the marines delivered by Jolly Greens earlier, pulled alongside the *Mayaguez* and the boarding party climbed aboard to find the ship abandoned. The *Holt* then began towing it away from Poulo Wai island.[94]

As these events unfolded, the crew of the *Mayaguez* was making its way seaward from where they had been held. As the Thai fishing boat approached the destroyer USS *Robert L. Wilson,* the *Mayaguez* crewmen stripped off their underwear to make white flags. On board the *Wilson* battle stations had sounded before anyone saw the skivvies flying from the mast of the fishing boat. Within an hour the crew of the *Mayaguez* was safely aboard.[95]

An hour after the assault began, there were fifty-four marines and Air Force crewmen pinned down on the two beaches at Koh Tang. Three helicopters had been shot down and two others severely damaged. So far fourteen Americans were dead or missing.

With the crew of the *Mayaguez* safe, the operation became one of disengaging the fifty-four members of the rescue force stranded on Koh Tang. To do that additional forces had to be landed. Accordingly, three more Jolly Greens prepared to deliver their marines. Two made it on their second try, but the marines were put down in separate locations, one south of the landing zone and the other on a small patch of sand 1000 yards from the other group. The third Jolly Green was repeatedly driven off by enemy fire. By 8:30 A.M. there were 109 marines and airmen on Koh Tang.[96] With the *Mayaguez* crewmen safe, A-7s, F-4s, and AC-130s could blast enemy positions on the island more freely.

U.S. Marines from USS *Harold E. Holt* board the *Mayaguez* following its recovery from the Cambodians.

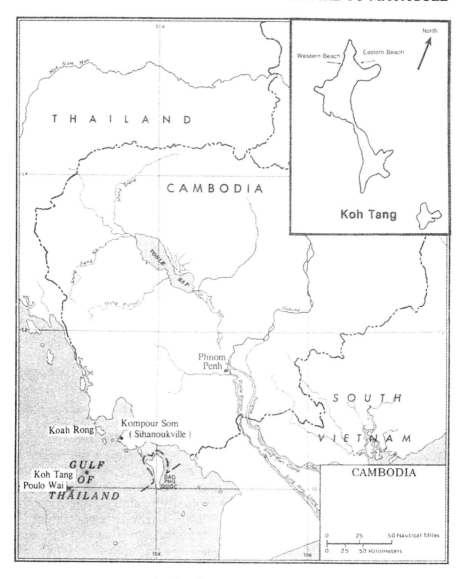

Landing Zones on Koh Tang

For the next hour and a half under heavy enemy fire, choppers landed reinforcements. Jolly Green 41 moved toward Koh Tang at ten o'clock. Lts. Thomas D. Cooper and David W. Keith, pilot and copilot of Jolly Green 41, made four attempts to land their troops but were driven away each time. Finally they called in an AC-130 gunship to hit enemy positions with 20-mm and 40-mm fire. Then Jolly 41 shot up the jungle near the beach. Jolly 41 flew in to drop off the five remaining marines. A mortar round exploded nearby before Cooper could pull clear of the landing zone, seriously damaging the chopper. Jolly Green 41 retreated toward Utapao.[97]

But enemy forces were still too strong to allow the marines to disengage and be safely removed. Cricket, the airborne command post, marshalled its still airworthy choppers (all five of them) for this final reinforcement effort. Two CH-53s, Knife 51, Knife 52, and one HH-53 (Jolly Green 43) were in the first wave. Jolly Green 11 and Jolly Green 12 formed the second wave. Knife 51 landed nineteen marines and carried out five wounded. Jolly Green 43 put in another twenty-eight marines. As Knife 52 approached the landing zone enemy fire ripped into its fuel tank. The aircraft commander, 1st Lt. Richard C. Brims, aborted the landing and returned the marines to Utapao. Jolly Green 43, having landed its load of troops, refueled and then orbited just in case an aircrew recovery situation developed. The second wave, Jolly Greens 11 and 12, unloaded their marines to bring the total to 222 Americans on Koh Tang.[98]

In early afternoon, with enemy resistance still heavy on Koh Tang and the leathernecks pinned down in their landing zones or on the beaches, the controllers aboard Cricket turned their attention to withdrawal. Jolly Green 43, flown by Capt. Roland W. Purser and Jolly Green 11 commanded by Capt. Donald R. Backlund, refueled at 2:30 in the afternoon and then orbited near Koh Tang while A-7s, F-4s, and OV-10s strafed, bombed, and dropped tear gas canisters on enemy positions. After this pounding, Jolly Green 43 moved toward the eastern beach where an isolated group of marines was fighting a persistent Khmer force. As the chopper approached the shore, heavy ground fire disabled one engine. Captain Purser continued on, landed and took on a very full load of fifty-four marines. Jolly Green 43 skipped over the waves to make an emergency landing on the aircraft carrier *Coral Sea*. Captain Backlund escorted the damaged chopper to the ship and then pointed Jolly Green 11 toward Koh Tang.

Three choppers remained operational, Jolly Greens 11 and 12, and Knife 51. Another helicopter, Jolly Green 44, previously out of commission at Nakhon Phanom, was being repaired in a hurry. By 4:00 P.M. it was rushing to Utapao.[99]

Meanwhile, Cricket and the forward air controllers directed tactical strikes against Khmer Rouge positions. On the *Coral Sea,* Captain Purser and his men worked with rubber tubes and borrowed clamps to repair Jolly Green 43's disabled engine and ruptured fuel lines. At 5:30 Purser's chopper rejoined Backlund off Koh Tang. Together they greeted Jolly Green 44, freshly arrived from the mainland.[100]

Before the evacuation effort resumed, an Air Force C-130 cargo plane lumbered over Koh Tang to drop a 15,000-pound bomb on the center of the island. The bomb devastated an area the size of a football field. Anyone inside a fifty-yard radius of the explosion died from the concussion.[101]

After the smoke from the explosion cleared, a forward air controller directed Backlund to make a final run to get the marines off the eastern beach. Backlund knew that those isolated men would probably not survive the night. Jolly Green 11 came under heavy enemy fire as soon as it neared the beach. Captain Backlund, who had been flying since before dawn, backed his chopper to the water's edge and tried to hover a foot above the surf. "I was pretty tired and scared and it was very noisy," said Backlund, "the ramp was moving up and down two, three, to four feet up off the rocks and then it would come crashing down."[102]

Under intense fire, the marines began boarding the chopper, two-by-two. A pair would rise from their position near the trees, fire a few rounds into the jungle, dash to the chopper's ramp, turn and empty their M-16s at the enemy infested underbrush, then toss their rifles into the helicopter and scramble toward the front. One of the first pair of leathernecks aboard, in a hurry to get to the forward part of the cabin, ripped out the intercom system. From that point Captain Backlund, working the controls, had no way of communicating with his pararescuemen and flight mechanics supervising the loading in the rear. SSgt. Harry W. Cash, the flight mechanic manning the rear ramp minigun, was blasting the jungle to provide covering fire for the retreating marines. He yelled into his intercom when the last two leathernecks leaped aboard. In the cockpit Backlund heard nothing. He held the precarious hover. Cash and the other crewmen in the rear yelled into their dead headsets for Backlund to pull up and away. Up front Captain Backlund wondered what was taking so long as he listened to enemy bullets pelting his chopper. Sergeant Cash saw black clad figures emerging from the jungle and swung his minigun to chop them down. One of the figures drew back to toss a grenade. As his arm started forward Cash's stream of fire sliced him in two. The grenade rolled toward the helicopter and exploded. With that Backlund decided that loaded or not it was time to go. Jolly Green 11 moved forward a few yards and then climbed.[103]

At dark there were three helicopters still operating and 202 marines to be evacuated. Knife 51 flew through a hail of small arms fire to pick up 41 of them. Jolly Green 43 followed to carry out 54 more. Then Jolly 44 moved to the beach to load up 34 leathernecks. The remaining 73 men had withdrawn to hold positions only a short sprint from the landing zone. OV-10s and A-7s strafed the nearby jungle, but the Khmer Rouge pressed their attack. At 7:25 P.M. the Marine commander on the island reported that he thought his men would be overrun within fifteen minutes. As an

AC-130 blasted the dark tree-line beyond the leathernecks, Jolly Green 44 returned from the *Coral Sea*. The marines set up a strobe light to guide the chopper to them. Jolly 44 followed the light to the beach, picked up 40 marines, and headed for the *Coral Sea*.[104]

Knife 51 spotted the strobe light. Above the light an OV-10 orbited, occasionally turning on its landing lights to draw enemy fire away from the approaching chopper. Knife 51 settled into the landing zone, picked up the remaining marines, then took off.[105]

During the action on Koh Tang, approximately 230 men were landed on the island and then withdrawn. Total U.S. casualties were fifteen killed, three missing and forty-nine wounded. Of the fifteen helicopters that participated, four were destroyed and nine were damaged.[106]

America's involvement in the fighting in Southeast Asia was over, and the Aerospace Rescue and Recovery Service had remained in action even as the last shots were fired. After the *Mayaguez* incident, events moved rapidly to the final withdrawal of all rescue forces from Thailand in January 1976. There were no combat saves after the 3d Aerospace Rescue and Recovery Group was credited with thirty during the action on Koh Tang. From late in the spring of 1975, the missions flown by rescue units in Thailand were no different from those flown by rescue units throughout the world. These included medical evacuation missions, searches for missing boats, and an aircrew recovery sortie for the two-man crew of a Royal Thai Air Force T-28 which made a forced landing near Ubon.[107]

Rescue forces were among the very last to leave Thailand. As bases closed, rescue units were moved to maintain a continuing search and rescue capability. On October 1, 1975, the last American units left Nakhon Phanom, and the 3d Aerospace Rescue and Recovery Group moved to Utapao. The Joint Rescue Coordination Center transferred with them to continue coordinating rescue forces as they were reduced in numbers by returning helicopters to the United States.[108]

When the 3d Aerospace Rescue and Recovery Group left Nakhon Phanom, the 40th Aerospace Rescue and Recovery Squadrons moved to Korat. There they were co-located with the remaining HC-130Ps and the A-7Ds of the 3d Tactical Fighter Squadron. On October 15 the 56th Aerospace Rescue and Recovery Squadron was inactivated, and its four HC-130Ps became part of the 40th Aerospace Rescue and Recovery Squadron. The HH-53 and the HC-130P crews coordinated with the A-7 pilots of the 3d Tactical Fighter Squadron to maintain a reduced alert posture. Also, one HH-53 remained at Udorn on a temporary basis to provide a search and rescue capability in northern Thailand.[110]

Meanwhile, packing and crating of equipment continued. On December 15, 1975, the Joint Rescue Coordination Center closed.[111] Six weeks later, on January 31, 1976, Lt. Col. Cleveland F. Forrester, last commander of the 3d Aerospace Rescue and Recovery Group, cased the unit flag. The same day, the 40th Aerospace Rescue and Recovery Squadron was inactivated at Korat.[112] Thus ended an era of unparalleled valor in which the Aerospace Rescue and Recovery Service gallantly upheld its motto, "That Others May Live."

During its involvement in the wars of Southeast Asia, the U.S. Air Force lost 2,254 aircraft in combat and in normal operations. Aircrew members killed, captured, or missing totaled 1,763. Throughout the war the Aerospace Rescue and Recovery Service became the greatest combat aircrew recovery force in the history of aerial warfare, saving 3,883 lives.[113] For those flyers who went down, whether in combat or by accident, the best hope of survival was in a quick recovery by air-sea rescue forces.

The air war in Southeast Asia shifted often, varying its intensity, location, and focus as Americans fought enemy forces that ranged along the warfare spectrum from insurgency to protracted and, finally, conventional action. Rescue forces remained flexible to counter each threat and meet every challenge. Wisely, the Aerospace Rescue and Recovery Service never followed hard and fast rules or established rigid regulations defining how much effort was enough. The rescue crews gave each mission all they had. Nevertheless, when enemy antiaircraft fire was too intense, there was only so much the helicopters (even the giant HH-53s with their armor plate and impressive firepower) could take. As discussed earlier, during the Linebacker II operations of December 1972, not one aircrew member was picked up from North Vietnam's heartland because the targets were in densely populated, highly-defended areas.[114] Furthermore, during the operations on Koh Tang in connection with the *Mayaguez* incident, the entrenched Khmer Rouge force, armed with automatic weapons, a few heavy machine guns, rocket launchers, and perhaps one mortar, destroyed four helicopters and damaged nine others, at least five seriously.[115] The inherent limitations of the helicopter, slow speed and large size, made it highly vulnerable in a high threat environment.

Almost every modern military organization has, at one time or another, been accused of attempting to fight its present war as it fought its last war. If true, it would seem that we should ignore the lessons of history to concentrate on discovering inventive alternatives to previous tactics and policies. But one should study history to learn from, rather than to repeat, the past.

Those involved in rescue can learn some valuable lessons from the Southeast Asia experience. The most important lesson can be summed up in the concept of readiness. Peacetime rescue forces must be ready to perform combat search and rescue in a variety of situations. Perhaps too much has been made of the lack of preparedness in the Air Rescue Service prior to the Vietnam war. Rescue was no less ready for the very different and difficult kinds of warfare in Indochina than any other organization in the Air Force, or the entire U.S. military. Nevertheless, it would appear that the old Air

Rescue Service maxim that combat search and rescue was an extension of peacetime operations was finally superseded by events.

Second, the search and rescue task force evolved to overcome the problems of combat aircrew recovery peculiar to Southeast Asia. As a team, the search and rescue task force triumphed over nature and the enemy to save hundreds of aircrew members down in the jungles of Vietnam, Laos, and Cambodia. Many of the tactics employed by search and rescue task forces could be used again if the Air Force found itself involved in operations against lightly armed forces fighting in an area with geographic features resembling those of Southeast Asia.

The usefulness of search and rescue task forces in future conflicts will be determined by such factors as the geographic and demographic nature of the battlefield and, of course, enemy defenses. It is questionable that an armada of HH-53s, A-7s, HC-130s and forward air controllers would be able to operate in the highly defended, relatively open areas of Europe, over the flat sands of the Middle East, or above the barren hills of Korea. A future enemy could possess technologically advanced air defenses including modern jet fighters able to detect and destroy aircraft flying at low altitudes, the SA-3, SA-6, SA-11, and a host of smaller, hand-held missiles like the SA-7, and the deadly ZSU-23-4 radar-directed, fully-mobile antiaircraft gun. These weapons would prove vastly more formidable than those in the 1950s vintage air defense system the Air Force faced in North Vietnam.

The Aerospace Rescue and Recovery Service was ultimately successful in Southeast Asia in saving 3,883 human beings from death, suffering, or captivity because innovation and imagination brought rescue from the SA-16/HC-54 era to the search and rescue task force of the late 1960s. Imagination and innovation within a system receptive to change brought improvement through the introduction of novel tactics and new equipment. Flexibility and readiness in the peacetime Aerospace Rescue and Recovery Service will be the key to future success in combat aircrew rescue. That flexibility will require a continuation of the same spirit of innovation and ingenuity that made combat rescue successful in the wars of Southeast Asia.

Right: A–37s near Bien Hoa;
below: HH–53 equipped with
limited night recovery system.

157

Above: U–10 takes off over two O–1E forward air control aircraft; HH–53 refueling in flight.

Above: Aircrews head for their helicopters at Nakhon Phanom Air Base, Thailand; left: a U.S. Marine Corps wounded being evacuated during Mayaguez incident.

U.S. Navy Photo

Above: HC-130H of the Air Rescue Service; center: Ambassador Jonathan Dean, carrying the embassy flag, arrives at Utapao during Operation Eagle Pull in the evacuation of Phnom Penh, April 12, 1975; bottom: evacuees of Phnom Penh in Operation Eagle Pull.

159

"25 Hours Later, North Vietnam—The Rescue of Lt. Ken Thomas." Art by Woodie Ishmael, 1966.

Notes

Chapter I

1. Carroll V. Glines and Jimmy W. Kilbourne, eds, *Escape and Evasion, 17 True Stories of Downed Pilots Who Made it Back* (New York, 1973), pp 134-136.
2. Maj Jimmy W. Kilbourne, "Only One Returned," *The Airman* XIII (Mar 1969), p 12.
3. Glines and Kilbourne, *Escape and Evasion,* p 138.
4. *Ibid.,* p 139.
5. Kilbourne, "Only One Returned," p 12.
6. Maj Carroll S. Shershun, "It's the Greatest Mission of Them All," *Aerospace Historian* XIV (Autumn 1969), p 13.
7. Brig Gen Joseph A. Cunningham, "Wherever Men Fly," *Air Force and Space Digest* XLIII, No 5 (Mar 1960), p 89.
8. Lt Col Carl Hess, (Luftwaffe, Ret), "The Air-Sea Rescue Service of the Luftwaffe in World War II" (Unpublished manuscript, Air University, 1955), pp 2-3.
9. *Ibid.,* pp 6-7.
10. *Ibid.,* pp 32-33.
11. *Ibid.,* pp 40-41.
12. *Ibid.*
13. Denis Richards, *Royal Air Force 1939-1945,* Vol I: *The Fight at Odds* (London, 1953), p 159.
14. John L. Vandegrift, Jr., ed, *A History of the Air Rescue Service* (Winter Park, Fla., 1959), p 7.
15. *Ibid.,* p 8.
16. *Ibid.*
17. Winston S. Churchill, *Their Finest Hour,* Book 2, Vol II, *The Second World War,* (6 Vols, New York, 1962), p 284.
18. Richards, *The Fight at Odds,* p 159.
19. Derek Wood and Derek Dempster, *The Narrow Margin, The Battle of Britain and the Rise of Air Power, 1930-1940* (New York, 1961), p 297.
20. Denis Richards and Hilary St. George Saunders, *Royal Air Force 1939-1945,* Vol II: *The Fight Avails* (London, 1954), pp 87-88.
21. *Ibid.,* p 88.
22. Hess, "The Air-Sea Rescue Service of the Luftwaffe," Appendix, p 170.
23. Wesley Frank Craven and James Lea Cate, eds, *The Army Air Forces in World War II,* Vol VII: *Services Around the World* (Chicago, 1958), p 480.
24. *Air Sea Rescue, 1941-1952* (USAF Historical Study 95, Maxwell AFB, Ala., 1954), p 1.
25. Vandegrift, *Air Rescue Service,* p 10.
26. Craven and Cate, Vol VII, *Army Air Forces in World War II,* p 477.
27. Vice Adm Sir Arthur Hezlet, *Aircraft and Sea Power* (New York, 1970), p 11.
28. Leonard Bridgman and C.G. Grey, eds, *Jane's All the World's Aircraft, 1937* (London, 1937), p 283.
29. Craven and Cate, Vol VII, *Army Air Forces in World War II,* p 493.
30. Vandegrift, *Air Rescue Service,* p 50. 1300
31. *Ibid.,* pp 35-36.
32. Craven and Cate, *Army Air Forces in World War II,* Vol VII, pp 478-479.
33. *Ibid.,* pp 481-482.
34. For further discussion of the effectiveness of air-sea rescue operations in World War II, see: USAF Historical Study 95, p 175; Craven and Cate, Vol VII, pp 481-483; Vandegrift, pp 10 and 34.
35. USAF Historical Study 95, pp 175-76.
36. Vandegrift, *Air Rescue Service,* pp 67-68.
37. USAF Historical Study 95, p 175.
38. Vandegrift, *Air Rescue Service,* p 72.
39. Gen Matthew B. Ridgway, *The Korean War* (New York, 1967), p 9.
40. Robert F. Futrell, Brig Gen Lawson S. Mosley, and Albert F. Simpson, *The United States Air Force in Korea, 1950-1953* (New York, 1961), p 9.
41. *United States Air Force Operations in the Korean Conflict, 1 November 1950-June 1952* (USAF Historical Study 72, Maxwell AFB, Ala., 1953), p 24.
42. Futrell, *Korea, 1950-1953,* p 539.
43. Robert F. Futrell, *Development of Aeromedical Evacuation in the USAF, 1909-1960* (USAF Historical Study 23, Maxwell AFB, Ala., 1953), p 564.
44. Hist, *A Day by Day History of Far East*

Air Forces Operations, Vol I, 25 June-31 October 1950. Prepared by the Combat Operations Division, Directorate of Operations, Headquarters, Far East Air Forces, pp 166-69.

45. Futrell, *Korea, 1950-1953,* p 539.

46. Vandegrift, *Air Rescue Service,* p 80.

47. *United States Air Force Operations in the Korean Conflict, 1 July 1952-27 July 1953* (USAF Historical Study 127, Maxwell AFB, Ala., 1956), pp 302-303.

48. Walter G. Hermes, *The United States Army in the Korean War, Vol II: Truce Tent and Fighting Front* (Washington, 1966), p 184.

49. USAF Historical Study 23, p 591.

50. *Helicopters in Korea, 1 July 1951-August 1953,* 8086 Army Unit Military History Detachment, Seoul, Korea, 1954, pp 36-40.

51. Futrell, *Korea, 1950-1953,* p 538.

52. Robert Jackson, *Air War Over Korea* (London, 1973), p 110.

53. Futrell, *Korea, 1950-1953,* pp 539-540.

54. *Ibid.,* p 541.

55. USAF Historical Study 95, pp 170-172.

56. Leonard Bridgman, *Jane's All the World's Aircraft, 1951* (London, 1951), p 282c.

57. Jackson Historical Study 127, p 303.

58. USAF Historical Study 127, p 303.

59. *Ibid.,* p 298.

60. Bridgman, *Jane's, 1951,* p 239c.

61. Futrell, *Korea, 1950-1953,* pp 539-540.

62. Vandegrift, *Air Rescue Service,* p 88.

63. *Lessons of the War in Indochina,* Vol II (A translation from the French), (RM-119, Santa Monica, 1967), p 299.

64. *Ibid.,* p 300-301.

65. *Ibid.*

66. Vandegrift, *Air Rescue Service,* p 94.

67. USAF Historical Study 23, pp 690-691.

68. *Ibid.,* pp 727-728.

69. Vandegrift, *Air Rescuce Service,* p 94.

70. *Ibid.*

71. Hist, 3904th Composite Wing, 1 Aug-31 Aug 1953, pp 3-5.

72. Vandegrift, *Air Rescue Service,* pp 94-95.

73. Military Airlift Service, Special Order 121, Jul 15, 1954.

74. Hist, Air Rescue Service (MATS), 1 Jan-31 Dec 1960, p 41.

75. Ltr, USAF to MATS, subj: Reorganization of ARS, dtd Sep 26, 1958.

76. Vandegrift, *Air Rescue Service,* p 170.

77. *Ibid.,* pp 96-97.

78. *Ibid.,* p 98.

79. Leonard Bridgman, ed. *Jane's All the World's Aircraft, 1955-56,* (New York, 1956), p 302.

80. Vandegrift, *Air Rescue Service,* p 171.

81. Hist, Air Rescue Service (MATS), 1 Jan-31 Dec 1960, p 13.

82. *Ibid.,* pp 34-35.

83. ARS Special Plan 522-61, Subj: Implementing Plan for Transfer of National SAR Centers and Local Base Rescue to ARS (MATS), Dec 20, 1960. In, Hist, Air Rescue Service (MATS), 1 Jul-31 Dec 1961, p 37.

84. Hist, Military Air Transport Service, 1 Jan-31 Dec 1961, p 37.

85. *Ibid.*

86. Ltr, Brig Gen Joseph A. Cunningham, Comdr ARS, to Lt Gen J.W. Kelly, CINCMAC, Oct 31, 1961.

87. MATS Special Plan 138-61, subj: National SAR and Local Base Rescue Implementing Plan, Mar 1, 1961.

88. Hist, Air Rescue Service (MATS), 1 Jan-31 Jun 1961, p 5.

Chapter II

1. Post Report, Laos, U.S. Embassy, Vientiane, Laos, 1974, p 1.

2. Brian Crozier, *Southeast Asia in Turmoil* (London, 1965), p 119.

3. Post Report, p 1.

4. Crozier, *Southeast Asia,* pp 120-125.

5. Bernard B. Fall, *Anatomy of a Crisis: The Laotian Crisis of 1960-1961* (New York, 1969), p 128; *Time,* Mar 17, 1961, p 24.

6. Arthur J. Dommen, *Conflict in Laos,*

the Politics of Neutralization (New York, 1971), p 410; *New York Times,* Dec 2, 1960, p 8.

7. Dommen, *Conflict in Laos,* p 178.

8. Intvw, Lt Col Robert G. Zimmerman with Lt Col Butler B. Jr., Nov 18, 1974, pp 20-21.

9. Arthur M. Schlesinger, Jr., *A Thousand Days* (New York, 1965), p 311.

10. Intvw, Lt Col Robert G. Zimmerman with Col William Vonplatten, May 10, 1975, pp 53-55; "U.S. Aircraft in Laos Missing," *New York Times,* Mar 26, 1961, p 6; Dommen, *Conflict in Laos,* p 183; Fall, *Anatomy of a Crisis,* p 215.

11. Corona Harvest, Report (SAFEO), *USAF Search and Rescue in Southeast Asia, 1954-11 March 1968,* Jan 31, 1969, pp 12-13.

12. Vandegrift, *Air Rescue Service,* p 168.

13. Schlesinger, *Thousand Days,* pp 309-11.

14. Robert F. Futrell and Martin Blumenson, *The United States Air Force in Southeast Asia: The Advisory Years, to 1965* (Washington, 1980), pp 128-30; Schlesinger, *Thousand Days,* pp 311-12; "U.S. Sending Laos 16 'Copters to Improve Mobility in Jungle," *New York Times,* Mar 25, 1961; Dommen, *Conflict in Laos,* p 189.

15. Maj Victor B. Anthony and Lt Col Richard R. Sexton, "A History of U.S. Air Force Operations in Northern Laos" (Office of AF Hist, unpublished manuscript), p 3.

16. JCS 2339/120, to SECDEF, subj: Steps to Improve the Situation in Southeast Asia with Particular Reference to Laos, Feb 26, 1962, pp 1-2; Anthony and Sexton, "Air Operations in Northern Laos," Ch III.

17. Corona Harvest Report (SAFEO), *Chronology of Significant Airpower Events in Southeast Asia, 1950-1968,* May 1, 1967, p 11.

18. Ltr (S), Lt Gen Thomas S. Moorman, VCINCPACAF to Korat RTAFB, Thailand, Sep 15, 1962, CH0219438.

19. Theodore C. Sorensen, *Kennedy* (New York, 1965), pp 548-49.

20. State Department Bulletin, Jan 23, 1961, p 155.

21. For a discussion of helicopter hover characteristics see: United States General Accounting Office, "Report on the Review of the Development and Procurement of Similar Type Helicopters Within the Department of Defense," June 1961, SAFS File 218-61. Also see: Memorandum for Deputy Assistant Secretary of Defense, subj: Air Force Position on GAO Report on HH-43, Aug 11, 1961. For an account of the disastrous results

of attempting to hover under unfavorable conditions see: Intvw, unk interviewer with Major Alan W. Saunders, Commander Det 3, Pacific Air Rescue Center, Jul 1, 1964.

22. Department of the Army Pamphlet No. 550-40, U.S. Army Area Handbook for Vietnam, Oct 1964, pp 31-52.

23. For discussion of the impact of the war on the people and culture of Vietnam see: Francis Fitzgerald, *Fire in the Lake: The Vietnamese and the Americans in Vietnam* (Boston, 1972).

24. Hal Kosut and Lester A. Sobel, eds., *South Vietnam,* Vol I: *U.S. Communist Confrontation in Southeast Asia, 1961-1965* (New York, 1966), p 5.

25. *The Pentagon Papers as Published by the New York Times.* (New York, 1971), p 72.

26. Memo, CSAF for SECAF, subj: Farm Gate Activity Report in South Vietnam, Feb 13, 1962, tab 3, p 23.

27. Hist, 2d Air Division, 15 Nov 1961-8 Oct 1962, I, pp xvii-xviii. Detachment 7 of the 13th Air Force was known unofficially as 2d ADVON from the beginning. It was officially renamed 2d ADVON in June 1962 and redesignated 2d Air Division in October 1962.

28. Memo, CSAF for SECAF, subj: Farm Gate Activity Report, Feb 13, 1962.

29. Intvw, author with Maj Alan Saunders, Oct 15, 1976.

30. Vandergrift, *Air Rescue Service,* p 168.

31. Corona Harvest, Report (SAFEO), *Evaluation of Airpower in Southeast Asia, 1954-1964,* Vol I, *1954-1961,* pp 5-11.

32. Corona Harvest, *USAF Search and Rescue, 1954-1968,* pp 13-14.

33. Futrell, *The Advisory Years,* p 141; Report of the Air Force Study Group on Vietnam, Office of the Secretary of the Air Force, Washington, D.C., May 1, 1964, A II, pp 3-5.

34. Msg, CHMAAG Vietnam to CINCPAC, 120820Z Feb 62 (Press release no. 2883); Msg, 2d ADVON to COFS USAF, 111535Z Feb 62.

35. Memo, Farm Gate Activity Report, Feb 13, 1962, tab 3m, pp 2-3.

36. JCS 2343/351-6, JCS to SECDEF, subj: Additional Aircraft for the Republic of Vietnam, Apr 16, 1962.

37. Jacob Van Staaveren, *USAF Plans and Policies in South Vietnam 1961-63,* (Washington, 1965), p 38.

38. Background paper, subj: USAF Operations in RVN, nd [ca Apr 64].

39. MATS SO G-27, Mar 23, 1962.

40. Memo, Farm Gate Activity Report, Feb 13, 1962, pp 2-3.

41. Joint Vietnamese/U.S. Search and Rescue Agreement, nd [ca spring 1962], signed by Gen Paul D. Harkins, Commander, MACV and Lt Gen Le Van Ty, Chief of the General Staff, Army of the Republic of Vietnam, p 1. (Hereafter cited as Joint Vietnam/U.S. SAR Plan).

42. *Ibid.*

43. *Ibid.,* p 2.

44. Corona Harvest, *USAF Search and Rescue, 1954-1968,* p 25.

45. Saunders intvw, Jul 1, 1964; Ltr, Lt Col E.J. Trexler to Col Gordon W. Crozier, subj: Corona Harvest Study, quoted in Corona Harvest, *USAF Search and Rescue, 1954-1968,* p 19.

46. Saunders intvw, p 4.

47. Msg, 34 TACT Gp, Bien Hoa to Det 3, PARC AOC SARCC TSW 081330Z Oct 63; Msg, Det 3, PARC AOC SARCC to Hdq ARC 181535Z Oct 63; Msg, Det 3, PARC AOC SARCC to Hdq ARS, 201710Z Oct 63; Msg, Det 3, PARC AOX SARCC to Hdq ARS, 231010Z Oct 63.

48. Study, Det 3, PARC SARCC Second Air Division SAR Requirement Study for Republic of Vietnam, Sep 1, 1963, p 8. (Hereafter cited as Second Air Division SAR Requirements Study).

49. Saunders Intvw, p 10.

50. Msg, COMUSMACV to AIG 24, 240806Z, Jan 64.

51. Saunders intvw, p 10.

52. Msg, COMUSMACV to AIG 24, 240806Z Jan 64.

53. Franz Schurmann, *The Logic of World Power: An Inquiry Into the Origins, Currents, and Contradictions of World Politics* (New York, 1974), p 496.

54. Van Staaveren, *USAF Plans and Policies, 1961-1963,* pp 46-48.

55. *Ibid.,* p 46.

56. *Ibid.,* p 48.

57. Msg, 13AF to PACAF, 240807Z Oct 62.

58. Second Air Division SAR Requirements Study.

59. *Ibid.,* Tab B.

60. Msg, 2d ADVON TO CSAF, 150540Z May 64.

61. Saunders Intvw, p 7.

62. Second Air Division SAR Requirements Study.

63. Ltr, Maj Gen Rollen H. Anthis to 13AF and PACAF, subj: Requirements for Professional Rescue Forces in the Republic of Vietnam, Nov 7, 1963; see Note 48.

64. Capt B. Conn Anderson, *USAF Search and Rescue in Southeast Asia (1961-66),* (Hq PACAF, Proj CHECO, Oct 24, 1966), p 16. (Hereafter cited as Anderson, *USAF SAR in SEA, 1961-66).*

65. *Ibid.;* Ltr, Col Walter F. Derck, Comdr PARC to Brig Gen Adriel N. Williams, Comdr ARS, Mar 23, 1964; Hist 2d Air Division, Jan-Jun 1964, p 108.

66. Anderson, *USAF SAR in SEA, 1961-1966,* p 16.

67. *Ibid.,* pp 16-18; Corona Harvest, *USAF Search and Rescue, 1954-1968,* p 51; Memorandum for the Record Lt Col N.V. Rudrud, Directorate of Operations, USAF, Subj: SAR Force, Aug 3, 1964.

68. Joseph J. Zasloff, *The Pathet Lao Leadership and Organization* (Lexington, Mass, 1973), p 70.

69. Msg, 6010 TFG to PACAF, date time group unreadable, Aug 14, 1962.

70. Msg, 6010 TFG to PACAF, 02100Z Aug 62.

71. 2d Air Division Manual 55-1, p 7.

72. JCS 2353/13, Note by the Secretaries to the Joint Chiefs of Staff on the Military Buildup in Thailand, Apr 21 1963.

73. Anthony and Sexton, "Air Operations in Northern Laos", ch V.

74. Capt Mark E. Smith, *USAF Reconnaissance in Southeast Asia* (1961-1966), (Hq PACAF, Proj CHECO, Oct 25, 1966), pp 19-22.

75. Corona Harvest, *USAF Search and Rescue, 1954-1968,* p 47.

76. *Ibid.*

77. Msg, USAIRA Vientiane to JCS, 070635Z Jun 64.

78. Msg, Maj J.H. Moore to Lt Gen Sam Maddux, 061250Z Jun 64.

79. Msg, 13AF to 2AD, 060745Z Jun 64; msg, Maj Gen J.H. Moore to RAdm Pringle, Jun 7, 1964; Msg, Det 3, PARC to Hq USAF, 061135Z Jun 64. Klusmann escaped in Sep 1964. At his debriefing he praised the Air America rescue attempt in the face of intense ground fire.

80. Msg, Det 3, PARC to Hdq USAF, 071050Z Jun 64.

81. Msg, Det 3, PARC to Hdq USAF 071533Z Jun 64.

82. Anthony and Sexton, "Air Operations in Northern Laos", ch VI.

83. Msg, Ambassador Martin to CSAF, 111010Z Jun 64.

84. Corona Harvest, *USAF Search and Rescue, 1954-1968,* pp 54-55.

85. *Ibid.,* pp 54-64.

86. Ltr, Lt Col F.W. Hartley to Comdr

ARS, Subj: Report on Conditions Existing in SEA, nd (ca Jun 1964).

87. Corona Harvest, *USAF Search and Rescue, 1954-1968*, pp 54-65.

88. Memorandum for the Chairman, JCS, subj: Helicopter Requirements, in Laos, Sep 12, 1964.

89. Background Paper, Helicopters for Air America, JCS 2344/97-1, Oct 29, 1964.

90. Memorandum for the Secretary of Defense, subj: Helicopter Requirements in Laos, Nov 4, 1964, p. 1.

91. MSgt Robert T. Helmka and TSgt Beverly Hale, *USAF Operations From Thailand, 1964-1965,* (Hq PACAF, Proj CHECO, Aug 10, 1966), p 122.

92. *Ibid.,* p 123.

93. Msg, AMEMB, Vientiane 325 to SECSTATE, Aug 19, 1964; Msg, AMEMB, Vientiane 337 to SECSTATE, Aug 20, 1964; 2ADM 55-1, p 7.

94. Msg, CINCPAC to 2d Air Div, 011940Z 20 Aug 64.

95. Ltr, ARRS Historian to 3ARRGp, Jun

29, 1966; Atch 3, "Chronological Buildup in SEA," doc 3.

96. End of tour report, Capt Philip Prince, Cmdr, Det 4 (Prov), ARS, Jan 18, 1965.

97. Msg, PACAF to CSAF, 190042Z Sept 64; Anderson, *USAF SAR in SEA, 1961-66,* pp 19-20.

98. Hist, 38th Air Rescue Squadron, Oct-Dec 65, p 4; Msg, Det 3 to Det Prov First, 260330Z Dec 64.

99. Msg, Dep Cmdr 2AD to Hdq 2AD, 181900Z Nov 64.

100. Hist, 313th Air Division, 1 Jul 64-30 Jun 65, pp 324-325; Msg, 333 ABRON to 2AD, 191215Z Nov 64.

101. *Ibid.*

102. Msg, USAIRA, Vientiane to CSAF, 190820Z Nov 64.

103. Robert F. Futrell, *Chronology of Significant Airpower Events in Southeast Asia, 1954-1967* (Corona Harvest, Aerospace Studies Institute, Maxwell AFB, Ala, Dec 15, 1967), p 46; Msgs AMEMB, Vientiane, 783 & 784 to SECSTATE, Nov 21, 1964.

Chapter III

1. Anderson, *USAF SAR In SEA, 1961-66,* pp 18-19.

2. *Ibid;* Hist, History of Air Rescue Service, 1 Jan-31 Dec 1965, p 87.

3. Anderson, *USAF SAR in SEA, 1961-66,* p 19.

4. Intvw, author with Col James V. Berryhill, former HH-43F pilot, 2 May 1977.

5. Anderson, *USAF SAR in SEA, 1961-66,* p 20.

6. John W.R. Taylor, ed., *Jane's All the World's Aircraft, 1964-65,* (New York, 1966), p 241; Anderson, *USAF SAR in SEA, 1961-1966,* p 21; Intvw, author with Major John Guilmartin, Aug 22, 1978.

7. Ltr, Comdr PARC to Comdr ARS, Mar 23, 1964, p 1.

8. PACAF Study, HH-3C Helicopter Requirements in the Pacific Command Dec 3, 1964, pp 3-4.

9. Corona Harvest, *Local Base Rescue (LBR) in Southeast Asia, 1954-31 March 1968,* Mar 20, 1969, pp 41-42.

10. ARS OPLAN 510, Hq ARS, Local Base Rescue Contingency Force, Oct 31, 1964.

11. *Ibid.*

12. Ltr, AFCCS, Gen Curtis E. LeMay to SAF-OS, Nov 16, 1964.

13. Robert F. Futrell, Corona Harvest, *Chronology of Significant Airpower Events in Southeast Asia, 1954-1967* (Maxwell AFB, Ala., Dec 15, 1967), p 54; Corona Harvest, *LBR in SEA,* p 44; Carl Berger, ed., *The United States Air Force in Southeast Asia: An Illustrated History* (Washington, 1977), p 35.

14. Berryhill intvw, May 2, 1977.

15. Ltr, Brig Gen Adriel N. Williams, Comdr ARS to CSAF, Sep 8, 1964.

16. Msg, Det 3 to ARS 040620Z Nov 64; Msg, Det 3 to ARS 040925Z Nov 64; and Ltr, PARC to 7AF, Jul 12, 1966, Atch 13.

17. Hist, 2d Air Div, Jul 64-Dec 64, p 33; Anderson, *USAF SAR in SEA, 1961-66,* p 11.

18. Corona Harvest Report, *Aircrew Recovery in Southeast Asia, 1965-31 March 1968,* May 20, 1969, p 44. (Hereafter cited as Corona Harvest, *ACR in SEA).*

19. Anderson, *USAF SAR in SEA,*

1961-66, p 18.

20. Study, Hq ARS, *HH-43 and HU-16 Operations in SEA, 17 Jan 64,* Tab C, pp 2-4.

21. Aerospace Rescue and Recovery Service (ARRS) Command Briefing, 1968, p 7.

22. Vandegrift, *Air Rescue Service,* p 97; Leonard Bridgman, ed., *Jane's All the World's Aircraft, 1955-56* (New York, 1956), p 256.

23. Anderson, *USAF SAR in SEA, 1961-66,* pp 42-43.

24. Project Corona Harvest, Special Report No. 78-18, Col P.Y. Williams, *Aerospace Rescue and Recovery in Southeast Asia,* April 1969, Maxwell AFB, Ala., p 14; Talking Papers, SEA Actions, Hq ARRS, Atch 4, Aug 7, 1965; Anderson, *USAF SAR in SEA, 1961-66,* pp 42-43; Corona Harvest, *ACR in SEA,* pp 67 and 78.

25. Hess, The Air-Sea Rescue Service of the Luftwaffe, pp 2-3; Vandegrift, *Air Rescue Service,* pp 6-7.

26. Msg, SECSTATE to AMEMB, Vientiane, Aug 26, 1964.

27. Francis K. Mason and Martin C. Windrow, *Know Aviation: Seventy Years of Man's Endeavor* (Garden City, N.Y., 1973), p 183.

28. Helmka and Hale, *USAF Operations from Thailand, 1964-1965,* p 122.

29. Hist, 313th Air Division, 1 July 64-30 Jun 65, pp 324-325; Msg, 333 ABRON to 2d AD, 191215Z Nov 65; and Berryhill Intvw, May 2, 1977.

30. Chronology, 2d Air Division, Jan-Dec 1964; Steve Birdsall, *The A-1 Skyraider,* (New York, 1970), pp 8-12; Mason and Windrow, *Know Aviation,* p 178.

31. Msg, CSAF to PACAF, May 24, 1965; Msg, AMEMB Vientiane to AMEMB Bangkok, 180744Z May 65.

32. OPORD 431-66, Jan 15, 1966; Anderson, *USAF SAR in SEA, 1961-66,* p 37.

33. Msg, 623d TFW to PACAF, 241049Z Jun 65.

34. Msg, 6235 Combat Support Group, Takhli to PACAF, 201411Z Sep 65; Msg, Det 1, 38th ARS NKP to CSAF, 201410Z Sep 65; Msg, 062250Z Jul 66; and Intvw, author with Lt Col Thomas J. Curtis, July 27, 1975.

35. Msg, USAIRA to CSAF, May 14, 1965.

36. Msg, CINCUSARPAC to CINCPAC, 300056Z May 65.

37. Msg, COMUSMACV to AMEMB

Bangkok, 300532Z Jun 66; Msg, CINCPACAF to CINCPAC, 041029Z Feb 66; and Msg, CINCPACAF to CINCPAC, 041029Z Feb 66.

38. *Ibid.*

39. Hist, Hq United States Military Assistance Command, Vietnam, 1968, Annex F, p F-XI-4. On Jan 8, 1966, the name of the Air Rescue Service was officially changed to Aerospace Rescue and Recovery Service. As part of a world wide reorganization, the 3d Aerospace Rescue and Recovery Group was established at Tan Son Nhut and given control of the 37th Aerospace Rescue and Recovery Squadron at Da Nang and the 38th ARRSq at Tan Son Nhut. The 37th ARRSq was activated concurrently with the establishment of the 3d ARRGp.

40. Msg, CINCPACAF to COMUSMACTHAI, 222016Z Jul 65.

41. Anderson, *USAF SAR in SEA, 1961-66,* p 37.

42. Hist, Air Rescue Service 1 Jan-31 Dec 1965, Vol I, p 26.

43. USAF Aircraft Characteristics Summary, (AFG-1, Addn 103, Nov 72), HH-3E Section; Anderson, *USAF SAR in SEA, 1961-66,* pp 41-42.

44. Anderson, *USAF SAR in SEA, 1961-66,* pp 41-42.

45. Talking Papers, SEA Actions, ARS, 1965, Atch 3.

46. Anderson, *USAF SAR in SEA, 1961-66,* pp 41-42.

47. Walter F. Lynch, *USAF Search and Rescue in Southeast Asia,* 1 Jul 69-31 Dec 70 (Hq PACAF, Project CHECO, Apr 23,71), pp 88-89. (Hereafter cited as Lynch, *USAF SAR in SEA, 1 Jul 69-31 Dec 70.*

48. *Ibid.,* p 90.

49. Hist, 38th ARSq, 1 Oct-31 Dec 65, p 8.

50. *Ibid;* PACAF CC Daily Operations Summary, Nov 7, 1965.

51. Hist, 38th ARSq, 1 Oct-31 Dec 65, p 8.

52. Working Paper 67/14, Dec 1, 1967, "Aircraft and Aircrew Member Loss Analysis", 7th Air Force, p 27.

53. Corona Harvest, *Joint Search and Rescue Center (JSARC) in Southeast Asia,* Vol II, *1954-31 March 1968,* Mar 20, 1969, pp 158-59 (Hereafter cited as Corona Harvest, *JSARC in SEA).* On January 8, 1966, when the 3d Aerospace Rescue and Recovery Group was activated at Tan Son Nhut, the JSARC became part of that unit as did the rescue control centers at Da Nang and

Udorn.

54. Corona Harvest, *JSARC in SEA*, pp 138-59; and Col P.Y. Williams, *Aerospace Rescue and Recovery in Southeast Asia: A Special Report*, Corona Harvest, (Maxwell AFB, Ala., Apr 1969), p 19 (Hereafter cited as Williams, *Rescue in SEA: Special Report*).

55. *Anderson, USAF SAR in SEA, 1961-66*, p 73.

56. Msg, CINCPAC to CINCPACFLT, 270047Z Dec 65.

57. Ltr, 3d ARRGp to Comdr ARRS, subj: Commander's Letter, Aug 11, 1967, p 1.

58. Corona Harvest, *JSARC in SEA*, pp 158-59.

59. USAF Management Summary Southeast Asia, Jan 7, 1966, p 27.

60. Anderson, *USAF SAR in SEA, 1961-66*, p 80.

61. Williams, *Rescue in SEA: Special Report*, p 19.

62. McConnell Papers, Item No. 317, Briefing by General Estes, Oct 28, 1965.

63. Hist, History of the Air Rescue Service, 1 Jan-31 Dec 1965, Vol I, p 23.

64. Williams, *Rescue in SEA: Special Report*, p 19.

65. Hist, Aerospace Rescue and Recovery Service, 1 Jan-30 Jun 66, Vol I, pp 121-123.

66. Don Little, "Chronology of Aerospace Rescue and Recovery Service, 1946-1976," Mar 1976, unpublished manuscript and unnumbered pages.

67. Anderson, *USAF SAR in SEA, 1961-66*, p 43.

68. Williams, *Rescue in SEA: Special Report*, p 21.

69. Lynch, *USAF SAR in SEA, 1969-70*, p 93.

70. Hq PACAF, *Summary of Air Operations in Southeast Asia*, Vol XXIX, Dec 1966, tab 6-2.

Chapter IV

1. ARRS Briefing, Airpower Effectiveness Evaluation, SEA (Project Loyal Look), Jan 26, 1967, p 3.

2. Lynch, *USAF SAR in SEA, 1 Jul 69-31 Dec 70*, p 94.

3. Hq ARRS, Analysis of SEA Combat ACR for Validation of Revision of Requirements for Development (RAD 7-39-1), Jan 31, 1967, pp 2-3.

4. End of tour report, Maj Joseph B. Ferrell, Det 1, 40 ARRSq Rescue Crew Commander (1 July 67-26 Jun 68), Oct 29, 1968, p 2.

5. See footnote 3 above.

6. Maj Richard A. Durkee, *USAF Search and Rescue in Southeast Asia, July 1966-November 1967*, (Hq PACAF, Project CHECO, Jun 19, 1968), pp 20-21. (Hereafter cited as Durkee, *USAF SAR in SEA, Jul 66-Nov 67.*)

7. Michael L. Yaffee, "Composite Aircraft Seen Emerging as Next Basic VTOL," *Aviation Week and Space Technology*, May 1, 1967, pp 60-67.

8. See footnote 3 above.

9. Durkee, *USAF SAR in SEA, Jul 66-Nov 67*, pp 4-5.

10. Intvw, Capt Art Smith, HH-53 Rescue Crew Commander, 40th ARRSq, Udorn RTAF, Thailand, May 21, 1969; Intvw, Col Philip Stambaugh, former CH-3C Rescue Crew Commander, Nov 21, 1978.

11. Intvw, author with Col Harry P. Dunn, (USAF ret), HH-3E/HH-53 Systems Project Office, 1964-72, Oct 19, 1977.

12. *Ibid.*

13. ARRS Briefing, Airpower Effectiveness Evaluation, SEA (Project Loyal Look), Jan 26, 1967, p 3; John W.R. Taylor, ed., *Jane's All the World's Aircraft, 1964-65* (New York, 1965), p 251; John W.R. Taylor, ed., *Jane's All the World's Aircraft, 1976-77* (New York, 1977), p 318.

14. Hist, History of the Aerospace Rescue and Recovery Service, 1 Jul-31 Dec 66, Vol I, p 35.

15. Msg, Hq ARRS to Hq MAC, 082100Z Nov 6; and Lynch, *USAF SAR in SEA, 1 Jul 69-31 Dec 70*, p 96.

16. Little, "Chronology", p 60.

17. Hist, History of the Aerospace Rescue and Recovery Service, 1 Jan 1967-30 Jun 1970, Vol I, pp 193-194.

18. *Ibid.*, p 195.

19. Durkee, *USAF SAR in SEA, Jul 66-Nov 67*, pp 8-9.

20. *Ibid.,* p 9.

21. *Ibid.,* pp 9-10, fig. 8.

22. Briefing, HC-130 Operations, Gen Brooks, to Gen Estes, Mar 29, 1967, pp 11-12.

23. Hist, 3d ARRGp, 1 Jul-30 Sep 67, Atch 3; and Durkee, *USAF SAR in SEA, Jul 66-Nov 67,* p 13.

24. Williams, *Rescue in SEA: Special Report,* p 20.

25. Hist, History of the Aerospace Rescue and Recovery Service, 1 Jul-31 Dec 66, p 132.

26. 37th ARRSq Narrative Report on Mission Number 1-3-24/12 Feb 67, Feb 20, 1967, pp 1-3; Hist, 3d ARRGp, 1 Jan-31 Mar 67, pp 11-12.

27. Intvw, author with Lt Col Alan R. Vette, former Commander 37th ARRSq, Apr 22, 1978.

28. Hist, ARRS, 1 Jan 67-30 Jun 70, pp 52-54.

29. Hist, 3d ARRGp 1 Apr-30 Jun 66, p 55; Little, "Chronology", p 56.

30. Little, "Chronology", p 59.

31. 37th ARRSq Narrative Report on Mission Number 1-3-42/13 Mar 67, Mar 15, 1967, pp 1-2.

32. Little, "Chronology", p 59.

33. Hist, ARRS, 1 Jan 67-30 Jun 70, pp 51-55.

34. End of tour report, Maj Joseph B. Ferrell, p 2.

35. Taylor, ed., *Jane's,* 1976, p 129.

36. Bill Gunston, *The Encyclopedia of the World's Combat Aircraft* (Secaucus, N.J., 1977), p 199.

37. Corona Harvest, *Aircrew Recovery in Southeast Asia, 1965-31 March 1968,* Vol IV, p 145.

38. Hist, ARRS, 1 Jul-31 Dec 66, p 41.

39. Little, "Chronology", p 61.

40. Ltr, Gen B.K. Holloway, Vice Chief of Staff, USAF to Gen Howell M. Estes, Jr. Comdr, MAC, subj: Appreciation for HH-53B Demonstration, Jun 26, 1967.

41. Ltr, Col Paul E. Lesk, Comdr, 3d ARRGp, to Lt Col Harold Sweifel, 536 TAS, Sep 21, 1967.

42. Durkee, *USAF SAR in SEA, Jul 66-Nov 67,* p 6.

43. Intvw, author with Col Harry P. Dunn, Feb 6, 1979.

44. Intvw, unk interviewer with Lt Col Chester R. Ratclift, Comdr 40th ARRSq, 20 May 69, Doc 9.

45. Lynch, *USAF SAR in SEA, 1 Jul 69-31 Dec 70,* p 43.

46. *Ibid.,* p 44.

47. ARRS Briefing, Loyal Look, Jun 26, 1967, p 3.

48. Corona Harvest, *Aircrew Recovery in Southeast Asia, 1965-31 March 1969,* Vol IV, p 50.

49. End of tour report, Lt Col Donald F. Coymer, HC-130P pilot, 39 ARRSq, (20 Mar 68-25 Mar 69), Dec. 10, 1969, p 1.

50. Durkee, *USAF SAR in SEA, Jul 66-Nov 67,* pp 18-19.

51. Mission Report, 40th ARRSq, Dec 21, 1972.

52. Lynch, *USAF SAR in SEA, 1 Jul 69-31 Dec 70,* pp 18-19.

53. Durkee, *USAF SAR in SEA, Jul 66-Nov 67,* Appendix II, p 31.

54. End of tour report, Col Albert L. Colcomb, 37th ARRSq Comdr (17 Feb 70-12 Feb 71), Feb 10, 1971, pp 15-16.

55. Intvw, Lt Col LeRoy W. Lowe with Col Frederick V. Sohle, Jr., Comdr, 3d ARRGp, 1969-1970, Mar 2, 1972; Lt Col LeRoy W. Lowe, *Search and Rescue Operations in SEA, 1 January 1971-31 March 1972* (Hq PACAF, Project CHECO, Oct 17, 1972), p 44. (Hereafter cited as Lowe, *SAR Ops in SEA, 1 Jan 71-31 Mar 72.*

56. Lowe, *SAR Ops in SEA, 1 Jan 71-31 Mar 72,* pp 44-53.

57. *Ibid.,* pp 47-48.

58. Ltr, Col H.D. Wood, Assistant for Joint Matters, Command Planning Division, AFXPDWC2 to Lt Col Halstead, AFXPDWC2, subj: Use of Tear Gas in Vietnam, Oct 20, 1967; Directorate of Management Analysis, *USAF Management Summary Reference Data,* Oct 14, 1969, Ref Data 23.

59. MACV Directive 525-11, "Combat Operations Employment of Riot Control Agents and Defense Against Chemical, Biological Attack", Jul 24, 1967; JCS Memorandum Jun 29, 1971, USAF Uses of Riot Control Agents in Southeast Asia in Support of Combat Operations, p 5.

60. *Ibid.,* p 6.

61. *Ibid.,* p 7.

62. *Ibid.*

63. Maj James B. Overton, *USAF Search and Rescue, November 1967-June 1969,* (Hq PACAF, Project CHECO, Jul 30, 1969), pp 34-35. (Hereafter cited as Overton, *USAF SAR, Nov 67-Jun 69.)*

64. Maj John Schlight, *Rescue at Ban Phanop, 5-7 December 1969,* (Hq PACAF, Project CHECO, Feb 15, 1970), p 7. (Hereafter cited as Schlight, *Rescue at Ban Phanop.)*

65. *Ibid.,* p 16.

66. End of tour report, Lt Col William M.

Harris, IV, Comdr, 37th ARRSq (12 Jun 71-1 Jun 72), Jun 10, 1972, p 5; Overton, *USAF SAR, Nov 67-Jun 69,* pp 2-3.

67. Lynch, *USAF SAR in SEA, 1 Jul 69-31 Dec 70,* p 58, table 1.

Chapter V

1. Hist, Aerospace Rescue and Recovery Service, 1 July 1970-30 June 1971, Annex, William B. Karstetter, *The Son Tay Raid,* p 28, (hereafter cited as Karstetter, *Son Tay Raid*); Intvw, Dr Charles Hildreth and William J. McQuillen with Brig Gen Leroy J. Manor, USAF Joint Contingency Task Force Commander, Dec 31, 1970, fig 1.

2. Karstetter, *Son Tay Raid,* p 2.(Available documentation, including the Joint Chiefs of Staff histories, do not indicate whether the JCS consulted the Secretary of Defense or National Security Council before directing that training and planning begin.)

3. Benjamin F. Schemmer, *The Raid* (New York, 1976), pp 93-95; Intvw, author with Col Tom Curtis, former resident of Son Tay Prison, Apr 22, 1978; and Intvw, author with Lt Col Rick Woolfer, Chief, Escape and Evasion/Prisoner of War Branch, 7602d Intelligence Squadron, Ft. Belvoir, Va., Apr 14, 1978.

4. Defense Intelligence Information Report (DIIR), 2 237 0093 72, Incidents in North Vietnam, Aug 9, 1972, p 2; DIIR, 1 516 0639 71, The U.S. Raid on Son Tay PW Camp, Dec 10, 1971, pp 1-5. (Hereafter cited as DIIR 2 237 0093 72 and DIIR 1 516 0639 71.)

5. Schemmer, *The Raid,* pp 78-80.

6. Heather David, *Operation: Rescue* (New York, 1971), pp 67-68.

7. Manor intvw, Dec 31, 1970, pp 3-4.

8. Intvw, Lt Col V.H. Gallacher and Maj Lyn R. Officer with Col Royal A. Brown, Son Tay raider, Feb 9, 1973, pp 34-35; Intvw, author with Col Herbert R. Zehnder, Son Tay raider, Apr 22, 1978; Manor intvw, p 2.

9. Manor intvw, Dec 31, 1970, p 2.

10. *Ibid.,* pp 6-7.

11. David, *Operation: Rescue,* pp 99-100, and Schemmer, *The Raid,* p 92.

12. Manor intvw, Dec 31, 1970, pp 2-6.

13. *Ibid.,* pp 4-5.

14. *Ibid.,* p 5; Marvin Kalb and Bernard Kalb, *Kissinger* (Boston, 1974), p 174.

15. Brown intvw, Feb 9, 1973, p 36; Zehnder intvw, Apr 22, 1978; David, *Operation: Rescue,* p 100.

16. Manor intvw, Dec 31, 1970, pp 9-10.

17. *Ibid.,* p 10; Zehnder intvw, Apr 22, 1978.

18. *Ibid.*

19. Karstetter, *The Son Tay Raid,* p 25.

20. Intvw, author with Lt Col Alfred C. Montrem, Son Tay raider, May 22, 1978.

21. Brown intvw, Feb 9, 1973, p 38.

22. "Son Tay," *Air Operations Review* (SNF), Hq USAF, DCS/Plans and Operations, Vol 9, Sep 71, pp 1-12 - 1-13.

23. *Ibid.*

24. Manor intvw, Dec 31, 1970, pp 12-13.

25. *Ibid.,* p 13.

26. Schemmer, *The Raid,* p 201.

27. *Ibid.,* p 205; Zehnder intvw, Apr 22, 1978; Montrem intvw, May 22, 1978.

28. *Air Operations Review,* pp 1-11 - 1-12; David, *Operation: Rescue,* pp 11-14.

29. Karstetter, *The Son Tay Raid,* p 35; Schemmer, *The Raid,* pp 211-212; Zehnder intvw, Apr 22, 1978; Manor intvw, 31 Dec 1970, pp 14-15.

30. Defense Intelligence Information Report 1 516 0144 71, American Raid on Son Tay PW Camp, Mar 11, 1971, p 2.

31. Karstetter, *The Son Tay Raid,* p 39.

32. Brown intvw, Feb 9, 1973, p 40.

33. Karstetter, *The Son Tay Raid,* p 41.

34. Curtis intvw, Apr 22, 1978; Woolfer intvw, Apr 14, 1978.

35. Robert A. Devine, *Since 1945: Politics and Diplomacy in Recent American History* (New York, 1975), p 173.

36. Lynch, *USAF SAR in SEA, 1 Jul 69-31 Dec 70,* pp 76-78.

37. *Ibid.,* pp 103-104. After the 12th TFW disbanded and 72 fighters were no longer operating out of Cam Ranh AB, a local base rescue unit was not necessary. Det 1, 38th ARRSq at Phan Rang AB, 15 miles south, provided services for Cam Ranh.

38. *Ibid.,* p 50.

39. *Ibid.,* pp 4-5.

40. Hist, 3d ARRGp, 1 Jul-30 Sep 1971, p 9.

41. *Ibid.,* p 8.

42. Hist, 37th ARRSq, 1 Jul-30 Sep 1971, pp 22-23.

43. 7AF PAD 71-7-21, Phu Cat.

44. Hist, 3d ARRGp, 1 Oct-31 Dec 1971, pp 8-9.

45. PAD 72-7-10, 7th AF, Jan 6, 1972; PAC SO G-35, Jan 27, 1972.

46. Hist, 3d ARRGp, Jan-Mar 1972, pp 5-2 5-4.

47. *Ibid.*

48. Msg, CSAF to 7AF, 092056Z Feb 72.

49. Hist, 39th ARRSq, Jan-Mar 1972, p 1.

50. Hist, 3d ARRGp, Jan-Mar 1972, p 11.

51. Hist, 3d ARRGp, Jul-Sep 72, p 2-2.

52. Dave Richard Palmer, *Summons of the Trumpet: U.S. Vietnam in Perspective* (San Rafael, Calif., 1978), pp 218-219.

53. Fitzgerald, *Fire in the Lake,* pp 8-9; Lynch, *USAF SAR in SEA, 1 Jul 69-31 Dec 70,* pp 73-81.

54. Hist, 3d ARRGp, Jan-Mar 1970, pp 29-30.

55. Lynch, *USAF SAR in SEA, 1 Jul 69-31 Dec 70,* p 78.

56. Maj A.J.C. Lavalle, ed., *Airpower and the 1972 Spring Invasion,* USAF Southeast Asia Monograph Series, Vol II (Washington, 1976), pp 39-40. (Hereafter cited as Lavalle, *Airpower and the Spring Invasion).*

57. Capt David G. Francis and Maj David R. Nelson, *Search and Rescue Operations in SEA, 1 April 1972-30 June 1973* (Hq PACAF, Project CHECO, Nov 27, 1974), p 38. (Hereafter cited as Francis and Nelson, *SAR Ops in SEA, 1 Apr 72-30 Jun 73).*

58. David K. Mann, *The 1972 Invasion of Military Region I: Fall of Quang Tri and Defense of Hue* (Hq PACAF, Project CHECO, Mar 15, 1973), pp 22-24. (Hereafter cited as Mann, *The 1972 Invasion);* Lavalle, *Airpower and the Spring Invasion,* p 39.

59. *Ibid.,* p 25.

60. Intvw, author with Col Jack Allison, Son Tay raider and Vice Comdr ARRS, 21 Apr 78.

61. Francis and Nelson, *SAR Ops in SEA, 1 Apr 72-30 Jun 73,* p 38.

62. *Ibid.*

63. Lavalle, *Airpower and the Spring Invasion,* p 41.

64. Intvw, author with Brig Gen Richard T. Kight, Comdr, Air Rescue Service, 1946-1952, Apr 22, 1978.

65. Schlight, *Rescue at Ban Phanop,* pp 12-13.

66. Quoted in Francis and Nelson, *SAR Ops in SEA, 1 Apr 72-30 Jun 73,* p 39.

67. Lavalle, *Airpower and the Spring Invasion,* p 49.

68. *Ibid.,* pp 49-50; intvw, author with Col Baylor R. Haynes, Apr 22, 1978.

69. Hist, 37th ARRSq, 1 Jul 72-30 Jun 73,

Vol VI, p 8.

70. Ted R. Sturm, "Miracle Mission," *Airman Magazine,* (Aug 1973), pp 44-46.

71. USAF Management Summary: Southeast Asia, July 27, 1973, p 14.

72. Office of the Secretary of Defense, Southeast Asia Statistical Summary, Table 305A.

73. *Ibid.,* table 350.

74. USAF Management Summary: Southeast Asia, Jul 24, 1972, p 25; USAF Management Summary: Southeast Asia, Feb 23, 1973, p 23.

75. USAF Management Summary: Southeast Asia, Jan 5, 1968, pp 14, 23, 50; Overton, *USAF SAR, Nov 67-Jun 69,* p 66.

76. Francis and Nelson, *SAR Ops in SEA, 1 Apr 72-30 Jun 73,* pp 4-5.

77. Zehnder intvw, Apr 22, 1978.

78. Msg, 7AF to CINCPACAF, 071036Z Nov 71; and Msg, CINCPACAF to CSAF, 160148Z Nov 71, subj: Combat ROC 15-17, RHAW for ACR HH-53.

79. Msg, 7AF to CINCPACAF, 210030Z Mar 72, subj: Combat ROC 6-72, Electronic Counter Measures (ECM) for HC-130Ps and ACR HH-53s.

80. Lowe, *SAR Ops in SEA, 1 Jan 71-31 Mar 72,* p 30.

81. Francis and Nelson, *SAR Ops in SEA, 1 Apr 72-30 Jun 73,* p 19.

82. *Ibid.,* p 16.

83. *Ibid.,* p 17; Ray Bonds, ed., *The Soviet War Machine: An Encyclopedia of Russian Military Equipment and Strategy* (New York, 1977), p 215.

84. Francis and Nelson, *SAR Ops in SEA, 1 Apr 72-30 Jun 73,* pp 16-17.

85. Msg, Hq ASD to CINCPACAF, 192020Z May 72, subj: BPE for Combat ROC 6-72, ECM Capability for Aircrew Recovery HH-53.

86. Francis and Nelson, *SAR Ops in SEA, 1 Apr 72-30 Jun 73,* pp 21-22.

87. Steve Birdsall, *The A-1 Skyraider* (New York, 1970), pp 20-21; Zehnder intvw, Apr 22, 1978.

88. Hist, 56th Special Operations Wing, Vol I, Oct-Dec 1972, p 37.

89. Hist, 3d ARRGp, Jul-Sep 1972, pp 4-2 4-3.

90. Hist, 56th SOW, Jan-Mar 1972, p 160.

91. *Ibid.,* p 2.

92. Msg, CSAF to CINCPACAF, 302211Z Mar 72, subj: Transfer of A-1 Aircraft to VNAF.

93. Movement Order no. 15, Dec 5, 1972.

94. Francis and Nelson, *SAR Ops in SEA, 1 Apr 72-30 Jun 73,* pp 4-5.

95. Hist, 56th SOW, Oct-Dec 72, pp 41-43.

96. Francis and Nelson, *SAR Ops in SEA, 1 Apr 72-30 Jun 73*, p 22.

97. *Ibid.*, pp 42-47.

98. Hist, 56th SOW, Oct-Dec 72, p 56.

99. Francis and Nelson, *SAR Ops in SEA, 1 Apr 72-30 Jun 73*, p 25.

100. Hist, 3d Tactical Fighter Squadron, 1 Jan-31 Mar 74, p 4.

101. Francis and Nelson, *SAR Ops in SEA, 1 Apr 72-30 Jun 73*, p 25.

102. Hq 7th AF, Commando Hunt VII Report, Jun 1972, p 242.

103. Hist, 56th SOW, Oct-Dec 72, p 124.

104. Francis and Nelson, *SAR Ops in SEA, 1 Apr 72-30 Jun 73*, pp 25-26.

105. *Ibid.*

106. Kalb and Kalb, *Kissinger*, p 420.

107. Hist, 3d ARRGp, Oct-Dec 72, p 3-2; Hist, 3d ARRGp, Jan-Mar 73, p 3-1.

108. Hist, 3d ARRGp, Jan-Mar 73, p 3-1.

109. *Ibid.*

110. *Ibid.*, pp 3-2 - 3-3.

Chapter VI

1. USAF Management Summary: Southeast Asia, Jun 21, 1973, pp 17-23.

2. Southeast Asia Statistical Summary, Nov 28, 1973, table 304.

3. USAF Management Summary: Southeast Asia, Sep 9, 1970, p 24 and 29.

4. *Ibid.*, pp 14, 44.

5. Lowe, *SAR Ops in SEA, 1 Jan 71-31 Mar 72*, p 36.

6. Francis and Nelson, *SAR Ops in SEA, 1 Apr 72-30 Jun 73*, p 32.

7. Hist, 40th Aerospace Rescue and Recovery Squadron, Oct-Dec 1971, p 9.

8. USAF Management Summary: Southeast Asia, Sep 28, 1973, p 14.

9. USAF Management Summary: Southeast Asia, Nov 30, 1973, p 23.

10. Hist, 3d ARRGp, Apr-Jun 73, p 4.

11. Hist, 3d ARRGp, Jul-Sep 73, pp 9-11.

12. Hist, 388th Tactical Fighter Wing, 1 Jan-31 Mar 74, p 32.

13. Msg, USSAG/7AF to CINCPAC, 300307Z Apr 74, subj: Commando Scrimmage IV.

14. Hist, 388th TFW, 1 Apr-30 Jun 74, Vol I, p 32.

15. Ltr, Hq 388th TFW Directorate of Operations to Director of Information, subj: Historical Report, 1 Jan 74-31 Mar 74, p 15.

16. Hist, 3d ARRGp, 1 Jan-31 Mar 74, p 15.

17. *Ibid.*

18. Mission Report, 40th ARRSq, Dec 21, 1972.

19. Msg, 13th AF ADVON, Udorn to 13th AF DO, 300750Z Feb 75, subj: AC-130/HH-53 SAR Integration; Hist, 16th Special Operations Squadron, Apr-Jun 75, p 8; Hist, 3d Tactical Fighter Squadron, 1 Apr-30 Jun 74, pp 4-5.

20. Hist, 3d ARRGp, 1 Jan-30 Jun 75, pp 8-12.

21. *Ibid.*, p. 6.

22. Intvw, author with Lt Col W.W. Michael, former 56th SOS member, Apr 12, 1978.

23. *Ibid.*

24. Lowe, *SAR Ops in SEA, 1 Jan 71-31 Mar 72*, pp 34-35.

25. Intvw, Michael, Apr 12, 1978.

26. USSAG/7AF CONPLAN 5060C, Eagle Pull.

27. Hist, 3d ARRGp, Jul-Sep 73, p 9.

28. CONPLAN 5060C, Jun 27, 1973, pp 6-7.

29. *Ibid.*

30. "The Bombing Stops, the Wait Begins", *Newsweek*, Aug 27, 1973, pp 31-32; *Air Force Magazine,* Military Balance 1973/74, Dec 1973, pp 106-107.

31. Appendix to Annex N, CONPLAN 5060C, pp N-2-1 - N-2-2.

32. Hist, Aerospace Rescue and Recovery Service, 1 Jul 74-31 Dec 75, Narrative, p 74.

33. Msg, USSAG/7AF to AIG 8713, 020031Z Mar 75, subj: Eagle Pull Readiness.

34. Msg, USSAG/7AF to AIG 8713, 270536Z Mar 75, subj: USSAG/7AF OPLAN 5060C-1-75, Special Instruction Frag, p 52.

35. *Ibid.*, p 10.

36. *Ibid.*, p 52.

37. Hist, ARRS, 1 Jul 74-31 Dec 75, p 74.

38. Msg, USSAG/7AF to CINCPAC,

161100Z May 75, subj: After Action Report on Eagle Pull, p 5.

39. Hist, ARRS, 1 Jul 74-31 Dec 75, p 74.

40. Milton R. Benjamin and Paul Brinkley-Rogers, "Farewell to Phnom Penh," *Newsweek,* Apr 21, 1975, p 27.

41. Msg, After Action Report on Eagle Pull, pp 4-5.

42. Msg, USSAG/7AF to AIG 8713, 110841Z Apr 75, subj: Eagle Pull Execute Message.

43. Msg, After Action Report on Eagle Pull, p 6; "Farewell," *Newsweek,* Apr 21, 1975, p 23.

44. Hist, ARRS, 1 Jul 74-31 Dec 75, p 75; Msg, 40th ARRSq to Hq ARRS, 151400Z Apr 75, subj: Eagle Pull Recap.

45. *Ibid.*

46. "Farewell," *Newsweek,* Apr 21, 1975, p 28.

47. Ltr, Maj Gen Ralph K. Sanders, Comdr, ARRS to Col Harold W. Wallace, Jr., Comdr, 41st ARRWg, Apr 28, 1975; Ltr, Lt Gen P.K. Carlton to Maj Gen Ralph K. Sanders, Apr 24, 1975.

48. Gen Van Tien Dung, *Our Great Spring Victory: An Account of the Liberation of South Vietnam* (New York, 1977), pp 24-26.

49. Wayne G. Peterson, Capt Wayne A. Myers, and Steven G. Bradshaw, *The Fall and Evacuation of South Vietnam,* (Hq PACAF, Apr 30, 1978), p 14.

50. Hist, CINCPAC, 1975, Appendix IV, Frequent Wind, p 19.

51. Msg, USDA SGN RVN to USSAG NKP, 300640Z Mar 75, subj: Aircraft Incident, pp 1-2; Frank Snepp, *Decent Interval* (New York, 1978), pp 257-61.

52. Intvw, author with Lt Col Charles N. Wood, J-2 MACV Representative to the 1972 Evacuation Plan Committee, May 8, 1978.

53. CONPLAN 5060V, Talon Vise, Jul 31, 1974.

54. Ltr, Lt Col Charles E. Trapp, Jr., Comdr 3d ARRGp, May 12, 1975, Doc. 1.

55. Snepp, *Decent Interval,* p 243.

56. Hist, CINCPAC, Frequent Wind, p 32.

57. Hist, ARRS, 1 Jul 74-31 Dec 75, p 76.

58. *Ibid.*

59. Ltr, Maj James J. Dupre, 3d ARRGp Plans Officer, to Hq ARRS/XP subj: Frequent Wind Mission Summary, May 12, 1975.

60. Briefing, ARRS Participation in Frequent Wind, p 7.

61. *Ibid.,* p 12.

62. Diary of Maj John F. Guilmartin, Jr., p 32.

63. Ltr, Maj J.F. Guilmartin, Jr., to 40th

ARRS/CC, May 12, 1975, subj: After Action Report on Operation Frequent Wind, p 3.

64. Joker/3d ARRGp HF Radio Log, p 1; and Intvw, author with Maj J.F. Guilmartin, Jr., 8 May 1978.

65. Guilmartin, After Action Report, p 3. The Jolly Green crews reported more opposition than those of other evacuation helicopters. The reason is probably that the ARRS choppers carried a crew of six rather than four like the CH-53s. Also, these extra crewmen, like the other rescue crewmen, were trained to spot small arms and antiaircraft fire.

66. Guilmartin, diary, p 41.

67. *Ibid.,* p 42.

68. *Ibid.,* p 41.

69. Joker/3d ARRGp Log, 14 Jan 75-15 May 75, p 29/1631; and Intvw, Guilmartin, May 8, 1978.

70. Joker/3d ARRGp HF Radio Log, p 5.

71. *Ibid.,* p 9.

72. Lt Col Thomas G. Tobin, et al., *Last Flight from Saigon,* USAF Southeast Asia Monograph Series, vol IV, monograph 6 (Washington, 1977), pp 107-109.

73. Snepp, *Decent Interval,* p 562.

74. Joker/3d ARRGp Log, pp 29/2325-29/2359.

75. Dupre, Frequent Wind Mission Summary, p 5; Guilmartin, diary, p 40.

76. Guilmartin, diary, p 46.

77. Reports of the Comptroller General of the United States Submitted to the Subcommittee on International Political and Military Affairs (U.S. House of Representatives), *Seizure of the Mayaguez,* Part IV, Oct 4, 1976, p 117.

78. "Victory at Sea," *Newsweek,* May 26, 1975, p 19.

79. Maj A.J.C. Lavalle, ed., *Fourteen Hours at Koh Tang,* USAF Southeast Asia Monograph Series, Vol III, Mono 5, (Washington, DC, 1978) p 95.

80. Msg, CINCPAC to Hq ARRS, 13230Z May 75, subj: SS Mayaguez Surveillance Operation, p 1.

81. Hist, 388th Tactical Figher Wing, 1 Apr-30 Jun 75, pp 27-34.

82. Msg, 56th SOW to CINCPACAF, subj: Mission Narrative, 191200Z May 75; and Msg, JCS to CINCPAC, subj: Khmer Seizure of Mayaguez, 131510Z May 75.

83. Guilmartin diary, p 53; Joker/3d ARRGp Log, p 13/1333; Capt John B. Taylor, "Air Mission Mayaguez," *Airman,* Jan 1976, p 40.

84. 56th SOW Mission Narative, May 19,

1975, p 3.

85. Hist, 388th TFW, 1 Apr-30 Jun 75, pp 27-34.

86. *Newsweek,* May 26, 1975, pp 20-21.

87. Hist, 388th TFW, 1 Apr-30 June 75, pp 27-34.

88. Assault on Koh Tang, Hq PACAF, DCS Plans and Operations, Jun 23, 1975, p 1.

89. *Ibid.,* p 7.

90. *Ibid.,* p 9.

91. Lavalle, *Fourteen Hours at Koh Tang,* p 107.

92. Hq PACAF, Assault on Koh Tang, p 9.

93. *Ibid.,* p 11.

94. Lavalle, *Fourteen Hours at Koh Tang,* p 116.

95. *Newsweek,* May 26, 1975, p 25.

96. Lavalle, *Fourteen Hours at Koh Tang,* pp 118-120.

97. Hq PACAF, Assault on Koh Tang, p 20.

98. 56th SOW Mission Narrative, May 19, 1975, pp 17-20.

99. Hq PACAF, Assasult on Koh Tang, p 20.

100. Intvw, Unk interviewer with Capt Donald W. Backlund and Capt Roland W. Purser, nd, p 9, in Hist, Aerospace Rescue and Recovery Service, 1 Jul 74-31 Dec 75, Vol VI, Supporting Documents. (Hereafter cited as Intvw, Backlund.)

101. Taylor, "Air Mission Mayaguez," *Airman,* p 46.

102. Intvw, Backlund, p 15.

103. *Ibid.;* Intvw, author with SSgt Harry W. Cash, Apr 23, 1978.

104. Hq PACAF, "Assault on Koh Tang," pp 32-35.

105. Lavalle, *Fourteen Hours at Koh Tang,* p 149.

106. Msg, 56th SOW to CINCPACAF, Mission Narrative, 191200Z May 75, p 42.

107. Hist, 3d Aerospace Rescue and Recovery Group, 1 Jul 75-31 Jun 76, pp vii-viii.

108. *Ibid.,* p 13.

109. *Ibid.,* p 17.

110. *Ibid.,* pp 14-17; Little, "Chronology", pp 95-96.

111. Hist, 3d ARRGp, 1 Jul 75-31 Jan 76, p viii.

112. Little, "Chronology", p 96.

113. Carl Berger, ed., *The United States Air Force in Southeast Asia: An Illustrated History,* (Washington, 1977) p 243; USAF Management Summary: Southeast Asia, 28 Sep 73, p 13 and 24.

114. Intvw, Guilmartin, 2 Aug 78; USAF Management Summary: Southeast Asia, 24 Jul 72, p 25; USAF Management Summary: Southeast Asia, 23 Feb 73, p 27.

115. Lavalle, *Fourteen Hours at Koh Tang,* pp 95-151; Msg, 56th SOW to CINCPACAF, 192100Z May 75, Appendix, p 43; and Joker/3d ARRGp Log, see entries for 14-15 May.

Glossary

A-1	Propeller-driven, single-engine, land-or-carrier-based multipurpose aircraft capable of carrying heavy bombloads in an attack role. It was used as a rescue escort aircraft under the call sign "Sandy" until late 1972.
A-7	Single-engine, land-or-carrier-based multipurpose jet aircraft used as a rescue escort with the call sign "Sandy" after late 1972.
A-37	Cessna's light ground-attack jet aircraft designed for COIN operation.
AA	Antiaircraft
AAA	Antiaircraft Artillery
ABCCC	Airborne Command and Control Center
AC	Aircraft Commander
ACR	Aircrew Rescue
AFB	Air Force Base
AFM	Air Force Manual
AFR	Air Force Regulation
AFSC	Air Force Systems Command
AIRA	Air Attache
AMC	Airborne Mission Controller
AMEMB	American Embassy
AOC	Air Operations Center
ARMA	Army Attache
ARRGp	Aerospace Rescue and Recovery Group
ARRS	Aerospace Rescue and Recovery Service
ARRSq	Aerospace Rescue and Recovery Squadron
ARRTC	Aerospace Rescue and Recovery Training Center
ARRWg	Aerospace Rescue and Recovery Wing
ARS	Air Rescue Service
ATC	Air Training Command
Barrell Roll	United States air interdiction in eastern Laos (1964) and later limited to air activity in northern Laos.
Bell Tone	U.S. Air Force air defense detachment at Don Muang Royal Thai Air Force Base, Thailand.
BUFF	Big Ugly Friendly Fellow — name given to the Sikorsky HH-53 helicopter by the rescue crews. It became a rescue helicopter call sign.
C-47	Propeller-driven, twin-engine, low-wing monoplane used as a transport, cargo carrier, gunship (AC-47) and, under the designation SC-47, served in the Air Rescue Service in the 1950s.
C-130	A high-wing, all-metal, medium range, land-based monoplane used as a transport, cargo carrier, gunship (AC-130) and airborne command post. Under the designation HC-130P it flew as a rescue airborne command post and was modified to give it the capability to refuel helicopters.
CAP	Combat Air Patrol/Civil Air Patrol
CARA	Combat Aircrew Recovery Aircraft
CAS	Controlled American Source (C.I.A.)/Continental Air Services
CBU	Cluster Bomb Unit
CH-34	Sikorsky's "Choctaw" S-58 helicopter equipped with a four-blade main rotor and a tail stabilizer rotor. Also designated H-34, the Choctaw served in Southeast Asia with the U.S. Army, U.S. Marine Corps, Vietnamese Air Force, Royal Laotain Air Force, Royal Thai Air Force and Air America.
CH-47	Boeing's twin-turbine helicopter with two 3-blade tandem rotors. Used as a troop transport and heavy lift helicopter by the U.S. Army, U.S. Marines, and the ARVN.

CH-53	Sikorsky's large, twin-turbine helicopter with a single six-blade main rotor and a four-blade stabilizing tail rotor. Used by the U.S. Air Force and the U.S. Marines as a transport.
CHECO	Contemporary Historical Evaluation of Counterinsurgency Operations (1962); Contemporary Historical Evaluation of Combat Operations (1965); Contemporary Historical Examination of Current Operations (1970).
CIA	Central Intelligence Agency
CINC	Commander-in-Chief
CINCPAC	Commander-in-Chief Pacific
CINCPACAF	Commander-in-Chief Pacific Air Forces
CJCS	Chairman Joint Chiefs of Staff
CNO	Chief of Naval Operations
COFS	Chief of Staff
COIN	Counterinsurgency
COMUSMACV	Commander, United States Military Assistance Command, Vietnam.
Corona Harvest	U.S. Air Force evaluation of air operations in Southeast Asia.
COSVN	Central Office for South Vietnam (Viet Cong Headquarters)
Crown	Airborne rescue command post
CSAF	Chief of Staff, Air Force
DASC	Direct Air Support Center
Det	Detachment
DMZ	Demilitarized Zone
Duckbutt	An over-water, precautionary orbit flown by rescue aircraft.
Eagle Pull	Code name for the evacuation of Phnom Penh in 1975.
EB-66	Douglas twin-engine, high-wing, reconnaissance/bomber which had several configurations for ELINT or for electronic jamming to protect strike forces.
ECM	Electronic Countermeasures
ECM Pod	An aerodynamic container which housed multiple transmitters and associated electronic devices. It was carried on an aircraft externally and provided aircraft self-protection in penetration of enemy defenses.
E&E	Escape and Evasion
ELINT	Electronic Intelligence
EWO	Electronic Warfare Officer
F	Fighter
F-4	McDonnell-Douglas "Phantom II" twin-jet, low-wing, twin-place, fighter-bomber used extensively in both the air superiority and attack missions in Southeast Asia.
F-5	Northrop's single-seat, twin-engine jet fighter used briefly by the U.S. Air Force in South Vietnam. Eventually F-5A and twin-seat F-5B as well as more advanced F-5E fighters made up the backbone of the Vietnamese Air Force.
F-8	Ling-Temco-Vought's single-engine, high-wing, carrier-or-land based fighter-bomber used by the U.S. Navy and U.S. Marines in Southeast Asia.
F-51	North American's single-engine, single-seat, propeller-driven fighter developed at the beginning of World War II and used in the Korean War in the ground attack and rescue escort mission. Known as the "Mustang".
F-82	North American's "Twin Mustang". A twin-engine, twin-boom, two-place fighter comprised of two F-51 fuselages.
F-86	North American "Saber", a single-engine, swept wing, jet fighter and interceptor of the Korean War era.
F-100	North American "Super Saber", a supersonic, single-engine, single-place, air-superiority and ground attack fighter.
F-102	Convair (General Dynamics) single-engine, delta-wing, single-place jet interceptor based in South Vietnam and later at Udorn Royal Thai Air

	Force Base, Thailand. These planes flew some rescue combat air patrol missions.
F-104	Lockheed's single-engine, single-place jet interceptor. Used briefly in Vietnam in 1964 and 1965 in the air superiority and ground attack role.
F-105	Republic Aviation's "Thunderchief" was a single-engine, high wing, jet fighter-bomber. The "Thud", as it was affectionately called, carried the brunt of the air war to North Vietnam. In the two-seat F-105F version it flew surface-to-air-mission suppression missions.
FAC	Forward Air Controller
FANK	Forces Armées National Khmer (Cambodian Army)
FAR	Forces Armées du Royaume (Royal Laotian Army)
Farm Gate	Detachment 2, 4400th Combat Crew Training Squadron and later the U.S. Air Force air commando unit at Bien Hoa Air Base, Vietnam.
Fast movers	High performance aircraft
FEAF	Far East Air Force
FIR	Flight Information Region
Fishbed	Code name for the Soviet-built MiG-21 jet fighter
FM	Frequency Modulation
FNRS	Full Night Recovery System
FOL	Forward Operating Location
Fragmentary Operations Order	(Frag) The daily supplement to the standard operations orders governing the conduct of the air war. It contained mission numbers, targets, type of ordnance, time-on-target, and other instruction.
Frequent Wind	Code name for the evacuation of Saigon in April 1975.
Ftr	Fighter
FWMF	Free World Military Forces
GVN	Government of Vietnam
H-5	The Sikorsky S-51 was a single-engine with either a two-blade metal or a three-blade wood rotor and a two-blade tail stabilizing rotor. Designated the H-5 by the Air Force, this helicopter saw limited rescue action in Korea before being replaced by the H-19.
H-19	Sikorsky's all metal, semi-monocoque fuselage helicopter. It had one all-metal three-blade main rotor and an all-metal two-blade anti-torque tail rotor. The engine was mounted in front. The H-19 served in the Air Rescue Service from 1951 into the early 1960's but saw no action in Vietnam.
H-21	Piasecki's all-metal, semi-monocoque-constructed helicopter. It had two 3-blade, all-metal rotors arranged in tandem and turning in opposite directions. Used by the ARS in the 1950's.
H-34	See CH-34.
H/HH-43	Kaman Aircraft Corporation's twin-rotor, single-engine helicopter designed for crash-rescue operations and the local base rescue mission. Rotors are intermeshing, counter-rotating, each with two blades, mounted side-by-side.
H/HH-3	The Rescue version of the Sikorsky CH-3. See CH-3.
H/HH-53	The Rescue version of the Sikorsky CH-53. See CH-53.
HC-130	See C-130.
He-59	Heinkel's twin-engine, propeller-driven, biplane amphibian used by the *Seenotdienst* (German Air-Sea Rescue Service) in the World War II.
HF/DF	High Frequency/Direction Finding
HU-1	Bell Helicopter's "Huey" was a single-engine, 2-blade single rotor helicopter with a two blade tail rotor. It was used by the U.S. Army, U.S. Marines, ARVN, and Air America.
HU-16	Grumman's "Albatross" propeller-driven, twin-engine, high-wing, amphibious aircraft was used by the ARS and ARRS for search and rescue missions from 1949 through 1967.
IFF	Identification, Friend or Foe is a system that uses electronic transmis-

	sions to which equipment carried by friendly aircraft automatically responds by emitting impulses that distinguish them from enemy aircraft.
IR	Infrared
Iron Hand	Surface-to-air missile suppression mission.
JANAF	Joint Army Navy Air Force
JCS	Joint Chiefs of Staff
JCSM	Joint Chiefs of Staff Memorandum
Joker	Call sign for the Joint Rescue Coordination Center
Jolly Green Giant (JG)	Call sign and nickname for the HH-3E and HH-53 helicopter.
JRCC	Joint Rescue Coordination Center (previously JSARC)
JSARC	Joint Search and Rescue Center (later JRCC)
Jungle Jim	The 4400the Combat Crew Training Squadron and subsequent air commando activity at Eglin Air Force Base, Florida.
Khmer Rouge	Cambodian Communists
King	Call sign of the HC-130P SAR airborne command aircraft. (previously Crown)
Kts.	Knots
LBR	Local Base Rescue
Lbs	Pounds
Lima Site (LS)	Temporary landing strip in Laos
Lima Site 36	Located at Na Khang in northern Laos, LS 36 was a staging area for SAR operations and a resupply point for friendly guerrillas. It was lost to the enemy in March and April 1967.
LLLTV	Low Light Level Television
LNRS	Limited Night Recovery System
LOC	Lines of Communication
LORAN	Long Range Navigation (also loran)
Ltr	Letter
LZ	Landing Zone
MAAG	Military Assistance Advisory Group
MAC	Military Airlift Command
MACSOG	Military Assistance Command, Studies and Observation Group
MACTHAI	Military Assistance Command, Thailand
MACV	Military Assistance Command, Vietnam
MAP	Military Assistance Program
MATS	Military Air Transport Service (later Military Airlift Command)
Medevac	Medical Evacuation
Memo	Memorandum
MG	Machine Gun
Mig	Mikoyan and Gurevich, Soviet designers of a series of fighter aircraft.
Mig-15	Soviet-built, single-engine jet fighter of Korean War vintage.
Mig-17	Soviet-built, single-engine jet fighter used by North Vietnam and Cambodia.
Mig-19	Soviet-built, twin-engine jet fighter used by North Vietnam.
Mig-21	Soviet-built, single-engine jet fighter used by North Vietnam.
MIGCAP	Anti-Mig Combat Air Patrol
Mod	Modification
MR	Military Region/Memorandum for the Record
Msg	Message
Mule Team	Early logistical support in Vietnam
NAC	Non-aircrew
Nail	Call sign for a FAC aircraft of the 2nd TASS at Nakhon Phanom RTAF, Thailand, operating in Laos
Napalm	A petroleum jelly fire bomb
NASA	National Aeronautics and Space Administration
NBL	No Bomb Line
NCO	Non-commissioned Officer

NKP	Nakhon Phanom
NM/nm	Nautical Mile
NMCC	National Military Command Center
NRS	Night Recovery System
NVA	North Vietnamese Army
NVA/PL	North Vietnamese/Pathet Lao
NVN	North Vietnam(ese)
NVNAF	North Vietnamese Air Force
O-1	Cessna's "Bird Dog" was a single-engine, 2-place, closed cabin, high-wing, strut-braced liaison and observation aircraft.
OL	Operating Location
Oplan	Operations Plan
OSC	On-Scene-Commander
OSD	Office of the Secretary of Defense
Out-country	Operations in countries other than South Vietnam
OV-10	North American's "Bronco" was a twin-engine, turbo-prop, 2-place, twin-tail observation and attack aircraft used by FACs and in rescue operations toward the end of the war.
PACAF	Pacific Air Forces
PACAFLT	Pacific Fleet
PACOM	Pacific Command
PAD	Program Action Directive
PARC	Pacific Air Rescue Center
Pathet Lao	A Laotian communist force or person.
Pave Nail	The OV-10 Pave Spot program expanded to include integrated loran.
Pave Spot	An OV-10 night observation device with bore-sighted laser range designator.
PBY-5A	Consolidated's "Catalina" was a propeller-driven, twin-engine, high-wing, strut-braced, all metal flying boat used for air-sea rescue missions in World War II.
PCS	Permanent change of station.
PDJ	Plaines des Jars (Plain of Jars) A militarily strategic area north-northeast of Vientiane, Laos.
Pedro	The call sign of the HH-43 local base rescue helicopters.
POL	Petroleum, Oil and Lubricants
POW	Prisoner of War
PSP	Pierced Steel Planking
PZ	Pickup Zone (helicopters)
Queen	The call sign for the OL-A Rescue Coordination Center at Tan Son Nhut
RAF	Royal Air Force (United Kingdom)
Ranch Hand	C-123 defoliation and herbicide operations
Raven	U.S. Air Force FACs operating in Laos.
RCA	Riot Control Agents
RCC	Rescue Coordination Center
RESCAP	Rescue Combat Air Patrol
RESCORT	Rescue Escort
RF-4	Reconnaissance version of the McDonnell-Douglas F-4.
RF-101	Reconnaissance version of the McDonnell-Douglas F-101.
RHAW	Radar Homing and Warning
RLAF	Royal Laotian Air Force
RLG	Royal Laotian Government
ROE	Rules of Engagement, operating rules and restrictions on air operations
Rolling Thunder	The nickname assigned to air strikes against selected targets and lines of communications in North Vietnam (March 1965 - October 1968).
RT-33	Reconnaissance version of the Lockheed T-33 single-engine, two place jet trainer.
RTAF	Royal Thai Air Force

RTAFB	Royal Thai Air Force Base
RVN	Republic of Vietnam
RVNAF	Republic of Vietnam Armed Forces
RF-101	Reconnaissance version of the McDonnell F-101 twin-engine jet fighter.
SA-2	Soviet-built "Guideline" surface-to-air-missile (SAM) with a range of 25 miles. Provided the nucleus of NVN's SAM defense.
SA-3	Soviet-built "Goa" mobile low-altitude SAM system introduced in the later part of the war.
SA-7	The Soviet "Grail" hand-held heat-seeking missile provided to the NVA and the Khmer Rouge in 1972.
SA-16	See HU-16
SAC	Strategic Air Command
SACSA	Special Assistant to the Director, JCS Joint Staff for Counterinsurgency and Special Activities.
SAF	Secretary of the Air Force
SAFE Areas	Selected Areas For Evasion; areas in SEA which were relatively free of enemy influence.
SAM	Surface-to-Air Missile
Sandy	The call sign for A-1 rescue escort aircraft located at Nakhon Phanom RTAFB, Thailand.
SAR	Search and Rescue
SARCAP	Search and Rescue Combat Air Patrol
SARTF	Search and Rescue Task Force
SB-17	Boeing's four-engine, low-wing bomber converted for air-sea rescue missions. It served in the European Theater during World War II and continued in the ARS inventory into the 1950s.
SB-29	Boeing's four-engine, mid-wing bomber converted for air-sea rescue missions. It served in the Pacific Theater in World War II and continued in the ARS inventory to serve in the Korean War.
SC-54	Douglas' "Rescuemaster" was a four-engine, low-wing transport converted for rescue. It served through the 1950s and into the 1960s seeing limited duty in Vietnam in 1965.
SEA	Southeast Asia
SEAOR	Southeast Asia Operational Requirement
SEATO	Southeast Asia Treaty Organization
SECAF	Secretary of the Air Force
SECDEF	Secretary of Defense
SECSTATE	Secretary of State
Seenotdienst	German Air-Sea Rescue Service in World War II
SERE	Survival, Evasion, Resistance and Escape
SIGINT	Signal Intelligence
SOS	Special Operations Squadron
SOW	Special Operations Wing
Spad	Call sign for the A-1 SAR support aircraft at Da Nang AB, RVN (later called Sandy)
Spectre	Call sign for the AC-130 gunships
SPO	System Program Office
Steel Tiger (SL)	Geographic area of southern Laos designated by 7th Air Force to facilitate planning and operations.
SVN	South Vietnam
T	Trainer
T-28	North American's "Trojan" was a propeller-driven, single-engine, low-wing, all-metal monoplane with a crew of two. The T-28D version is an attack plane capable of carrying a variety of ordnance and was used by the Vietnamese Air Force, Royal Laotian Air Force and the Khmer Air Force.
TAC	Tactical Air Command
TACAIR	Tactical Air

180

TACAN	Tactical Air Navigation System
TACC	Tactical Air Control Center
Task Force Alpha (TFA)	A filter point for sensor information received from sensors emplanted along the Ho Chi Minh Trail. It was organized in 1967 under the command of 7th Air Force at Tan Son Nhut AB, Vietnam, and later moved to Nakhon Phanom RTAFB, Thailand.
TASS/TASSq	Tactical Air Support Squadron
TDY	Temporary Duty
TFG/TFGp	Tactical Fighter Group
TFS/TFSq	Tactical Fighter Squadron
TFW/TFWg	Tactical Fighter Wing
TS	Top Secret
TSN	Tan Son Nhut
TUOC	Tactical Unit Operations Center
Twenty Alternate (20A)	Major General Van Pao's Meo guerrilla and CIA headquarters in northern Laos. A forward operating location for rescue helicopters.
34 Alpha (34A Operations)	Clandestine operations against North Vietnam.
U	Utility Aircraft
(U)	Unclassified
UHF	Ultra High Frequency
Unk	Unknown
URC-64	A small survival radio carried by aircrews
US	United States
USA	United States Army
USAF	United States Air Force
USAIRA	United States Air Attache
USAmb	United States Ambassador
USMC	United States Marine Corps
USN	United States Navy
USSAG/7AF	US Support Activities Group/7Air Force
USSR	Union of Soviet Socialist Republics
VC	Viet Cong
VC/NVA	Viet Cong/North Vietnamese Army
VCS	Vice Chief of Staff
VFR	Visual Flight Rules
VHF	Very High Frequency
Viet Minh	Initial description of Vietnamese Communists. It was later applied to North Vietnamese forces who entered Laos prior to regular North Vietnamese Army troops. By the early 1960s the term had fallen into disuse.
VNAF	South Vietnamese Air Force
VP	Vang Pao (Laotian general)
V/STOL	Vertical and/or Short Takeoff and Landing
VTOL	Vertical Takeoff and Landing
Water Pump	Detachment 6, 1st Air Commando Wing (USAF) deployed to Thailand in 1964 and later applied to Detachment 1, 56th Special Operations Wing at Udorn RTAFB, Thailand.

Bibliographic Note

GOVERNMENTAL SOURCES

Sources located at The Air University's Albert F. Simpson Historical Research Center, Maxwell Air Force Base, Alabama, were of primary importance in writing the history of search and rescue operations in Southeast Asia. The Simpson Center holds both secondary and primary sources in original or "hard" copies and also has microfilm of most documents. Microfilm copies of original documents are available in the Office of Air Force History in Washington, D.C. However, these copies are of varying quality and are as yet incomplete.

In 1962 the U.S. Air Force began an extensive effort to identify and collect documents on its role in the conflicts of Southeast Asia by establishing the Project Contemporary Historical Evaluation of Counterinsurgency Operations (CHECO), later called Contemporary Historical Evaluation of Combat Operations. CHECO officers and historians worked with the Air Force commands and agencies in Southeast Asia to procure selected documents pertinent to historical research. Additionally, CHECO historians wrote accounts of operations which are of varying quality but useful as references for source documentation.

Anderson, Capt. B. Conn. *USAF Search and Rescue in Southeast Asia (1961-1966)*. Hq PACAF: Project CHECO, 1966.

Durkee, Maj. Richard A. *USAF Search and Rescue in Southeast Asia, July 1966-November 1967*. Hq PACAF: Project CHECO, 1968.

Francis, Capt. David G., and Nelson, Maj. David R. *Search and Rescue Operations in SEA, 1 April 1972-30 June 1973*. Hq PACAF: Project CHECO, 1974.

Hale, TSgt. Beverly, and Helmka, MSgt. Robert T. *USAF Operations From Thailand, 1964-1965*. Hq PACAF: Project CHECO, 1966.

Lowe, Lt. Col. LeRoy W. *Search and Rescue Operations in SEA, 1 January 1971-31 March 1972*. Hq PACAF: Project CHECO, 1972.

Lynch, Walter F. *USAF Search and Rescue in Southeast Asia, 1 July 1969-31 Dec 1970*. Hq PACAF: Project CHECO, 1971.

Mann, David K. *The 1972 Invasion of Military Region I: Fall of Quang Tri and Defense of Hue*. Hq PACAF: Project CHECO, 1973.

Overton, Maj. James B. *USAF Search and Rescue, November 1967-June 1969*. Hq PACAF: Project CHECO, 1970.

Schlight, Maj. John. *Rescue at Ban Phanop, 5-7 December 1969*. Hq PACAF: Project CHECO, 1970.

Smith, Capt. Mark E. *USAF Reconnaissance in Southeast Asia (1961-1966)*. Hq PACAF: Project CHECO, 1966.

Williams, P.Y. *Aerospace Rescue and Recovery in Southeast Asia*. Maxwell AFB, Ala.: Project CHECO Special Report, 1969.

Official histories and monographs, written from World War II through the Vietnam conflict, are generally available to qualified researchers and many have been published in unclassified form. Some of the official histories used in this book were still in manuscript form awaiting publication. Those official histories which have not been published are located in the Office of Air Force History and at the Albert F. Simpson Center. Project Corona Harvest documents, histories written in an effort to determine what "lessons could be learned" from on-going Air Force operations, are located in the Office of Air Force History.

Anthony, Maj. Victor B., and Sexton, Lt. Col. Richard R. "A History of U.S. Air Force Operations in Northern Laos." Washington, D.C.: Office of Air Force History, not yet published.

Berger, Carl. *The United States Air Force in Southeast Asia: An Illustrated History.* Washington, D.C.: Office of Air Force History, 1972.

Craven, Wesley Frank and Cate, James Lea. eds. *The Army Air Forces in World War II. Vol. VII: Services Around the World.* Chicago: University of Chicago Press, 195 .

Crozier, Lt Col Gordon W. *USAF Search and Rescue in Southeast Asia.* Vol. 1: *1954 - 31 March 1968.* Scott AFB, Ill.: Hq ARRS, Project Corona Harvest, 1969.

Crozier, Lt Col Gordon W.; Jacobs, Lt Col Robert F.; and Shrigley, Robert F. *USAF Search and Rescue in Southeast Asia.* Vol II: *Joint Search and Rescue Center (JSARC) in Southeast Asia, 1954-31 March 1968.* Scott AFB, Ill.: Hq ARRS, Project Corona Harvest, 1969.

Crozier, Lt Col Gordon W.; Jacobs, Lt Col Robert F.; and Shrigley, Robert F. *USAF Search and Rescue in Southeast Asia.* Vol III: *Local Base Rescue (LBR) in Southeast Asia, 1954-31 March 1968.* Scott AFB, Ill.: Hq ARRS, Project Corona Harvest, 1968.

Crozier, Lt Col Gordon W.; Jacobs, Lt Col Robert F.; and Shrigley, Robert F. *USAF Search and Rescue in Southeast Asia.* Vol IV: *Aircrew Recovery in Southeast Asia, 1965 - 31 March 1968.* Scott AFB, Ill.: Hq ARRS, Project Corona Harvest, 1968.

Futrell, Robert F.; Mosley, Brig Gen Lawson S.; and Simpson, Albert F. *The United States Air Force in Korea, 1950-1953.* (New York: Duell, 1961).

Futrell, Robert F. "The United States Air Force in Southeast Asia: The Assistance and Combat Advisory Years, 1950-1965." Washington, D.C.: Office of Air Force History draft manuscript, 1975.

Futrell, Robert F. and Blumenson, Martin. *"The Air Force in Southeast Asia: The Advisory Years, to 1965."* Washington, D.C.: Office of Air Force History, 1980.

Futrell, Robert F. *Evolution of Airpower in Southeast Asia.* Vol I: *1954-1961.* Maxwell AFB, Ala.: Project Corona Harvest, 1968.

Futrell, Robert F. *Chronology of Significant Airpower Events in Southeast Asia, 1950-1968.* Maxwell AFB, Ala.: Aerospace Studies Institute, Project Corona Harvest, 1968.

Hess, Lt Col Carl (Luftwaffe, Ret.). "The Air-Sea Rescue Services of the Luftwaffe in World War II." Maxwell AFB, Ala.: unpublished manuscript, 1955.

Hermes, Walter G. *The United States Army in the Korea War.* Vol. II: *Truce Tent and Fighting Front.* Washington, D.C.: Office of the Chief of Military History, United States Army, 1966.

Lavalle, Maj A.J.C., ed. *Airpower and the Spring Invasion.* Vol. II, USAF Monograph Series. Washington, D.C.: Government Printing Office, 1976.

Lavalle, Maj A.J.C., ed. *Fourteen Hours at Koh Tang.* Vol. III, USAF Monograph Series. Washington, D.C.: Government Printing Office, 1977.

Little, Donald D. "Chronology of Aerospace Rescue and Recovery Service, 1946-1976." Scott AFB, Ill.: Military Airlift Command History Office, draft manuscript, 1976.

Tobin, Lt Col Thomas G., et. al. *Last Flight From Saigon*. Vol. IV, USAF Monograph Series, Washington, D.C.: Government Printing Office, 1977.

Van Staaveren, Jacob. *USAF Plans and Policies in South Vietnam, 1961-1963*. Washington, D.C.: Office of Air Force History, 1965.

USAF Historical Study 95, *Air-Sea Rescue, 1945-1952*. Maxwell AFB, Ala.: Research Studies Institute, 1954.

USAF Historical Study 72, *United States Air Force Operations in the Korean Conflict, 1 November 1950-June 1952*. Maxwell AFB, Ala.: Research Studies Institute, 1956.

USAF Historical Study 127, *United States Air Force Operations in the Korean Conflict, 1 July 1952-27 July 1953*. Maxwell AFB, Ala.: Research Studies Institute, 1956.

Office of the Chief of Military History, United States Army. *Helicopters in Korea, 1 July 1951-31 August 1953*. Seoul, Korea: 8086th Army Unit Military History Detachment, 1954.

Rand 2M-119, *Lessons of the War in Indochina*. Santa Monica, Cal.: Rand Corporation, 1967.

Study, "HH-43 and HU-16 Operations in SEA." Scott AFB, Ill.: Hq ARS, 1964.

The Office of Air Force History maintains a large and vital unit histories program which requires each Air Force unit to document its activities on a regular basis. Although unit histories are unpublished, they are of great importance in tracing the day-by-day development of Air Force operations. For this study of search and rescue operations, unit histories were obtained from the Albert F. Simpson Historical Research Center and the Historical Office of the Military Airlift Command to supplement those held in the Office of Air Force History.

Quality of the unit histories varies greatly. Generally, the major command and wing histories are detailed, well written, and comprehensive. Histories written at the squadron and detachment level tended to be repetitive and lacking in overall professional quality.

Second Air Division, 15 November 1961-8 October 1962.

313th Air Division, 1 July 1964-30 June 1965.

Headquarters, United States Military Assistance Command, Vietnam, 1968, Annex F.

CINCPAC, 1975, Appendix IV, Frequent Wind.

Military Air Transport Service, 1 January-31 December, 1961.

Air Rescue Service (MATS), 1 January-31 December 1960.

Air Rescue Service (MATS), 1 January-31 June 1961.

Air Rescue Service, 1 January-31 December 1965.

Aerospace Rescue and Recovery Service, Vol. I, 1 January-30 June 1966.

Aerospace Rescue and Recovery Service, 1 July-31 December 1966.

Aerospace Rescue and Recovery Service, Vol. I, 1 January-30 June 1970.

Aerospace Rescue and Recovery Service, 1 July 1970-30 June 1971, Annex, "The Son Tay Raid."

Aerospace Rescue and Recovery Service, 1 July 1974-31 December 1975.

3904th Composite Wing, 1 August-31 August 1953.

56th Special Operations Wing, 1 January-31 March 1972.

56th Special Operations Wing, 1 October-31 December 1972.

388th Tactical Fighter Wing, 1 January-31 March 1974.

388th Tactical Figher Wing, 1 April-30 June 1974.

388th Tactical Figher Wing, 1 April-30 June 1975.

3d Aerospace Rescue and Recovery Group, 1 April-30 June 1966.

3d Aerospace Rescue and Recovery Group, 1 July-30 September 1967.

3d Aerospace Rescue and Recovery Group, 1 January-31 March 1970.
3d Aerospace Rescue and Recovery Group, 1 July-30 September 1971.
3d Aerospace Rescue and Recovery Group, 1 October-31 December 1971.
3d Aerospace Rescue and Recovery Group, 1 January-31 March 1972.
3d Aerospace Rescue and Recovery Group, 1 July-30 September 1972.
3d Aerospace Rescue and Recovery Group, 1 January-31 March 1973.
3d Aerospace Rescue and Recovery Group, 1 April-30 June 1973.
3d Aerospace Rescue and Recovery Group, 1 July-30 September 1973.
3d Aerospace Rescue and Recovery Group, 1 January-30 June 1975.
3d Aerospace Rescue and Recovery Group, 1 July 1975-31 January 1976.
37th Aerospace Rescue and Recovery Squadron, 1 July-30 September 1971.
37th Aerospace Rescue and Recovery Squadron, 1 July 1972-30 June 1973.
39th Aerospace Rescue and Recovery Squadron, 1 January-31 March 1972.
40th Aerospace Rescue and Recovery Squadron, 1 October-31 December 1971.
3d Tactical Fighter Squadron, 1 January-31 March 1974.

End of Tour Reports and interviews are important documents because they provide the human insights which escape formal documentation. The U.S. Air Force established a Southeast Asia End of Tour Report program in 1962 to offer senior officers completing a tour of duty in an area threatened by insurgency the opportunity to summarize their experiences in their own words. Under Pacific Air Forces and the Office of Air Force History, the End of Tour Report program was expanded to allow virtually all officers the same opportunity to critique their Southeast Asia experience.

The Southeast Asia Oral History Program, started in 1967, attempted to obtain tape-recorded interviews with key personnel involved in the war. Most of these interviews have been transcribed and are located in the Office of Air Force History and in the Alfred F. Simpson Historical Research Center. The author conducted an extensive interview program in an attempt to talk to as many people who flew rescue missions as he possibly could in the time allowed. Sometimes these interviews were conducted over the telephone. Attendance at the Jolly Green Giants Helicopter Pilot's annual reunion greatly enhanced this process. Together with End of Tour Reports, interviews help to fill the gap in official documentation and provide useful insights that are normally excluded from the formal reporting systems.

Allison, Col John V. Son Tay Raider and Vice Commander, ARRS. Interviewed by the Ft. Walton Beach, Fla., April 21, 1978.
Berryhill, Col James V. HH-43F pilot. Interviewed by the author, Maxwell AFB, Ala., May 2, 1977.
Brown, Col Royal A. Son Tay Raider. Interviewed by Lt Col V.H. Gallacher and Maj. Lynn R. Officer, Eglin AFB, Fla., February 9, 1973.
Cash, SSgt Harry W. Parajumper on the Mayaguez Rescue Mission. Interviewed by the author, Ft. Walton Beach, Fla., April 23, 1978.
Colcomb, Col Albert L. Commander, 37th ARRSq, End of Tour Report, February 10, 1971.
Coymer, Lt Col Donald F. HC-130P pilot, 39th ARRSq, End of Tour Report, December 10, 1969.
Curtis, Col Thomas. Former Prisoner of War at the Son Tay camp. Interviewed by the author, Ft. Walton Beach, Fla., April 22, 1972.

Dunn, Col Harry P. HH-3/HH-53 Systems Project Officer, 1964-1972. Interviewed by the author, Rockville, Md., October 19, 1977 and February 6, 1979.

Ferrell, Maj Joseph B. Rescue Crew Commander, Detachment 1, 40th ARRSq, End of Tour Report, October 29, 1968.

Harris, Lt Col William M., IV. Commander, 37th ARRSq, End of Tour Report, June 10, 1972.

Haynes, Col Baylor R. Commander, 37th ARRSq. Interviewed by the author, Ft. Walton Beach, Fla., April 22, 1978.

Kight, Brig Gen Richard T. Commander, Air Rescue Service, 1946-1952. Interviewed by the author, Ft. Walton Beach, Fla., April 22, 1978.

Manor, Brig Gen Leroy J. USAF Joint Contingency Task Force Commander. Interviewed by Dr Charles Hildreth and William J. McQuillen, Eglin AFB, Fla., December 31, 1970.

Michael, Lt Col W.W. 56th SOSq navigator. Interviewed by the author, Washington, D.C.: April 12, 1978.

Montrem, Lt Col Alfred C. Son Tay raider. Interviewed by the author, Ft. Walton Beach, Fla., April 22, 1978.

Ratcliffe, Lt Col Chester R. Commander, 40th ARRSq. Unknown interviewer, Udorn RTAFB, Thailand, May 20, 1969.

Saunders, Maj Alan W. Commander of the first rescue detachment in Vietnam. Unknown interviewer, Saigon, RVN, July 1, 1964.

Smith, Capt Arthur E. Rescue Crew commander. Unknown interviewer, Udorn RTAFB, Thailand, November 21, 1968.

Sohle, Col Frederick V., Jr. Commander, 3d ARRGp, 1969-1970. Interviewed by Lt. Col. Leroy W. Lowe, Saigon, RVN, March 2, 1972.

Stambaugh, Col Philip. Rescue Crew commander. Interviewed by the author, Washington, D.C., November 21, 1978.

Toland, Col Butler B., Jr. Air Attache to Laos. Interviewed by Lt. Col. Robert G. Zimmerman, Washington, D.C., November 18, 1974.

Vette, Lt Col Alan R. Commander, 37th ARRSq. Interviewed by the author, Ft. Walton Beach, Fla., April 22, 1978.

Von Platten, Col William. Air Attache to Laos. Interviewed by Lt. Col. Robert G. Zimmerman, Washington, D.C., May 10, 1975.

Wood, Lt Col Charles N. J-2 MACV Representative to the 1972 Evacuation Plan Committee. Interviewed by the author, Washington, D.C., May 8, 1978.

Woolfer, Lt Col Rick L. Chief, Escape and Evasion/Prisoner of War Branch, 7602nd Interviewed by the author, Ft. Belvoir, Va., April 14, 1978.

Articles appearing in the Air Force's *Airman Magazine,* used in this book are:

Kilbourne, Maj Jimmy W. "Only One Returned." *Airman Magazine,* March 1970, pp 11-13.

Strum, Ted R. "Miracle Mission." *Airman Magazine,* August 1973, pp 43-46.

Taylor, John B. "Air Mission Mayaguez."*Airman Magazine,* January 1976, pp 38-44.

A great portion of the research for this study was based on messages, plans, reports and other miscellaneous documents. Research in these documents was accomplished at the Washington National Records Center at Suitland, Maryland, at the Alfred F. Simpson Historical Research Center, and by using microfilm in the Office of Air Force History.

All these various documents have been indexed into the computerized Data Base Inventory (DABIN) System which is maintained by the Technical Systems Branch of the Alfred F. Simpson Historical Research Center.

SEARCH AND RESCUE

DABIN identifies source documents including single-page messages, reports, orders, and interviews giving pertinent details as to title, author, date, general subject, and significant key words in the titles. Moreover, DABIN reveals the location of the sources by repository and tells the researcher how to obtain those documents. A listing of each of the documents used in researching this study would only serve to repeat the footnotes. Below is a representative selection.

Defense Intelligence Agency. Defense Intelligence Information Report 2 237 009372, "Incidents in North Vietnam," 9 August 1972.
Defense Intelligence Agency. Defense Intelligence Information Report 1 516 0639 72, "The U.S. Raid on Son Tay PW Camp," 10 December 1971.
Diary of Maj John F. Guilmartin. Major Guilmartin's personal papers. (Not listed on DABIN).
Hq 7th Air Force. Commando Hunt VII, June 1972.
Joint Vietnamese/U.S. Search and Rescue Agreement.[undtd, c.a. Spring 1962].
Joker/3d ARRGp Mission Log, 1973-1975. (Not listed in DABIN).
MATS Special Plan 138-61, National SAR and Local Base Rescue Implementing Plan.
Memorandum, Chief of Staff for the Secretary of the Air Force," "Farmgate Activity Report," 13 February 1962.
Papers of Gen Joseph P. McConnell, Chief of Staff, U.S. Air Force, Item No. 317, "Briefing by General Estes," 28 October 1965.
Second Air Division Manual 55-1.
United States Support Activities Group/7th Air Force. Contingency Plan 5060C, Eagle Pull.

NON-GOVERNMENTAL SOURCES

Birdsall, Steve. *The A-1 Skyraider*. New York: Arco Books, 1970.
Bonds, Ray, ed. *The Soviet War Machine: An Encyclopedia of Russian Military Equipment and Strategy*. New York: Chartwell Books, Inc., 1977.
Bridgman, Leonard and Grey, C.G., eds. *Jane's All the World's Aircraft, 1937*. London: Sampson and Low, 1937.
Bridgman, Leonard, ed. *Jane's All The World's Aircraft, 1951-52*. London: Sampson and Low, 1952.
Bridgman, Leonard, etc. *Jane's All the World's Aircraft, 1955-56*. New York: McGraw Hill, 1956.
Butterfield, Fox; Kenworthy, E.W.; Sheehan, Neil; and Smith, Hedrick. *The Pentagon Papers*. New York: Quadrangle Books, 1971.
Churchill, Winston S. *Their Finest Hour*. Book 2, Vol. II, *The Second World War*, 6 vols. New York: Bantam Books, 1962.
Crozier, Brian.*Southeast Asia in Turmoil*. London: Penguin Books, 1965.
David, Heather. *Operation: Rescue*. New York: Pinnacle Books, 1971.
Devine, Robert A. *Since 1945: Politics and Diplomacy in Recent American History*. New York: John Wiley and Sons, Inc., 1975.
Dommen, Arthur J. *Conflict in Laos: The Politics of Neutralization*. New York: Frederick A. Praeger Publishers, 1971.
Dung, Gen. Van Tien. *Our Great Spring Victory: An Account of the Liberation of South Vietnam*. New York: Monthly Press Review, 1977.
Fall, Bernard B. *Anatomy of a Crisis: The Laotian Crisis of 1960-1961*. New York: Frederick A. Praeger, 1969.

Fitzgerald, Francis. *Fire in the Lake: The Vietnamese and the Americans in Vietnam.* Boston: Little, Brown, and Company, 1971.

Glines, Carroll V. and Kilbourne, Jimmy W., eds. *Escape and Evasion: 17 True Stories of Downed Pilots Who Made it Back.* New York: Macmillan, 1973.

Gunston, William. *The Encyclopedia of the World's Combat Aircraft.* Seacaucus, N.Y.: Chartwell Books Inc., 1977.

Hezlet, Vice Admiral Sir Arthur. *Aircraft and Sea Power.* New York: Stein and Day, 1970.

Jackson, Robert. *Air War Over Korea.* New York: Scribner, 1975.

Kalb, Bernard and Kalb, Marvin. *Kissinger.* Boston: Little, Brown, and Company, 1974.

Kosut, Hal and Sobel, Lester A., eds. *South Vietnam,* Vol. I: *U.S.-Communist Confrontation in Southeast Asia, 1961-1965.* New York: Facts on File, Inc., 1966.

Mason, Francis K. and Windrow, Martin C. *Know Aviation: Seventy Years of Man's Endeavor.* Garden City, N.Y.: Doubleday, 1973.

Palmer, Richard Dave. *Summons of the Trumpet: U.S. Vietnam in Perspective.* San Rafael, Cal.: Presidio Press, 1978.

Richards, Denis. *Royal Air Force 1939-1945,* Vol. I, *The Fight at Odds.* London: Her Majesty's Stationary Office, 1953.

Richards, Denis, and Saunders, Hilary St. George. *Royal Air Force 1939-1945,* vol. II, *The Fight Avails.* London: Her Majesty's Stationary Office, 1954.

Ridgway, Gen. Matthew B. *The Korean War.* New York: Doubleday and Company, 1967.

Schemmer, Benjamin F. *The Raid.* New York: Harper and Row, 1976.

Schurmann, Franz. *The Logic of World Power: An Inquiry Into the Origins, Currents, and Contradictions of World Politics.* New York: Pantheon Books, 1974.

Schlesinger, Arthur M., Jr. *The Thousand Days.* Boston: Houghton Mifflin Company, 1965.

Snepp, Frank. *Decent Interval.* New York: Random House, 1978.

Sorensen, Theodore C. *Kennedy.* New York: Harper and Row, 1965.

Taylor, John W.R., ed.*Jane's All the World's Aircraft, 1964-65.* New York: McGraw-Hill, 1965.

—————————. *Jane's All the World's Aircraft, 1976-77.* New York: Franklin Watts, 1977.

Vandegrift, John L., Jr. *A History of the Air Rescue Service.* Winter Park, Fla.: Archeon Books, 1959.

Wood, Derek and Dempster, Derek. *The Narrow Margin: The Battle of Britain and the Rise of Air Power, 1930-1940.* New York: McGraw-Hill, 1961.

Zasloff, Joseph J. *The Pathet Lao Leadership and Organization.* Lexington, Mass.: D.C. Heath and Company, 1973.

Articles

Benjamin, Milton R. and Brinkley-Rogers, Paul. "Farewell to Phnom Penh," *Newsweek,* 21 April 1975.

Cunningham, Brig. Gen. Joseph A. "Wherever Men Fly," *Air Force and Space Digest,* March 1960, pp 88-89.

Shershun, Maj. Carrol S. "It's the Greatest Mission of them All," *Aerospace Historian,* Autumn 1969, pp 10-15.

Yaffee, Michael L. "Composite Aircraft Seen Emerging as Next Basic VTOL," *Aviation Week and Space Technology,* 1 May 1967, pp 60-67.

"The Bombing Stops, the Wait Begins," *Newsweek,* 27 August 1973.

"Victory at Sea," *Newsweek,* 26 May 1975.

Index

SEARCH AND RESCUE

SEARCH AND RESCUE

English Channel: 3-6, 8, 65
Equipment *(see also by name)*
    in search and rescue: 4, 7-8, 16-17, 43, 63, 112, 122-123
    shortages in deficiencies in: 46, 50
Escapes. *See* Evasions and escapes
Escort missions: 17, 37-41, 49, 51-52, 54-55, 63, 65-68, 72, 94, 117, 124-126
Estes, Howell M., Jr.: 75, 89
Evasions and escapes: 2, 67
Everest, Frank K.: 103

Farm Gate (code name): 36-42, 46
Felt, Harry D.
    and aircraft availability and assignment: 52
    and commitments to Laos: 34
    and rescue operations control: 33, 45, 74
    and training programs: 45
Field Goal (code name): 35
Fighter-Bomber Squadron, 35th: 9
Fighter Squadrons
    3d Tactical: 125, 135
    510th Tactical: 35
    602d (Commando): 66
Fighter Wings
    12th Tactical: 113
    388th Tactical: 139
First-aid kits, in search and rescue: 4, 43, 84
Flak traps. *See* Ambushes, by enemy
Flares, in search and rescue: 37, 42-43, 49, 67, 84, 109, 111, 123, 145
Flight Control Command: 8
Flight record, longest by rotary-winged: 85
Floats, in search and rescue: 4
Food supplies, in search and rescue: 7, 51
Forby, Willis E.: 67
Ford, Gerald R.: 147-148
Formosa crisis (1958). *See* Taiwan crisis (1958)
Forrester, Cleveland F.: 154
Fort Bragg: 104
Forward air controllers. *See* Air controllers
France
    German occupation of: 3-4
    search and rescue experience: 14-15
Free World forces: 98
Frequent Wind, Operation. *See* Civilians, evacuation of
Frisbie, Norman H.: 104
Fuel supplies, consumption rates and shortages: 51, 70
Fuel tanks: 60, 64, 70, 126

Geneva Agreement on Indochina (1954): 15, 37
Geneva Agreements on Laos (1961-62): 33, 35, 46-47, 83
Germany, search and rescue experience: 3-4, 7, 65, 95
Glotz, Konrad: 3
Godley, G. McMurtrie: 124
Goering, Hermann: 3

198

Lightning Source UK Ltd.
Milton Keynes UK
UKHW031134170220
358851UK00010B/2383

9 781782 664284